THE POWER OF IDEAS

Isaiah Berlin was born in Riga, capital of Latvia, in 1909.
When he was six, his family moved to Russia: there in 1917,
in Petrograd, he witnessed both the Social Democratic and
the Bolshevik Revolution.

In 1921 his family came to England, and he was educated
at St Paul's School and Corpus Christi College, Oxford. At
Oxford he was a Fellow of All Souls, a Fellow of New College, Professor of Social and Political Theory and founding
President of Wolfson College. He also held the Presidency of
the British Academy. In addition to *The Power of Ideas*, his
published work includes *Karl Marx, Four Essays on Liberty,
Russian Thinkers, Concepts and Categories, Against the
Current, Personal Impressions, The Crooked Timber of Humanity, The Sense of Reality, The Proper Study of Mankind,
The Roots of Romanticism* and *Three Critics of the Enlightenment*. As an exponent of the history of ideas he was
awarded the Erasmus, Lippincott and Agnelli Prizes; he also
received the Jerusalem Prize for his lifelong defence of civil
liberties. He died in 1997.

Henry Hardy, a Fellow of Wolfson College, Oxford, is one
of Isaiah Berlin's Literary Trustees. He has edited several
other books by Berlin, and is currently preparing his letters
and his remaining unpublished writings for publication.

For further information about Isaiah Berlin visit
http://berlin.wolf.ox.ac.uk/

Also by Isaiah Berlin

✻

THE POWER OF IDEAS

ISAIAH BERLIN

Edited by Henry Hardy

Princeton University Press
Princeton and Oxford

Published in the United States by Princeton University Press, 41 William Street, Princeton, New Jersey 08540

In the United Kingdom, published by Chatto & Windus in 2000

'My Intellectual Path' © The Isaiah Berlin Literary Trust and Henry Hardy 1998
'The Search for Status' © The Isaiah Berlin Literary Trust 2000
Other essays copyright Isaiah Berlin 1947, 1951, 1953, 1954, 1956,
© Isaiah Berlin 1960, 1962, 1966, 1968, 1969, 1972, 1975, 1978, 1979, 1995
Editorial matter © Henry Hardy 2000

Second printing, and first paperback printing, 2002
Paperback ISBN 0-691-09276-1

The cloth edition of this book has been cataloged as follows

Library of Congress Catalog Card Number 99–068984
ISBN 0-691-05018-X

Printed on acid free paper. ∞

www.pup.princeton.edu

Printed in the United States of America

2 4 6 8 10 9 7 5 3

ISBN-13: 978-0-691-09276-8

ISBN-10: 0-691-09276-1

For Wolfson College, Oxford

CONTENTS

EDITOR'S PREFACE

Over a hundred years ago, the German poet Heine warned the French not to underestimate the power of ideas: philosophical concepts nurtured in the stillness of a professor's study could destroy a civilisation.

Isaiah Berlin, *Two Concepts of Liberty*, 1958[1]

THE THEME that links the contents of this volume of Isaiah Berlin's shorter, more introductory pieces is the same as that of three earlier volumes of his longer essays, namely the crucial social and political role – past, present and future – of ideas, and of their progenitors.[2] Within the confines of this theme a rich variety of subject-matters is represented, and the appositeness of Heine's warning is exemplified on a broad front. It was a warning that Berlin often referred to, and provides one kind of answer (there are naturally others) to those who ask, as from time to time they do, why intellectual history matters.

I have had it in mind for over twenty years to publish a collection of this kind. In the mid-1970s, in the process of devising a scheme for the publication of the first four volumes of my edition of Berlin's writings, I read everything he had written, so far as I could track it down at the time, and it quickly became clear that there ought at some point to be a volume comprising his briefer, rather more popular, pieces. Not that he ever wrote anything unpopular, so to speak: indeed, it is surely one of the attractions of

---

[1] In this pithy summary Berlin characteristically sharpens the expression of the original passage, the most relevant part of which may be rendered thus: 'Note this, you proud men of action, you are nothing but the unconscious tools of the men of thought, who in humble stillness have often drawn up your most definite plans of action.' See Heinrich Heine, *Zur Geschichte der Religion und Philosophie in Deutschland* (1834), book 3: vol. 7, p. 294, in *Heinrich Heines sämtliche Werke*, ed. Oskar Walzel (Leipzig, 1911–20). Berlin's remark is on p. 192 of *The Proper Study of Mankind: An Anthology of Essays* (London, 1997; New York, 1998).

[2] In order to preserve a reasonable degree of thematic unity I have excluded some excellent short pieces that belong less naturally in this company, reserving them for other contexts.

his work that he was constitutionally incapable of writing with the opacity of the specialist.

When I had drawn up a possible list of contents for such a volume, and refined it in discussion with one or two colleagues, I proposed the result to Berlin, who unhesitatingly rejected it, at any rate as an immediate prospect – characteristically, he did not quite close the door permanently. He was influenced, he explained, by the recent appearance of one or two collections by other writers that seemed to him too indiscriminately inclusive. Books made up of short book reviews and other pieces of ephemeral journalism, he believed, did not reflect credit on their authors: it was vanity to think that everything one had written deserved preservation in volume form simply because of its authorship, and he did not wish to be guilty of a book of this character.

It would be hard to disagree with this view of Berlin's, expressed at any rate in these terms, but he was mistaken, in my opinion, if he truly thought that his own shorter writings constituted a case in point. It might be possible to construct an assemblage of minor Berliniana open to such strictures, but there exist nevertheless, intermediate between items of this kind and his more substantial essays, numerous pieces of writing whose concision in no way affects their durability; indeed, they often provide introductory overviews that are usefully complementary to his longer explorations of the same or similar topics.

At all events, I took Berlin's reservations to heart, and have borne them in mind in choosing the contents of the present volume, which I prepared for publication before he died, expecting to have to persuade him to sanction it before I could go ahead. Had this hurdle not been before me, I should probably have chosen somewhat more freely, and indeed I hope to include other short pieces in future volumes.

I had told Berlin that I was engaged on this volume (in what turned out to be the last year of his life), and he made no objection, though we unfortunately never got to the point of discussing my final selection. Nevertheless, I have deliberately not added further pieces since his death – with two exceptions explained below – in the belief that the book can accordingly be regarded, if only to this limited extent, as the last of those I put together with his specific acquiescence ('approval', as always, would be too strong a term). The exceptions apart, I think it unlikely that he would have wished to modify the list of contents substantially, if at all.

The first exception is 'My Intellectual Path', a retrospective autobiographical survey which serves as an introduction. In February 1996, in his eighty-seventh year, Berlin received a letter from Ouyang Kang, Professor of Philosophy at Wuhan University in China, inviting him to provide a summary of his ideas for translation into Chinese and inclusion in a volume designed to introduce philosophers and students of philosophy in China to contemporary Anglo-American philosophy, hitherto largely unavailable to them in Chinese. Berlin had written nothing substantial since 1988, when he published his intellectual *credo*, 'On the Pursuit of the Ideal', a response to the award of the first Agnelli Prize for his contribution to ethics.[1] Although his intellect was undiminished, and he had continued to compose short occasional pieces, it seemed clear that – reasonably enough in his eighties – he had in effect laid down his authorial pen.

But the Chinese project caught his imagination; he regarded this new readership as important, and felt an obligation to address it. He told the Professor that he would try to write something. With a single sheet of notes before him, he dictated a first draft on to cassette. The transcript was at times rough-hewn, and stood in need of the editing he invited, but no intellectual additives were needed to produce a readable text. When he had approved my revised version, making a few final insertions and adjustments, he said, with his characteristic distaste for revisiting his work, that he did not wish to see the piece again. It was to be the last essay he wrote. It was published in the *New York Review of Books* in the year after his death, and now fittingly joins the corpus of his collected essays.

The other exception is 'Jewish Slavery and Emancipation', the classic statement of Berlin's Zionist views. Although this piece made a mark when it first appeared (in 1951), and has often been sought out and discussed since, Berlin always declined to have it included in one of my collections in his lifetime. What he had to say proved controversial – perhaps more so than he expected – and he was reluctant to expose himself to another round of public argument by reissuing the essay and thus by implication reaffirming its contents. Nevertheless, he did not materially change his

---

[1] This piece is included in *The Crooked Timber of Humanity: Chapters in the History of Ideas* (London, 1990; New York, 1991) and in *The Proper Study of Mankind* (see p. ix above, note 1).

opinions on the topic, and I have no doubt that it is now right to add this canonical statement of them to his permanent *oeuvre*. Towards the end of his life, moreover, he asked me, if I ever republished the piece, to restore some remarks about T. S. Eliot and anti-Semitism that he had removed, after representations from Eliot, from the version published in *Hebrew University Garland* in 1952. On reconsideration he felt that he had been too obliging to Eliot. The essay is longer than the others, certainly, but not otherwise out of place, and the desirability of gathering it in without undue delay seemed to me decisive.

One of the procedural rules I usually follow is not to duplicate items from one volume in another. Here I have allowed myself one exception to this rule. 'The Purpose of Philosophy' belongs archetypically in its present company, and deserves to be read more widely than by the professional philosophers who comprise the principal readership of *Concepts and Categories*, the other volume in which it appears.[1]

Another such rule is not to alter individual essays in an attempt to eliminate any duplication in pieces that were independently conceived. Here the most notable overlap is between 'The Purpose of Philosophy' and 'The Philosophers of the Enlightenment'; but it did not seem to me to be great enough to warrant exclusion of either item, since each also has its distinctive contribution to make.

The original publication details of the pieces I have included are as follows:

'My Intellectual Path': *New York Review of Books*, 14 May 1998 (this piece was written for a volume edited by Ouyang Kang and Steve Fuller, *Contemporary British and American Philosophy and Philosophers*, to be published first in Chinese translation by The People's Press, Beijing, and subsequently in English)

'The Purpose of Philosophy': *Insight* (Nigeria) 1 No 1 (July 1962)

'The Philosophers of the Enlightenment': Introduction to his *The Age of Enlightenment: The Eighteenth-Century Philosophers* (Boston, 1956: Houghton Mifflin; New York, 1956: New American Library; Oxford, 1979: Oxford University Press)

'One of the Boldest Innovators in the History of Human Thought': *New York Times Magazine*, 23 November 1969

---

[1] *Concepts and Categories: Philosophical Essays* (London, 1978; New York, 1979).

'Russian Intellectual History': Introduction to Marc Raeff (ed.), *Russian Intellectual History* (New York/Chicago/Burlingame, 1966: Harcourt, Brace and World; Hassocks, 1978: Harvester; New York, 1978: Humanities Press)

'The Man Who Became a Myth': *Listener* 38 (1947)

'A Revolutionary without Fanaticism': Introduction to Alexander Herzen, *From the Other Shore* and *The Russian People and Socialism* (London, 1956: Weidenfeld and Nicolson; with revisions, Oxford, 1979: Oxford University Press); reprinted with postscript in *New York Review of Books*, 19 April 1979 (I have here incorporated some other revisions made by the author before 1979 on a copy of the original version that has only recently come to light)

'The Role of the Intelligentsia': *Listener* 79 (1968)

'Liberty': in Ted Honderich (ed.), *The Oxford Companion to Philosophy* (Oxford, 1995: Oxford University Press) (this item was first drafted in preparation for IB's appearance on 11 February 1962 in an Associated Television film on freedom of speech, the first of a series of five programmes collectively entitled *The Four Freedoms*)

'The Philosophy of Karl Marx': as 'Marx' in J. O. Urmson (ed.), *Concise Encyclopedia of Western Philosophy and Philosophers* (London, 1960: Hutchinson; 2nd ed. 1975)

'The Father of Russian Marxism' (broadcast on the Third Programme of the BBC on 11 December 1956 to mark the centenary of Plekhanov's birth): *Listener* 56 (1956); reprinted as 'Father of Russian Socialism' in *New Leader* (USA), 4 February 1957

'Realism in Politics', *Spectator* 193 (1954)

'The Origins of Israel': as 'Israel – A Survey' in *The State of Israel* (London, 1953: Anglo-Israel Association); reprinted (*a*) as 'The Face of Israel' in *Jewish Frontier* 21 No 5 (May 1954), (*b*) in *Israel: Some Aspects of the New State* (London, 1955: Anglo-Israel Association), (*c*) as 'The Origins of Israel' in Walter Z. Laqueur (ed.), *The Middle East in Transition* (London, 1958: Routledge and Kegan Paul)

'Jewish Slavery and Emancipation', *Jewish Chronicle*, 21 and 28 September, 5 and 12 October 1951; reprinted (with alterations here reversed) in Norman Bentwich (ed.), *Hebrew University Garland* (London, 1952: Constellation Books)

'Chaim Weizmann's Leadership': as 'Men Who Lead' in *Jerusalem Post*, 2 November 1954; reprinted as 'The Anatomy of Leadership' in *Jewish Frontier* 21 No 12 (December 1954)

'The Search for Status': previously unpublished talk (the last of a series of four), broadcast on the BBC's European Service on 20 July 1959, closely based on part of *Two Concepts of Liberty*, the author's

Inaugural Lecture as Chichele Professor of Social and Political Theory at Oxford (Oxford, 1958: Clarendon Press)

'The Essence of European Romanticism': Preface to H. G. Schenk, *The Mind of the European Romantics* (London, 1966: Constable; New York, 1967: Frederick Ungar; Oxford, 1979: Oxford University Press)

'Meinecke and Historicism': Foreword to Friedrich Meinecke, *Historism: The Rise of a New Historical Outlook*, trans. J. E. Anderson (London, 1972: Routledge and Kegan Paul)

'General Education': Foreword to Michael Yudkin (ed.), *General Education: A Symposium on the Teaching of Non-Specialists* (Harmondsworth, 1969: Allen Lane/Penguin); reprinted as 'General Education' in *Oxford Review of Education* 1 (1975)

In some cases it is relevant to bear in mind the dates of publication in this list, since several of the pieces bear the signs, here and there, of having been written some time ago: in particular, all the essays but the first date from before the demise of the Soviet Union, which the author left in 1920 and visited in 1945–6 and 1956; and the two essays on Israel were written within three or four years of the establishment of that State in 1948. I have not attempted to edit out these signs (even where this would have been possible).[1] I did consider printing dates of first publication either at the beginning or at the end of each item, but decided against, principally because much of the writing, and many whole items, have the comparatively timeless quality that is characteristic of most of Berlin's work, and I did not want to detract from this by giving undue prominence to information that is seldom crucial. But I have added a note when it seemed helpful to draw attention to the relevant date *in situ*.

I must record, as always, a debt of gratitude to the specialists who have assisted me in tracking down the sources of (most of) Berlin's quotations. In the case of this volume my main obligations of this kind are to Linda Armstrong, Andrew Fairbairn, Aileen Kelly, Hartmut Pogge von Strandmann and Helen Rappaport. I shall be grateful to be told of any sources I have failed to identify. Roger Hausheer has once again been an invaluable source of advice, and has helped in numerous specific ways, not least by

---

[1] I have, however (as in previous volumes), filled out or adapted a handful of passages which, though appropriate to the original contexts of the pieces in which they occurred, would have been disproportionately distracting if left unattended to here.

suggesting a natural running-order for the pieces I have selected. Otherwise I am indebted, as before, to my benefactors, and to the patiently hospitable Oxford College that Berlin founded. This last, substantial and growing, debt I signal by the warmly felt dedication that appears on an earlier page.

Wolfson College, Oxford   HENRY HARDY
September 1999

Note to the paperback edition

In this edition I have corrected a few small errors that came to light after the book was first published.

I am also now able to give a more precise source for 'interested error' than that offered on p. 135 below, note 1. It seems most likely that IB took this phrase from an excessively free passage in a translation of Holbach's *Système de la nature*. In part 1, chapter 1, 'De la nature', Holbach writes: 'recourons à nos sens, que l'on nous a faussement fait regarder comme suspects'. In his 1820 translation Samuel Wilkinson renders this as 'let us recover our senses, which interested error has taught us to suspect'. H. D. Robinson borrows Wilkinson's invention in his 1868 version: 'let us fall back on our senses, which errour, interested errour, has taught us to suspect'.

However creative this Englishing may be, the sentiment is thoroughy Holbachian, as the quotations in the note on p. 135 illustrate.

I am grateful to Roger Hausheer for putting me on to the trail of this hitherto elusive phrase – one of which Berlin was fond.

H. H.

MY INTELLECTUAL PATH

I

MY INTEREST in philosophical issues started when I was an undergraduate at Oxford in the late 1920s and early 1930s, because philosophy was part of the course which at that time a great many students in Oxford pursued. As a result of a continuing interest in this field I was appointed in 1932 to teach philosophy, and my views at that time were naturally influenced by the kind of discussions that my philosophical contemporaries held in Oxford. There were plenty of other issues in philosophy, but as it happens the topics which my colleagues and I concentrated on were the fruits of a return to empiricism which began to dominate British philosophy before the First World War, under the influence mainly of two celebrated Cambridge philosophers, G. E. Moore and Bertrand Russell.

Verificationism

The first topic which occupied our attention in the middle and late 1930s was the nature of meaning – its relation to truth and falsehood, knowledge and opinion, and in particular the test of meaning in terms of the verifiability of the propositions in which it was expressed. The impulsion towards this topic came from the members of the Vienna School, themselves disciples of Russell and greatly influenced by thinkers such as Carnap, Wittgenstein and Schlick. The fashionable view was that the meaning of a proposition was the way in which it was verifiable – that if there was no way whatever of verifying what was being said, it was not a statement capable of truth or falsehood, not factual, and therefore either meaningless or a case of some other use of language, as seen in commands or expressions of desire, or in imaginative literature, or in other forms of expression which did not lay claim to empirical truth.

I was influenced by this school in the sense of being absorbed in the problems and theories which it generated, but I never became a true disciple. I always believed that statements that could be true or false or plausible or dubious or interesting, while indeed they did relate to the world as empirically conceived (and I have never conceived of the world in any other way, from then to the present day), were nevertheless not necessarily capable of being verified by some simple knock-down criterion, as the Vienna School and their logical positivist followers asserted. From the beginning I felt that general propositions were not verifiable in that way. Statements, whether in ordinary use or in the natural sciences (which were the ideal of the Vienna School), could be perfectly meaningful without being strictly verifiable. If I said 'All swans are white', I would never know if I knew this about all the swans there were, or whether the number of swans might not be infinite; a black swan no doubt refuted this generalisation, but its positive verification in the full sense seemed to me unattainable; nevertheless it would be absurd to say that it had no meaning. The same was true about hypothetical propositions, and still more so about unfulfilled hypotheticals, of which it was plainly paradoxical to maintain that they could be shown to be true or false by empirical observation; yet they were clearly meaningful.

I thought of a great many other statements of this kind, which clearly had meaning in the full sense of the word, but whose meaning escaped the narrow criterion proposed, that of direct empirical observation – the world of the senses. Consequently, though I took a lively part in these discussions (indeed, what later came to be called Oxford Philosophy began in my rooms in the evenings, at gatherings attended by such later celebrated philosophers as A. J. Ayer, J. L. Austin and Stuart Hampshire, influenced as they all were by Oxford empiricism, and to some degree by Oxford realism – that is, the belief that the external world is independent of human observers), nevertheless I remained a heretic, though a friendly one. I have never departed from the views I held at that time, and still believe that while empirical experience is all that words can express – that there is no other reality – nevertheless verifiability is not the only, or indeed the most plausible, criterion of knowledge or beliefs or hypotheses.

This has remained with me for the rest of my life, and has coloured everything else that I have thought.

Another topic which I offered for the attention of my young colleagues was the status of such propositions as 'This pink (shade) is more like this vermilion than it is like this black.' If generalised, it was clear that this was a truth which no experience was likely to refute – the relations of visible colours being fixed. At the same time the general proposition could not be called a priori because it did not proceed formally from any definitions, and did not therefore belong to the formal disciplines of logic or mathematics, in which alone a priori propositions, then regarded as tautologies, belong. So we had found a universal truth in the empirical sphere. What were the definitions of 'pink', 'vermilion' and the rest? They had none. The colours could be recognised only by looking, so that their definitions were classified as ostensive, and from such definitions nothing logically followed. This came close to the old problem of Kant's synthetic a priori propositions, and we discussed this and its analogues for many months. I was convinced that my proposition was, if not strictly a priori, self-evidently true, and that its contradictory was not intelligible. Whether my colleagues ever raised the matter again I do not know, but the topic entered formally into the discussions held by us at the time. It corresponded to a view of Russell's embodied in a work called *The Limits of Empiricism*.

Phenomenalism

The other main topic that my contemporaries discussed was phenomenalism – that is, the question of whether human experience was confined to that provided by the senses, as was taught by the British philosophers Berkeley and Hume (and in some of their writings by Mill and Russell), or whether there existed a reality independent of sensible experience. For some philosophers, like Locke and his followers, there was such a reality, although it was not directly accessible to us – a reality which caused the sensible experiences which are all that we can directly know. Other philosophers held that the external world was a material reality which could be perceived directly, or misperceived as the case might be: this was called realism, as opposed to the view that our world was entirely created by human faculties – reason, imagination and the like – which was called idealism, in which I never believed. I have never believed in any metaphysical truths – whether rationalist truths, as expounded by Descartes, Spinoza, Leibniz and, in his own very different fashion, Kant, or the truths of (objective) idealism, the fathers of which are Fichte, Friedrich Schelling and Hegel, who still have their disciples. Thus meaning, truth and the nature of the external world were the topics which I thought about, and to some extent wrote about – and some of my views on them have been published.[1]

One of the intellectual phenomena which made the greatest impact on me was the universal search by philosophers for absolute certainty, for answers which could not be doubted, for total intellectual security. This from the very beginning appeared to me to be an illusory quest. No matter how solidly based, widespread, inescapable, 'self-evident' a conclusion or a direct datum may seem to be, it is always possible to conceive that something could modify or indeed upset it, even if one cannot at the moment imagine what this might be. And this suspicion that a great deal of philosophy was set on an illusory path later came to dominate my ideas in a quite new and different connection.

While thus engaged in teaching and discussing the kind of philosophy I have outlined, I was commissioned to write a biography of Karl Marx. Marx's philosophical views never appeared to me to be particularly original or interesting, but my study of his views led me to investigate his predecessors, in particular the French *philosophes* of the eighteenth century – the first organised adversaries of dogmatism, traditionalism, religion, superstition, ignorance, oppression. I acquired an admiration for the great task which the thinkers of the French Encyclopaedia had set themselves, and for the great work which they did to liberate men from darkness – clerical, metaphysical, political and the like. And although I came in due course to oppose some of the bases of their common beliefs, I have never lost my admiration for and sense of solidarity with the Enlightenment of that period: what I came to be critical of, apart from its empirical shortcomings, are some of its consequences, both logical and social; I realised that Marx's dogmatism, and that of his followers, in part derived from the certainties of the eighteenth-century Enlightenment.

---

[1] See the author's *Concepts and Categories* (op. cit., p. xii above, note 1).

II

HISTORY OF IDEAS AND POLITICAL THEORY

During the War I served as a British official. When I came back to Oxford to teach philosophy, I became preoccupied with two central problems. The first was monism – the central thesis of Western philosophy from Plato to our day – and the second, the meaning and application of the notion of freedom. I devoted a good deal of time to each, and they shaped my thought for a good many years to come.

Monism

Dazzled by the spectacular successes of the natural sciences in their own century and its predecessors, men such as Helvétius, Holbach, d'Alembert, Condillac, and propagandists of genius such as Voltaire and Rousseau, believed that, provided the right method was discovered, truth of a fundamental kind could be uncovered about social, political, moral and personal life – truth of the kind that had scored such triumphs in the investigations of the external world. The Encyclopaedists believed in scientific method as the only key to such knowledge; Rousseau and others believed in eternal truths discovered by introspective means. But however they differed, they belonged to a generation which was convinced that it was on the path to the solution of all the problems that had plagued mankind from its beginnings.

A wider thesis underlay this: namely, that to all true questions there must be one true answer and one only, all the other answers being false, for otherwise the questions cannot be genuine questions. There must exist a path which leads clear thinkers to the correct answers to these questions, as much in the moral, social and political worlds as in that of the natural sciences, whether it is the same method or not; and once all the correct answers to the deepest moral, social and political questions that occupy (or should occupy) mankind are put together, the result will represent the final solution to all the problems of existence. Of course, we may never attain to these answers: human beings may be too confused by their emotions, or too stupid, or too unlucky, to be able to arrive at them; the answers may be too difficult, the means may be lacking, the techniques too complicated to discover; but however

truths as an external reality

this may be, provided the questions are genuine, the answers must exist. If we do not know, our successors may know; or perhaps wise men in antiquity knew; and if they did not, perhaps Adam in Paradise knew; or if he did not, the angels must know; and if even they do not know, God must know – the answers must be there.

If the answers to social, moral and political questions are discovered, then, knowing them for what they are – the truth – men cannot fail to follow them, for they would have no temptation to do otherwise. And so a perfect life can be conceived. It may not be attainable, but in principle the conception must be capable of being formed – indeed, the possibility of discovering the only true answers to the great questions must in principle be believed in.

This creed was certainly not confined to the thinkers of the Enlightenment, though the methods recommended by others differ. Plato believed that mathematics was the route to truth, Aristotle, perhaps, that it was biology; Jews and Christians sought the answers in sacred books, in the pronouncements of divinely inspired teachers and the visions of mystics; others believed that the laboratory and mathematical methods could settle things; still others believed, like Rousseau, that only the innocent human soul, the uncorrupted child, the simple peasant would know the truth – better than the corrupt inhabitants of societies ruined by civilisation. But what they all agreed about, as did their successors after the French Revolution, who may have supposed the truth more difficult to obtain than their more naïve and optimistic predecessors,[1] was that the laws of historical development could be – and by then had been – discovered, that the answers to the questions of how to live and what to do – morality, social life, political organisation, personal relationships – are all capable of being organised in the light of the truths discovered by the correct methods, whatever those may be.

moral optimism

This is a *philosophia perennis* – what men, thinkers, have believed from the pre-Socratics to all the reformers and revolutionaries of our own age. It is the central belief on which human thought has rested for two millennia. For if no true answers to questions exist, how can knowledge ever be attainable in any

[1] Fourier, an early socialist, and Saint-Simon believed in a scientifically organised society. For Saint-Simon it was to be headed by bankers and scientists, and inspired by artists and poets. Their successors were the French socialists, such as Cabet, Pecqueur, Louis Blanc and the terrorist Blanqui, and, in the end, Marx and Engels and their followers.

province? This was the heart of European rational, and indeed spiritual, thought for many ages. [No matter that people differ so widely, that cultures differ, moral and political views differ; no matter that there is a vast variety of doctrines, religions, moralities, ideas – all the same there must somewhere be a true answer to the deepest questions that preoccupy mankind.]

Niebuhr's critique

I do not know why I always felt sceptical about this almost universal belief, but I did. It may be a matter of temperament, but so it was.

Giambattista Vico

What first shook me was my discovery of the works of the eighteenth-century Italian thinker Giambattista Vico. He was the first philosopher, in my view, to have conceived the idea of cultures. Vico wanted to understand the nature of historical knowledge, of history itself: it was all very well to lean on the natural sciences as far as the external world was concerned, but all they could provide us with was an account of the behaviour of rocks or tables or stars or molecules. In thinking about the past, we go beyond behaviour; we wish to understand how human beings lived, and that means understanding their motives, their fears and hopes and ambitions and loves and hatreds – to whom they prayed, how they expressed themselves in poetry, in art, in religion. We are able to do this because we are ourselves human, and understand our own inner life in these terms. We know how a rock, or a table, behaves because we observe it and make conjectures and verify them; but we do not know why the rock wishes to be as it is – indeed, we think it has no capacity for wishing, or for any other consciousness. But we do know why we are what we are, what we seek, what frustrates us, what expresses our inmost feelings and beliefs; we know more about ourselves than we shall ever know about rocks or streams.

[True knowledge is knowledge of why things are as they are] not merely what they are; and the more we delve into this, the more we realise that the questions asked by the Homeric Greeks are different from the questions asked by the Romans, that the questions asked by the Romans differ from those asked in the Christian Middle Ages or in the seventeenth-century scientific culture or Vico's own eighteenth-century days. The questions differ, the answers differ, the aspirations differ; the use of language, of symbols, differs; and the answers to one set of questions do not answer, do not have much relevance to, the questions of other cultures. Of course Vico was a pious Roman Catholic, and he believed that the Church alone could provide the answers. But be that as it may, it did not prevent him from formulating the original idea that cultures differ, that what matters to a fifth-century Greek is very different from what matters to a Red Indian or a Chinese or a scientist in an eighteenth-century laboratory; and therefore their outlooks differ, and there are no universal answers to all their questions. Of course there is a common human nature, otherwise men in one age could not understand the literature or the art of another, or, above all, its laws, about which Vico, as a jurist, knew most. But that did not prevent there being a wide variety of cultural experience, so that activity of one kind was relevant to activity of some other kind within a single culture, but did not share such close links with the parallel activity in another culture.

culture is the death knell of universal truth [handwritten marginal note]

J. G. Herder

Then I read a far more relevant thinker, namely the German philosopher and poet Johann Gottfried Herder. Herder was not the first (his teacher, Johann Georg Hamann, has that honour) to deny the doctrine of his French contemporaries that there are universal, timeless, unquestionable truths which hold for all men, everywhere, at all times; and that the differences are simply due to error and illusion, for the truth is one and universal – 'quod ubique, quod semper, quod ab omnibus creditum est'.[1] Herder believed that different cultures gave different answers to their central questions. He was more interested in the humanities, the life of the spirit, than in the external world; and he became convinced that what was true for a Portuguese was not necessarily true for a Persian. Montesquieu had begun to say this kind of thing, but even he, who believed that men were shaped by environment, by what he called 'climate', was in the end a universalist – he believed that the central truths were eternal, even if the answers to local and ephemeral questions might be different.

---

[1] 'What is believed everywhere, always, by everyone.' Vincent of Lérins, *Commonitorium* 2. 3.

Herder laid it down that every culture possesses its own 'centre of gravity';[1] each culture has its own points of reference; there is no reason why these cultures should fight each other – universal toleration must be possible – but unification was destruction. Nothing was worse than imperialism. Rome, which crushed native civilisations in Asia Minor in order to produce one uniform Roman culture, committed a crime. The world was a great garden in which different flowers and plants grew, each in its own way, each with its own claims and rights and past and future. From which it followed that no matter what men had in common – and of course, again, there was a common nature to some degree – there were no universally true answers, as valid for one culture as for another.

cultural nationalism

Herder is the father of cultural nationalism. He is not a political nationalist (that kind of nationalism had not developed in his time), but he believed in the independence of cultures and the need to preserve each in its uniqueness. He believed that the desire to belong to a culture, something that united a group or a province or a nation, was a basic human need, as deep as the desire for food or drink or liberty; and that this need to belong to a community where you understood what others said, where you could move freely, where you had emotional as well as economic, social and political bonds, was the basis of developed, mature human life. Herder was not a relativist, though he is often so described: he believed that there were basic human goals and rules of behaviour, but that they took wholly different forms in different cultures, and that consequently, while there may have been analogies, similarities, which made one culture intelligible to another, cultures were not to be confused with each other – mankind was not one but many, and the answers to the questions were many, though there might be some central essence to them all which was one and the same.

universal NEED?

Romanticism and its offspring

This idea was developed further by the romantics, who said something wholly new and disturbing: that ideals were not objective truths written in heaven and needing to be understood, copied, practised by men; but that they were created by men.

[1] *Herder's sämmtliche Werke*, ed. Bernhard Suphan (Berlin, 1877–1913), vol. 5, p. 509.

Values were not found, but made; not discovered, but generated –
that is what some of the German romantics certainly believed, as
against the objectivist, universalising tendency of the superficial
French. Uniqueness mattered. A German poet writes poetry in
German, in language which, in the course of writing, he to some
degree creates: he is not simply a writer in German. The German
artist is a maker of German paintings, poems, dances – and so in all
other cultures. A Russian thinker, Alexander Herzen, once asked,
'Where is the song before it is sung?'[1] Where indeed? 'Nowhere'
is the answer – one creates the song by singing it, by composing it.
So, too, life is created by those who live it, step by step. This is an
aesthetic interpretation of morality and of life, not an application of
eternal models. Creation is all.

From this sprang all kinds of diverse movements – anarchism,
romanticism, nationalism, Fascism, hero-worship. I make my own
values, maybe not consciously: and besides, who is 'I'? For
Byronic romantics, 'I' is indeed an individual, the outsider, the
adventurer, the outlaw, he who defies society and accepted values,
and follows his own – it may be to his doom, but this is better than
conformity, enslavement to mediocrity. But for other thinkers 'I'
becomes something much more metaphysical. It is a collective – a
nation, a Church, a Party, a class, an edifice in which I am only a
stone, an organism of which I am only a tiny living fragment. *It* is
the creator; I myself matter only in so far as I belong to the
movement, the race, the nation, the class, the Church; I do not
signify as a true individual within this super-person to whom my
life is organically bound. Hence German nationalism: I do this not
because it is good or right or because I like it – I do it because I am
a German and this is the German way to live. So also modern
existentialism – I do it because I commit myself to this form of
existence. Nothing makes me; I do not do it because it is an
objective order which I obey, or because of universal rules to
which I must adhere; I do it because I create my own life as I do;
being what I am, I give it direction and I am responsible for it.
Denial of universal values, this emphasis on being above all an
element in, and loyal to, a super-self, is a dangerous moment in
European history, and has led to a great deal that has been

[1] See A. I. Gertsen, *Sobranie sochinenii v tridtsati tomakh* (Moscow, 1954–66)
[hereafter SS], vol. 6, pp. 33 and 335. Subsequent references to this edition are by
volume and page, thus: SS vi 33.

destructive and sinister in modern times; this is where it begins, in the political ruminations and theories of the earliest German romantics and their disciples in France and elsewhere.[1]

I never for a moment accepted the idea of these super-egos, but I recognised their importance in modern thought and action. Slogans like 'Not I but the Party', 'Not I but the Church', 'My country right or wrong, but my country' have inflicted a wound on the central faith of human thought as I outlined it above – that the truth is universal, eternal, for all men at all times – from which it has never recovered. Mankind not as an object but as a subject, an ever-moving spirit, self-creating and self-moving, a self-composed drama in many acts, which, according to Marx, will end in some kind of perfection – all this issues from the romantic revolution. While I reject this huge metaphysical interpretation of human life *in toto* – I remain an empiricist, and know only what I am able to experience, or think I could experience, and do not begin to believe in supra-individual entities – nevertheless I own that it made some impact on me, in the following way.

Pluralism

I came to the conclusion that there is a plurality of ideals, as there is a plurality of cultures and of temperaments. I am not a relativist; I do not say 'I like my coffee with milk and you like it without; I am in favour of kindness and you prefer concentration camps' – each

---

[1] The romantics viewed their notion of self-moving centres of historical activity, thrusting forward on their own terms, as ultimately subjective. These were arbitrary entities – whether Byronic, somewhat satanic figures at war with society, or heroes who mould around themselves groups of followers (robbers, in the case of Schiller's play) or entire nations (Lycurgus, Moses – nation-builders so much admired by Machiavelli – to whom there are certainly modern parallels) – creating in accordance with freely invented patterns. This view was sternly opposed by such thinkers as Hegel and Marx, who taught, each in his own fashion, that progress must conform to the iron laws of historical development – whether material development, as in Marx, or spiritual, as in Hegel. Only thus can the emancipation of human powers from irrational drives be achieved, and a reign be ushered in of total justice, freedom, virtue, happiness and harmonious self-realisation. This idea of inexorable progress is inherited from the Judaeo-Christian tradition, but without the notions of the inscrutable divine will or the Last Judgement of mankind – the separation of the satisfactory sheep from the unsatisfactory goats – conducted after death.

of us with his own values, which cannot be overcome or integrated. This I believe to be false. But I do believe that there is a plurality of values which men can and do seek, and that these values differ. There is not an infinity of them: the number of human values, of values which I can pursue while maintaining my human semblance, my human character, is finite – let us say 74, or perhaps 122, or 26, but finite, whatever it may be. [And the difference this makes is that if a man pursues one of these values, I, who do not, am able to understand why he pursues it or what it would be like, in his circumstances, for me to be induced to pursue it. Hence the possibility of human understanding.]

pluralism of ideals

finity → understanding

I think these values are objective – that is to say, their nature, the pursuit of them, is part of what it is to be a human being, and this is an objective given. The fact that men are men and women are women and not dogs or cats or tables or chairs is an objective fact; and part of this objective fact is that there are certain values, and only those values, which men, while remaining men, can pursue. If I am a man or a woman with sufficient imagination (and this I do need), I can enter into a value-system which is not my own, but which is nevertheless something I can conceive of men pursuing while remaining human, while remaining creatures with whom I can communicate, with whom I have some common values – for all human beings must have some common values or they cease to be human, and also some different values else they cease to differ, as in fact they do.

That is why pluralism is not relativism – the multiple values are objective, part of the essence of humanity rather than arbitrary creations of men's subjective fancies. Nevertheless, of course, if I pursue one set of values I may detest another, and may think it is damaging to the only form of life that I am able to live or tolerate, for myself and others; in which case I may attack it, I may even – in extreme cases – have to go to war against it. But I still recognise it as a human pursuit. I find Nazi values detestable, but I can understand how, given enough misinformation, enough false belief about reality, one could come to believe that they are the only salvation. Of course they have to be fought, by war if need be, but I do not regard the Nazis, as some people do, as literally pathological or insane, only as wickedly wrong, totally misguided about the facts, for example in believing that some beings are subhuman, or that race is central, or that Nordic races alone are truly creative, and so forth. I see how, with enough false education, enough widespread illusion and error, men can, while remaining men, believe this and commit the most unspeakable crimes.

If pluralism is a valid view, and respect between systems of values which are not necessarily hostile to each other is possible, then toleration and liberal consequences follow, as they do not either from monism (only one set of values is true, all the others are false) or from relativism (my values are mine, yours are yours, and if we clash, too bad, neither of us can claim to be right). My political pluralism is a product of reading Vico and Herder, and of understanding the roots of romanticism, which in its violent, pathological form went too far for human toleration.

So with nationalism: the sense of belonging to a nation seems to me quite natural and not in itself to be condemned, or even criticised. But in its inflamed condition – my nation is better than yours, I know how the world should be shaped and you must yield because you do not, because you are inferior to me, because my nation is top and yours is far, far below mine and must offer itself as material to mine, which is the only nation entitled to create the best possible world – it is a form of pathological extremism which can lead, and has led, to unimaginable horrors, and is totally incompatible with the kind of pluralism which I have attempted to describe.

It may be of interest to remark, incidentally, that there are certain values that we in our world accept which were probably created by early romanticism and did not exist before: for example, the idea that variety is a good thing, that a society in which many opinions are held, and those holding different opinions are tolerant of each other, is better than a monolithic society in which one opinion is binding on everyone. Nobody before the eighteenth century could have accepted that: the truth was one and the idea of variety was inimical to it. Again, the idea of sincerity, as a value, is something new. It was always right to be a martyr to the truth, but only to the truth: Muslims who died for Islam were poor, foolish, misled creatures who died for nonsense; so, for Catholics, were Protestants and Jews and pagans; and the fact that they held their beliefs sincerely made them no better – what was important was to be right. In discovering the truth, as in every other walk of life, success was what was important, not motive. If a man says to you that he believes that twice two is seventeen, and someone says,

'You know, he doesn't do it to annoy you, he doesn't do it because he wants to show off or because he has been paid to say it – he truly believes, he is a sincere believer', you would say, 'This makes it no better, he is talking irrational nonsense.' That is what Protestants were doing, in the view of Catholics, and vice versa. The more sincere, the more dangerous; no marks were given for sincerity until the notion that there is more than one answer to a question – that is, pluralism – became more widespread. That is what led value to be set on motive rather than on consequence, on sincerity rather than on success.

The enemy of pluralism is monism – the ancient belief that there is a single harmony of truths into which everything, if it is genuine, in the end must fit. The consequence of this belief (which is something different from, but akin to, what Karl Popper called essentialism – to him the root of all evil) is that those who know should command those who do not. Those who know the answers to some of the great problems of mankind must be obeyed, for they alone know how society should be organised, how individual lives should be lived, how culture should be developed. This is the old Platonic belief in the philosopher-kings, who were entitled to give orders to others. There have always been thinkers who hold that if only scientists, or scientifically trained persons, could be put in charge of things, the world would be vastly improved. To this I have to say that no better excuse, or even reason, has ever been propounded for unlimited despotism on the part of an élite which robs the majority of its essential liberties.

Someone once remarked that in the old days men and women were brought as sacrifices to a variety of gods; for these, the modern age has substituted new idols: -isms. To cause pain, to kill, to torture are in general rightly condemned; but if these things are done not for my personal benefit but for an -ism – socialism, nationalism, Fascism, Communism, fanatically held religious belief, or progress, or the fulfilment of the laws of history – then they are in order. Most revolutionaries believe, covertly or overtly, that in order to create the ideal world eggs must be broken, otherwise one cannot obtain the omelette. Eggs are certainly broken – never more violently or ubiquitously than in our times – but the omelette is far to seek, it recedes into an infinite distance. That is one of the corollaries of unbridled monism, as I call it – some call it fanaticism, but monism is at the root of every extremism.

Freedom

Political freedom is a topic to which I devoted two lectures during the 1950s. The later of these, entitled 'Two Concepts of Liberty',[1] inaugurated my Oxford Professorship, and its gist was to distinguish between two notions of liberty (or freedom – the terms are used interchangeably), negative and positive. By negative liberty I meant the absence of obstacles which block human action. Quite apart from obstacles created by the external world, or by the biological, physiological, psychological laws which govern human beings, there is lack of political freedom – the central topic of my lecture – where the obstacles are man-made, whether deliberately or unintentionally. The extent of negative liberty depends on the degree to which such man-made obstacles are absent – on the degree to which I am free to go down this or that path without being prevented from doing so by man-made institutions or disciplines, or by the activities of specific human beings.

It is not enough to say that negative freedom simply means freedom to do what I like, for in that case I can liberate myself from obstacles to the fulfilment of desire simply by following the ancient Stoics and killing desire. But that path, the gradual elimination of the desires to which obstacles can occur, leads in the end to humans being gradually deprived of their natural, living activities: in other words, the most perfectly free human beings will be those who are dead, since then there is no desire and therefore no obstacles. What I had in mind, rather, was simply the number of paths down which a man can walk, whether or not he chooses to do so. That is the first of the two basic senses of political freedom.

Some have maintained, against me, that freedom must be a triadic relationship: I can overcome or remove or be free from obstacles only in order to do something, to be free to perform a given act or acts. But I do not accept that. The basic sense of unfreedom is that in which we ascribe it to the man in jail, or the man tied to a tree; all that such a man seeks is the breaking of his chains, escape from the cell, without necessarily aiming at a particular activity once he is liberated. In the larger sense, of course, freedom means freedom from the rules of a society or its

---

[1] Delivered in 1958, and available in two collections of essays by the author: *Four Essays on Liberty* (London and New York, 1969) and *The Proper Study of Mankind* (see p. ix above, note 1).

institutions, from the deployment against one of excessive moral or physical force, or from whatever shuts off possibilities of action which otherwise would be open. This I call 'freedom from'.

The other central sense of freedom is freedom *to*: if my negative freedom is specified by answering the question 'How far am I controlled?', the question for the second sense of freedom is 'Who controls me?' Since we are talking about man-made obstacles, I can ask myself 'Who determines my actions, my life? Do I do so, freely, in whatever way I choose? Or am I under orders from some other source of control? Is my activity determined by parents, schoolmasters, priests, policemen? Am I under the discipline of a legal system, the capitalist order, a slave-owner, the government (monarchical, oligarchic, democratic)? In what sense am I master of my fate? My possibilities of action may be limited, but how are they limited? Who are those who stand in my way, how much power can they wield?'

These are the two central senses of 'liberty' which I set myself to investigate. I realised that they differed, that they were answers to two different questions; but, although cognate, they did not in my view clash – the answer to one did not necessarily determine the answer to the other. Both freedoms were ultimate human ends, both were necessarily limited, and both concepts could be perverted in the course of human history. Negative liberty could be interpreted as economic *laissez-faire*, whereby in the name of freedom owners are allowed to destroy the lives of children in mines, or factory-owners to destroy the health and character of workers in industry. But that was a perversion, not what the concept basically means to human beings, in my view. Equally it was said that it is a mockery to inform a poor man that he is perfectly free to occupy a room in an expensive hotel, although he may not be able to pay for it. But that, too, is a confusion. He is indeed free to rent a room there, but has not the means of using this freedom. He has not the means, perhaps, because he has been prevented from earning more than he does by a man-made economic system – but that is a deprivation of freedom to earn money, not of freedom to rent the room. This may sound a pedantic distinction, but it is central to discussions of economic versus political freedom.

The notion of positive freedom has led, historically, to even more frightful perversions. Who orders my life? I do. I? Ignorant, confused, driven hither and thither by uncontrolled passions and drives – is that all there is to me? Is there not within me a higher, more rational, freer self, able to understand and dominate passions, ignorance and other defects, which I can attain to only by a process of education or understanding, a process which can be managed only by those who are wiser than myself, who make me aware of my true, 'real', deepest self, of what I am at my best? This is a well-known metaphysical view, according to which I can be truly free and self-controlled only if I am truly rational – a belief which goes back to Plato – and since I am not perhaps sufficiently rational myself, I must obey those who are indeed rational, and who therefore know what is best not only for themselves but also for me, and who can guide me along lines which will ultimately awaken my true rational self and put it in charge, where it truly belongs. I may feel hemmed in – indeed, crushed – by these authorities, but that is an illusion: when I have grown up and have attained to a fully mature, 'real' self, I shall understand that I would have done for myself what has been done for me if I had been as wise, when I was in an inferior condition, as they are now.

In short, they are acting on my behalf, in the interests of my higher self, in controlling my lower self; so that true liberty for the lower self consists in total obedience to them, the wise, those who know the truth, the élite of sages; or perhaps my obedience must be to those who understand how human destiny is made – for if Marx is right, then it is a Party (which alone grasps the demands of the rational goals of history) which must shape and guide me, whichever way my poor empirical self may wish to go; and the Party itself must be guided by its far-seeing leaders, and in the end by the greatest and wisest leader of all.

There is no despot in the world who cannot use this method of argument for the vilest oppression, in the name of an ideal self which he is seeking to bring to fruition by his own, perhaps somewhat brutal and *prima facie* morally odious, means (*prima facie* only for the lower empirical self). The 'engineer of human souls', to use Stalin's phrase,[1] knows best; he does what he does

---

[1] Stalin used the phrase 'engineers of human souls' in a speech on the role of Soviet writers made at Maxim Gorky's house on 26 October 1932, recorded in an unpublished manuscript in the Gorky archive – K. L. Zelinsky, 'Vstrecha pisatelei s I. V. Stalinym' ('A meeting of writers with I. V. Stalin') – and published for the first time, in English, in A. Kemp-Welch, *Stalin and the Literary Intelligentsia, 1928–39* (Basingstoke and London, 1991), pp. 128–31: for this phrase see p. 131 (and, for the Russian original, 'inzhenery chelovecheskikh dush', I. V. Stalin, *Sochineniya* (Moscow, 1946–67), vol. 13, p. 410). Ed.

nearly
Rawlsian

not simply in order to do his best for his nation, but in the name of the nation itself, in the name of what the nation would be doing itself if only it had attained to this level of historical understanding. That is the great perversion which the positive notion of liberty has been liable to: whether the tyranny issues from a Marxist leader, a king, a Fascist dictator, the masters of an authoritarian Church or class or State, it seeks for the imprisoned, 'real' self within men, and 'liberates' it, so that this self can attain to the level of those who give the orders.

This goes back to the naïve notion that there is only one true answer to every question: if I know the true answer and you do not, and you disagree with me, it is because you are ignorant; if you knew the truth, you would necessarily believe what I believe; if you seek to disobey me, this can be so only because you are wrong, because the truth has not been revealed to you as it has been to me. This justifies some of the most frightful forms of oppression and enslavement in human history, and it is truly the most dangerous, and, in our century in particular, the most violent, interpretation of the notion of positive liberty.

This notion of two kinds of liberty and their distortions then formed the centre of much discussion and dispute in Western and other universities, and does so to this day.

Determinism

My other lecture on freedom was entitled 'Historical Inevitability'.[1] Here I stated that determinism was a doctrine very widely accepted among philosophers for many hundreds of years. Determinism declares that every event has a cause, from which it unavoidably follows. This is the foundation of the natural sciences: the laws of nature and all their applications – the entire body of natural science – rest upon the notion of an eternal order which the sciences investigate. But if the rest of nature is subject to these laws, can it be that man alone is not? When a man supposes, as most ordinary people do (though not most scientists and philosophers), that when he rises from the chair he need not have done so, that he did so because he chose to do so, but he need not have chosen – when he supposes this, he is told that this is an illusion, that even

---

[1] Delivered in 1953, and also included both in *Four Essays on Liberty* and in *The Proper Study of Mankind*.

though the necessary work by psychologists has not yet been accomplished, one day it will be (or at any rate in principle can be), and then he will know that what he is and does is necessarily as it is, and could not be otherwise. I believe this doctrine to be false, but I do not in this essay seek to demonstrate this, or to refute determinism – indeed, I am not sure if such a demonstration or refutation is possible. My only concern is to ask myself two questions. Why do philosophers and others think that human beings are fully determined? And, if they are, is this compatible with normal moral sentiments and behaviour, as commonly understood?

My thesis is that there are two main reasons for supporting the doctrine of human determinism. The first is that, since the natural sciences are perhaps the greatest success story in the whole history of mankind, it seems absurd to suppose that man alone is not subject to the natural laws discovered by the scientists. (That, indeed, is what the eighteenth-century *philosophes* maintained.) The question is not, of course, whether man is wholly free of such laws – no one but a madman could maintain that man does not depend on his biological or psychological structure or environment, or on the laws of nature. The only question is: Is his liberty totally exhausted thereby? Is there not some corner in which he can act as he chooses, and not be determined to choose by antecedent causes? This may be a tiny corner of the realm of nature, but unless it is there, his consciousness of being free, which is undoubtedly all but universal – the fact that most people believe that, while some of their actions are mechanical, some obey their free will – is an enormous illusion, from the beginnings of mankind, ever since Adam ate the apple, although told not to do so, and did not reply, 'I could not help it, I did not do it freely, Eve forced me to do it.'

The second reason for belief in determinism is that it does devolve the responsibility for a great many things that people do on to impersonal causes, and therefore leaves them in a sense unblameworthy for what they do. When I make a mistake, or commit a wrong or a crime, or do anything else which I recognise, or which others recognise, as bad or unfortunate, I can say, 'How could I avoid it? – that was the way I was brought up' or 'That is my nature, something for which natural laws are responsible' or 'I belong to a society, a class, a Church, a nation, in which everyone does it, and nobody seems to condemn it' or 'I am psychologically conditioned by the way in which my parents behaved to each other and to me, and by the economic and social circumstances in which I was placed, or was forced into, not to be able to choose to act otherwise' or, finally, 'I was under orders.'

Against this, most people believe that everyone has at least two choices that he can make, two possibilities that he can realise. When Eichmann says 'I killed Jews because I was ordered to; if I had not done it I would have been killed myself' one can say 'I see that it is improbable that you would have chosen to be killed, but in principle you could have done it if you had decided to do it – there was no literal compulsion, as there is in nature, which caused you to act as you did.' You may say it is unreasonable to expect people to behave like that when facing great dangers: so it is, but however unlikely it may be that they should decide to do so, in the literal sense of the word they *could* have chosen to do so. Martyrdom cannot be expected, but can be accepted, against whatever odds – indeed, that is why it is so greatly admired.

So much for the reasons for which men choose to embrace determinism in history. But if they do, there is a difficult logical consequence, to say the least. It means that we cannot say to anyone, 'Did you have to do that? Why need you have done that?' – the assumption behind which is that he could have refrained, or done something else. The whole of our common morality, in which we speak of obligation and duty, right and wrong, moral praise and blame – the way in which people are praised or condemned, rewarded or punished, for behaving in a way in which they were not forced to behave, when they could have behaved otherwise – this network of beliefs and practices, on which all current morality seems to me to depend, presupposes the notion of responsibility, and responsibility entails the ability to choose between black and white, right and wrong, pleasure and duty; as well as, in a wider sense, between forms of life, forms of government, and the whole constellations of moral values in terms of which most people, however much they may or may not be aware of it, do in fact live.

If determinism were accepted, our vocabulary would have to be very, very radically changed. I do not say that this is impossible in principle, but it goes further than what most people are prepared to face. At best, aesthetics would have to replace morality. You can admire or praise people for being handsome, or generous, or musical – but that is not a matter of their choice, that is 'how they are made'. Moral praise would have to take the same form: if I praise you for saving my life at your own risk, I mean that it is wonderful that you are so made that you could not avoid doing this, and I am glad that I encountered someone literally determined to save my life, as opposed to someone else who was determined to look the other way. Honourable or dishonourable conduct, pleasure-seeking and heroic martyrdom, courage and cowardice, deceitfulness and truthfulness, doing right against temptation – these would become like being good-looking or ugly, tall or short, old or young, black or white, born of English or Italian parents: something that we cannot alter, for everything is determined. We can hope that things will go as we should like, but we cannot do anything towards this – we are so made that we cannot help but act in a particular fashion. Indeed, the very notion of an act denotes choice; but if choice is itself determined, what is the difference between action and mere behaviour?

It seems to me paradoxical that some political movements demand sacrifices and yet are determinist in belief. Marxism, for example, which is founded on historical determinism – the inevitable stages through which society must pass before it reaches perfection – enjoins painful and dangerous acts, coercion and killing, equally painful at times both to the perpetrators and to the victims; but if history will inevitably bring about the perfect society, why should one sacrifice one's life for a process which will, without one's help, reach its proper, happy destination? Yet there is a curious human feeling that if the stars in their courses are fighting for you, so that your cause will triumph, then you should sacrifice yourself in order to shorten the process, to bring the birth-pangs of the new order nearer, as Marx said. But can so many people be truly persuaded to face these dangers, just to shorten a process which will end in happiness whatever they may do or fail to do? This has always puzzled me, and puzzled others.

All this I discussed in the lecture in question, which has remained controversial, and has been much discussed and disputed, and is so still.

The pursuit of the ideal

There is one further topic which I have written about, and that is the very notion of a perfect society, the solution to all our ills. Some of the eighteenth-century French *philosophes* thought the ideal society they hoped for would inevitably come; others were more pessimistic and supposed that human defects would fail to bring it about. Some thought that progress towards it was inexorable, others that only great human effort could achieve it, but might not do so. However this may be, the very notion of the ideal society presupposes the conception of a perfect world in which all the great values in the light of which men have lived for so long can be realised together, at least in principle. Quite apart from the fact that the idea had seemed Utopian to those who thought that such a world could not be achieved because of material or psychological obstacles, or the incurable ignorance, weakness or lack of rationality of men, there is a far more formidable objection to the very notion itself.

I do not know who else may have thought this, but it occurred to me that some ultimate values are compatible with each other and some are not. Liberty, in whichever sense, is an eternal human ideal, whether individual or social. So is equality. But perfect liberty (as it must be in the perfect world) is not compatible with perfect equality. If man is free to do anything he chooses, then the strong will crush the weak, the wolves will eat the sheep, and this puts an end to equality. If perfect equality is to be attained, then men must be prevented from outdistancing each other, whether in material or in intellectual or in spiritual achievement, otherwise inequalities will result. The anarchist Bakunin, who believed in equality above all, thought that universities should be abolished because they bred learned men who behaved as if they were superior to the unlearned, and this propped up social inequalities. Similarly, a world of perfect justice – and who can deny that this is one of the noblest of human values? – is not compatible with perfect mercy. I need not labour this point: either the law takes its toll, or men forgive, but the two values cannot both be realised.

Again, knowledge and happiness may or may not be compatible. Rationalist thinkers have supposed that knowledge always liber-ates, that it saves men from being victims of forces they cannot understand; to some degree this is no doubt true, but if I know that I have cancer I am not thereby made happier, or freer – I must choose between always knowing as much as I can and accepting that there are situations where ignorance may be bliss. Nothing is more attractive than spontaneous creativity, natural vitality, a free flowering of ideas, works of art – but these are not often compatible with a capacity for careful and effective planning, without which no even moderately secure society can be created. Liberty and equality, spontaneity and security, happiness and knowledge, mercy and justice – all these are ultimate human values, sought for themselves alone; yet when they are incompatible, they cannot all be attained, choices must be made, sometimes tragic losses accepted in the pursuit of some preferred ultimate end. But if, as I believe, this is not merely empirically but conceptually true – that is, derives from the very conception of these values – then the very idea of the perfect world in which all good things are realised is incomprehensible, is in fact conceptually incoherent. And if this is so, and I cannot see how it could be otherwise, then the very notion of the ideal world, for which no sacrifice can be too great, vanishes from view.

To go back to the Encyclopaedists and the Marxists and all the other movements the purpose of which is the perfect life: it seems as if the doctrine that all kinds of monstrous cruelties must be permitted, because without these the ideal state of affairs cannot be attained – all the justifications of broken eggs for the sake of the ultimate omelette, all the brutalities, sacrifices, brain-washing, all those revolutions, everything that has made this century perhaps the most appalling of any since the days of old, at any rate in the West – all this is for nothing, for the perfect universe is not merely unattainable but inconceivable, and everything done to bring it about is founded on an enormous intellectual fallacy.

- plurlism, not monism
- empirical responsibility, not utopia
- deontology

THE PURPOSE OF PHILOSOPHY

WHAT IS the subject-matter of philosophy? There is no universally accepted answer to this question. Opinions differ, from those who regard it as contemplation of all time and all existence – the queen of the sciences, the keystone of the entire arch of human knowledge – to those who wish to dismiss it as a pseudo-science exploiting verbal confusions, a symptom of intellectual immaturity, due to be consigned together with theology and other speculative disciplines to the museum of curious antiquities, as astrology and alchemy have long ago been relegated by the victorious march of the natural sciences.

Perhaps the best way of approaching this topic is to ask what constitutes the field of other disciplines. How do we demarcate the province of, say, chemistry or history or anthropology? Here it seems clear that subjects or fields of study are determined by the kind of questions to which they have been invented to provide the answers. The questions themselves are intelligible if, and only if, we know where to look for the answers.

If you ask someone an ordinary question, say 'Where is my coat?', 'Why was Kennedy elected President of the United States?', 'What is the Soviet system of criminal law?', he would normally know how to set about finding an answer. We may not know the answers ourselves, but we know that, in the case of the question about the coat, the proper procedure is to look on the chair, in the cupboard, and so forth. In the case of Kennedy's election or the Soviet system of law we consult writings or specialists for the kind of empirical evidence which leads to the relevant conclusions and renders them, if not certain, at any rate probable.

In other words, we know where to look for the answer: we know what makes some answers plausible and others not. What makes this type of question intelligible in the first place is that we think that the answer can be discovered by empirical means, that is,

by orderly observation or experiment, or methods compounded of
these, namely those of common sense or the natural sciences. There
is another class of questions where we are no less clear about the
proper route by which the answers are to be sought, namely the
formal disciplines: mathematics, for example, or logic, or grammar,
or chess or heraldry, defined in terms of certain fixed axioms and
certain rules of deduction and so on, where the answer to problems
is to be found by applying these rules in the manner prescribed as
correct.

We do not know the correct proof of Fermat's Theorem, for
example – no one is known to have found it – but we know along
what lines to proceed; we know what kind of methods will, and
what kind of methods will not, be relevant to the answer.[1] If
anyone thinks that answers to mathematical problems can be
obtained by looking at green fields or the behaviour of bees, or that
answers to empirical problems can be obtained by pure calculation
without any factual content at all, we would today think them
mistaken to the point of insanity. Each of these major types of _discipline_
question – the factual and the formal – possesses its own specialised _+_
techniques: discoveries by men of genius in these fields, once they _technique_
are established, can be used by men of no genius at all in a semi-
mechanical manner in order to obtain correct results.

The hallmark of these provinces of human thought is that once
the question is put we know in which direction to proceed to try to
obtain the answer. [The history of systematic human thought is
largely a sustained effort to formulate all the questions that occur _human_
to mankind in such a way that the answers to them will fall into _thought and_
one or other of two great baskets: the empirical, that is, questions _the formulation_
whose answers depend, in the end, on the data of observation; and _of questions_
the formal, that is, questions whose answers depend on pure
calculation, untrammelled by factual knowledge.] This dichotomy is
a drastically over-simple formulation – empirical and formal elements are not so easily disentangled – but it contains enough truth
not to be seriously misleading. The distinction between these two
great sources of human knowledge has been recognised since the
first beginnings of self-conscious thinking.

Yet there are certain questions that do not easily fit into this
simple classification. 'What is an okapi?' is answered easily enough

---

[1] Pierre de Fermat died in 1665. This essay was written in 1962. Fermat's Last
Theorem was finally proved by Andrew Wiles in 1994. Ed.

by an act of empirical observation. Similarly 'What is the cube root of 729?' is settled by a piece of calculation in accordance with accepted rules. But if I ask 'What is time?', 'Are all men truly brothers?', how do I set about looking for the answer? If I ask 'Where is my coat?' a possible answer (whether correct or not) would be 'In the cupboard', and we would all know where to look. But if a child asked me 'Where is the image in the mirror?' it would be little use to invite it to look inside the mirror, which it would find to consist of solid glass; or on the surface of the mirror, for the image is certainly not on its surface in the sense in which a postage stamp stuck on it might be; or behind the mirror (which is where the image looks as if it were), for if you look behind the mirror you will find no image there – and so on.

Many who think long enough, and intensely enough, about such questions as 'What is time?' or 'Can time stand still?', 'When I see double, what is there two of?', 'How do I know that other human beings (or material objects) are not mere figments of my own mind?', get into a state of hopeless frustration. 'What is the meaning of "the future tense"?' can be answered by grammarians by mechanically applying formal rules; but if I ask 'What is the meaning of "the future"?', where are we to look for the answer?

There seems to be something queer about all these questions – as wide apart as those about double vision, or number, or the brotherhood of men, or the purposes of life; they differ from the questions in the two baskets in that the question itself does not seem to contain a pointer to the way in which the answer to it is to be found. The other, more ordinary, questions contain precisely such pointers – built-in techniques for finding the answers to them. The questions about time, the existence of others and so on reduce the questioner to perplexity, and annoy practical people precisely because they do not seem to lead to clear answers or useful knowledge of any kind.

This shows that between the two original baskets, the empirical and the formal, there is at least one intermediate basket, in which all those questions live which cannot easily be fitted into the other two. These questions are of the most diverse nature; some appear to be questions of fact, others of value; some are questions about words and a few symbols; others are about methods pursued by those who use them: scientists, artists, critics, common men in the ordinary affairs of life; still others are about the relations between various provinces of knowledge; some deal with the presuppositions of thinking, some with the nature and ends of moral or social or political action.

The only common characteristic which all these questions appear to have is that they cannot be answered by either observation or calculation, by either inductive methods or deductive; and, as a crucial corollary of this, that those who ask them are faced with a perplexity from the very beginning – they do not know where to look for the answers; there are no dictionaries, encyclopaedias, compendia of knowledge, no experts, no orthodoxies which can be referred to with confidence as possessing unquestionable authority or knowledge in these matters. Moreover some of these questions are distinguished by being general and by dealing with matters of principle; and others, while not themselves general, very readily raise or lead to questions of principle.

Such questions tend to be called philosophical. Ordinary men regard them with contempt, or awe, or suspicion, according to their temperaments. For this reason, if for no other, there is a natural tendency to try to reformulate these questions in such a way that all or at any rate parts of them can be answered either by empirical or formal statements; that is to say, efforts, sometimes very desperate ones, are made to fit them into either the empirical or the formal basket, where agreed methods, elaborated over the centuries, yield dependable results whose truth can be tested by accepted means.

The history of human knowledge is, to a large degree, a sustained attempt to shuffle all questions into one of the two 'viable' categories; for as soon as a puzzling, 'queer' question can be translated into one that can be treated by an empirical or a formal discipline, it ceases to be philosophical and becomes part of a recognised science.[1] Thus it was no mistake to regard astronomy in, say, the early Middle Ages as a 'philosophical' discipline: so long as answers to questions about stars and planets were not determined by observation or experiment and calculation, but were dominated by such non-empirical notions as those, for example, of perfect bodies determined to pursue circular paths by their goals or inner essences, with which they were endowed by God or nature,

---

[1] The claims of metaphysics or theology to be sciences must rest on the assumption that intuition or revelation are direct sources of knowledge of facts about the world; since they claim to be forms of direct experience, their data, if their existence is allowed, belong, for our purposes, to the 'empirical' basket.

even if this was rendered improbable by empirical observation, it was not clear how astronomical questions could be settled: that is, what part was to be played by observing actual heavenly bodies, and what part by theological or metaphysical assertions which were not capable of being tested either by empirical or by formal means.

Only when questions in astronomy were formulated in such a manner that clear answers could be discovered by using and depending on the methods of observation and experiment, and these in their turn could be connected in a systematic structure the coherence of which could be tested by purely logical or mathematical means, was the modern science of astronomy created, leaving behind it a cloud of obscure metaphysical notions unconnected with empirical tests and consequently no longer relevant to the new science, and so gradually relegated and forgotten.

So, too, in our own time, such disciplines as economics, psychology, semantics, logic itself, are gradually shaking themselves free from everything that is neither dependent on observation nor formal; if and when they have successfully completed this process they will be finally launched on independent careers of their own as natural or formal sciences, with a rich philosophical past, but an empirical and/or formal present and future. The history of thought is thus a long series of parricides, in which new disciplines seek to achieve their freedom by killing off the parent subjects and eradicating from within themselves whatever traces still linger there of 'philosophical' problems, that is, the kind of questions that do not carry within their own structure clear indications of the techniques of their own solution.

That, at any rate, is the ideal of such sciences; in so far as some of their problems (for example, in modern cosmology) are not formulated in purely empirical or mathematical terms, their field necessarily overlaps with that of philosophy. Indeed, it would be rash to say of any developed high-level science that it has finally eradicated its philosophical problems. In physics, for instance, fundamental questions exist at the present time which in many ways seem philosophical – questions that concern the very framework of concepts in terms of which hypotheses are to be formed and observations interpreted. How are wave-models and particle-models related to one another? Is indeterminacy an ultimate feature of sub-atomic theory? Such questions are of a philosophical type; in particular, no deductive or observational programme leads at all directly to their solution. On the other hand, it is of course true that those who try to answer such questions need to be trained and gifted in physics, and that any answers to these questions would constitute advances in the science of physics itself. Although, with the progressive separation of the positive sciences, no philosophers' questions are physical, some physicists' questions are still philosophical.

This is one reason, but only one, why the scope and content of philosophy does not seem greatly diminished by this process of attrition. For no matter how many questions can be so transformed as to be capable of empirical or formal treatment, the number of questions that seem incapable of being so treated does not appear to grow less. This fact would have distressed the philosophers of the Enlightenment, who were convinced that all genuine questions could be solved by the methods that had achieved so magnificent a triumph in the hands of the natural scientists of the seventeenth and early eighteenth centuries.

It is true that even in that clear day men still appeared no nearer to the solution of such central, indubitably philosophical, because apparently unanswerable, questions as whether men and things had been created to fulfil a purpose by God or by nature, and if so what purpose; whether men were free to choose between alternatives, or on the contrary were rigorously determined by the causal laws that governed inanimate nature; whether ethical and aesthetic truths were universal and objective or relative and subjective; whether men were only bundles of flesh and blood and bone and nervous tissue, or the earthly habitations of immortal souls; whether human history had a discernible pattern, or was a repetitive causal sequence or a succession of casual and unintelligible accidents. These ancient questions tormented them as they had their ancestors in Greece and Rome and Palestine and the medieval West.

Physics and chemistry did not tell one why some men were obliged to obey other men and under what circumstances, and what was the nature of such obligations; what was good and what was evil; whether happiness and knowledge, justice and mercy, liberty and equality, efficiency and individual independence, were equally valid goals of human action, and, if so, whether they were compatible with one another, and if not, which of them were to be chosen, and what were valid criteria for such choices, and how we could be certain about their validity, and what was meant by the notion of validity itself; and many more questions of this type.

Yet – so a good many eighteenth-century philosophers argued – a similar state of chaos and doubt had once prevailed in the realm of the natural sciences too; yet there human genius had finally prevailed and created order.

> Nature, and Nature's laws lay hid in night.
> God said, *Let Newton be!* and all was light.[1]

If Newton could, with a small number of basic laws, enable us, at least in theory, to determine the position and motion of every physical entity in the universe, and in this way abolish at one blow a vast, shapeless mass of conflicting, obscure and only half-intelligible rules of thumb which had hitherto passed for natural knowledge, was it not reasonable to expect that, by applying similar principles to human conduct and the analysis of the nature of man, we should be able to obtain similar clarification and establish the human sciences upon equally firm foundations?

Philosophy fed on the muddles and obscurities of language; if these were cleared away, it would surely be found that the only questions left would be concerned with testable human beliefs, or expressions of identifiable, everyday human needs or hopes or fears or interests. These were the proper study of psychologists, anthropologists, sociologists, economists; all that was needed was a Newton, or series of Newtons, for the sciences of man; in this way the perplexities of metaphysics could once and for all be removed, the idle tribe of philosophical speculators eradicated and, on the ground thus cleared, a clear and firm edifice of natural science built.

This was the hope of all the best-known philosophers of the Enlightenment, from Hobbes and Hume to Helvétius, Holbach, Condorcet, Bentham, Saint-Simon, Comte, and their successors. Yet this programme was doomed to failure. The realm of philosophy was not partitioned into a series of scientific successor states. Philosophical questions continued (and continue) to fascinate and torment enquiring minds.

Why is this so? An illuminating answer to this problem was given by Kant, the first thinker to draw a clear distinction between, on the one hand, questions of fact, and, on the other, questions

---

[1] Alexander Pope, 'Epitaph: Intended for Sir Isaac Newton' (1730).

about the patterns in which these facts presented themselves to us – *facts vs. patterns*
patterns that were not themselves altered however much the facts
themselves, or our knowledge of them, might alter. These patterns
or categories or forms of experience were themselves not the
subject-matter of any possible natural science.

Kant was the first to draw the crucial distinction between facts –
the data of experience, as it were, the things, persons, events,
qualities, relations that we observed or inferred or thought about –
[and the categories in terms of which we sensed and imagined and
reflected about them.] These were, for him, independent of the
different cosmic attitudes – the religious or metaphysical frameworks that belonged to various ages and civilisations. Thus the
majority of Greek philosophers, and most of all Aristotle, thought
that all things had purposes built into them by nature – ends or
goals which they could not but seek to fulfil. The medieval
Christians saw the world as a hierarchy in which every object and
person was called upon to fulfil a specific function by the Divine
Creator; he alone understood the purpose of the entire pattern, and
made the happiness and misery of his creatures depend upon the
degree to which they followed the commandments that were
entailed by the differing purposes for which each entity had been
created – the purposes that in fulfilling themselves realised the
universal harmony, the supreme pattern, the totality of which was
kept from the creatures, and understood by the Creator alone.

The rationalists of the eighteenth and nineteenth centuries saw
no purpose in anything but what man himself had created to serve
his own needs, and regarded all else as determined by the laws of
cause and effect, so that most things pursued no purposes, but were
as they were, and moved and changed as they did, as a matter of
'brute' fact.

These were profoundly different outlooks. Yet those who held
them saw very similar items in the universe, similar colours, tastes,
shapes, forms of motion and rest, experienced similar feelings,
pursued similar goals, acted in similar fashions.

Kant, in his doctrine of our knowledge of the external world,
taught that the categories through which we saw it were identical
for all sentient beings, permanent and unalterable; indeed this is
what made our world one, and communication possible. But some
of those who thought about history, morals, aesthetics, did see
change and differences; what differed was not so much the
empirical content of what these successive civilisations saw or

heard or thought as the basic patterns in which they perceived them, the models in terms of which they conceived them, the category-spectacles through which they viewed them.

The world of a man who believes that God created him for a specific purpose, that he has an immortal soul, that there is an afterlife in which his sins will be visited upon him, is radically different from the world of a man who believes in none of these things; and the reasons for action, the moral codes, the political beliefs, the tastes, the personal relationships of the former will deeply and systematically differ from those of the latter.

Men's views of one another will differ profoundly as a very consequence of their general conception of the world: the notions of cause and purpose, good and evil, freedom and slavery, things and persons, rights, duties, laws, justice, truth, falsehood, to take some central ideas completely at random, depend directly upon the general framework within which they form, as it were, nodal points. Although the facts which are classified and arranged under these notions are not at all identical for all men at all times, yet these differences – which the sciences examine – are not the same as the profounder differences which wearing different sets of spectacles, using different categories, thinking in terms of different models, must make to men of different times and places and cultures and outlooks.

Philosophy, then, is not an empirical study: not the critical examination of what exists or has existed or will exist – this is dealt with by common-sense knowledge and belief, and the methods of the natural sciences. Nor is it a kind of formal deduction, as mathematics or logic is. Its subject-matter is to a large degree not the items of experience, but the ways in which they are viewed, the permanent or semi-permanent categories in terms of which experience is conceived and classified. Purpose versus mechanical causality; organism versus mere amalgams; systems versus mere togetherness; spatiotemporal order versus timeless being; duty versus appetite; value versus fact – these are categories, models, spectacles. Some of these are as old as human experience itself; others are more transient. With the more transient, the philosopher's problems take on a more dynamic and historical aspect. Different models and frameworks, with their attendant obscurities and difficulties, arise at different times. The case of contemporary problems in the explanatory framework of physics, already mentioned, is one example of this. But there are other examples, which affect the thought not just of physicists or other specialists, but of reflective men in general.

In politics, for example, men tried to conceive of their social existence by analogy with various models: Plato at one stage, perhaps following Pythagoras, tried to frame his system of human nature, its attributes and goals, following a geometrical pattern, since he thought it would explain all there was. There followed the biological pattern of Aristotle; the many Christian images with which the writings of the Fathers as well as the Old and New Testaments abound; the analogy of the family, which casts light upon human relations not provided by a mechanical model (say that of Hobbes); the notion of an army on the march with its emphasis on such virtues as loyalty, dedication, obedience, needed to overtake and crush the enemy (with which so much play was made in the Soviet Union); the notion of the State as a traffic policeman and night-watchman preventing collisions and looking after property, which is at the back of much individualist and liberal thought; the notion of the State as much more than this – as a great co-operative endeavour of individuals seeking to fulfil a common end, and therefore as entitled to enter into every nook and cranny of human experience, that animates much of the 'organic' thought of the nineteenth century; the systems borrowed from psychology, or from theories of games, that are in vogue at present – all these are models in terms of which human beings, groups and societies and cultures, have conceived of their experience.

These models often collide; some are rendered inadequate by failing to account for too many aspects of experience, and are in their turn replaced by other models which emphasise what these last have omitted, but in their turn may obscure what the others have rendered clear. The task of philosophy, often a difficult and painful one, is to extricate and bring to light the hidden categories and models in terms of which human beings think (that is, their use of words, images and other symbols), to reveal what is obscure or contradictory in them, to discern the conflicts between them that prevent the construction of more adequate ways of organising and describing and explaining experience (for all description as well as explanation involves some model in terms of which the describing and explaining is done); and then, at a still 'higher' level, to examine the nature of this activity itself (epistemology, philosophical logic, linguistic analysis), and to bring to light the concealed models that operate in this second-order, philosophical, activity itself.

If it is objected that all this seems very abstract and remote from daily experience, something too little concerned with the central interests, the happiness and unhappiness and ultimate fate, of ordinary men, the answer is that this charge is false. Men cannot live without seeking to describe and explain the universe to themselves. The models they use in doing this must deeply affect their lives, not least when they are unconscious; much of the misery and frustration of men is due to the mechanical or unconscious, as well as deliberate, application of models where they do not work. Who can say how much suffering has been caused by the exuberant use of the organic model in politics, or the comparison of the State to a work of art, and the representation of the dictator as the inspired moulder of human lives, by totalitarian theorists in our own times? Who shall say how much harm and how much good, in previous ages, came of the exaggerated application to social relations of metaphors and models fashioned after the patterns of paternal authority, especially to the relations of rulers of States to their subjects, or of priests to the laity?

If there is to be any hope of a rational order on earth, or of a just appreciation of the many various interests that divide diverse groups of human beings – knowledge that is indispensable to any attempt to assess their effects, and the patterns of their interplay and its consequences, in order to find viable compromises through which men may continue to live and satisfy their desires without thereby crushing the equally central desires and needs of others – it lies in the bringing to light of these models, social, moral, political, and above all the underlying metaphysical patterns in which they are rooted, with a view to examining whether they are adequate to their task.

The perennial task of philosophers is to examine whatever seems insusceptible to the methods of the sciences or everyday observation, for example, categories, concepts, models, ways of thinking or acting, and particularly ways in which they clash with one another, with a view to constructing other, less internally contradictory and (though this can never be fully attained) less pervertible metaphors, images, symbols and systems of categories. It is certainly a reasonable hypothesis that one of the principle causes of confusion, misery and fear is, whatever may be its psychological or social roots, blind adherence to outworn notions, pathological suspicion of any form of critical self-examination, frantic efforts to prevent any degree of rational analysis of what we live by and for.

This socially dangerous, intellectually difficult, often agonising and thankless but always important activity is the work of philosophers, whether they deal with the natural sciences or moral or political or purely personal issues. The goal of philosophy is always the same, to assist men to understand themselves and thus operate in the open, and not wildly, in the dark.

THE PHILOSOPHERS
OF THE ENLIGHTENMENT

PHILOSOPHICAL PROBLEMS arise when men ask questions of themselves or of others which, though very diverse, have certain characteristics in common. These questions tend to be very general, to involve issues of principle, and to have little or no concern with practical utility. But what is even more characteristic of them is that there seem to be no obvious and generally accepted procedures for answering them, nor any class of specialists to whom we automatically turn for the solutions. Indeed there is something peculiar about the questions themselves: those who ask them do not seem any too certain about what kind of answers they require, or indeed how to set about finding them.

To give an illustration: if we ask 'Were any ravens seen in Iceland in 1955?' we know how to set about answering such a question – the correct answer must obviously be based on observation, and the naturalist is the expert to whom we can appeal. But when men ask questions like 'Are there any material objects in the universe (or does it, perhaps, consist rather of minds and their states)?', what steps do we take to settle this? Yet outwardly there is a similarity between the two sentences. Or again, supposing I ask 'Did the battle of Waterloo take place in the seventeenth century?', we know how to look for the relevant evidence, but what are we to do when asked 'Did the universe have a beginning in time?'? We know how to answer 'Are you quite certain that he knows you?' But if someone wonders 'Can I ever be quite certain about what goes on in the mind of another?', how do we satisfy him? It is easier to reply to 'Why is Einstein's theory superior to Newton's?' than to 'Why are the predictions of scientists more reliable than those of witch-doctors?' (or vice versa), or to 'How many positive roots are there of the equation $x^2 = 2$?' than to 'Are there irrational numbers?', or to 'What is the exact meaning of the word "obscurantist"?' than to 'What is the exact meaning of the word "if"?' 'How should I mend this broken typewriter?' seems different in kind from 'How should I (or men in general) live?'

In each case the attempt to answer the second question of the pair somehow seems to encounter an obstacle. There is not, as there is for the first member of the pair, a well-attested, generally accepted method of discovering the solution. And yet questions of this kind seem definite enough, and have proved, to some men, very puzzling and indeed tormenting. Why, then, is there such difficulty in arriving at answers which settle the matter once and for all, so that the problems do not crop up afresh in each generation? This failure to provide definite solutions creates the impression that there is no progress in philosophy, merely subjective differences of opinion, with no objective criteria for the discovery of the truth.

The history of such questions, and of the means employed to provide the answers, is, in effect, the history of philosophy. The frame of ideas within which, and the methods by which, various thinkers at various times try to arrive at the truth about such issues – the very ways in which the questions themselves are construed – change under the influence of many forces, among them answers given by philosophers of an earlier age, the prevailing moral, religious and social beliefs of the period, the state of scientific knowledge, and, not least important, the methods used by the scientists of the time, especially if they have achieved spectacular successes, and have, therefore, bound their spell upon the imagination of their own and later generations.

One of the principal characteristics of such questions – and this seems to have become clearer only in our own day – is that, whatever else they may be, they are neither empirical nor formal. That is to say, philosophical questions cannot be answered by adducing the results of observation or experience, as empirical questions, whether of science or of common sense, are answered. Such questions as 'What is the supreme good?' or 'How can I be sure that your sensations are similar to mine? Or that I ever genuinely understand what you are saying, and do not merely seem to myself to do so?' cannot be, on the face of it, answered by either of the two great instruments of human knowledge: empirical investigation on the one hand, and, on the other, deductive reasoning as it is used in the formal disciplines – the kind of argument which occurs, for example, in mathematics or logic or grammar.

Indeed it might almost be said that the history of philosophy in its relation to the sciences consists, in part, in the disentangling of those questions which are either empirical (and inductive) or formal (and deductive) from the mass of problems which fill the minds of men, and the sorting out of these under the heads of the empirical or formal sciences concerned with them. It is in this way that, for instance, astronomy, mathematics, psychology, biology and the rest became divorced from the general corpus of philosophy (of which they once formed a part), and embarked upon fruitful careers of their own as independent disciplines. They remained within the province of philosophy only so long as the kinds of way in which their problems were to be settled remained unclear, so that they were liable to be confused with other problems with which they had relatively little in common, and their differences from which had not been sufficiently discerned. The advance both of the sciences and of philosophy seems bound up with this progressive allocation of the empirical and formal elements, each to its own proper sphere; always, however, leaving behind a nucleus of unresolved (and largely unanalysed) questions, whose generality, obscurity and, above all, apparent (or real) insolubility by empirical or formal methods gives them a status of their own which we tend to call philosophical.

Realisation of this truth (if it be one) was a long time in arriving. The natural tendency was to regard philosophical questions as being on a level with other questions, and answerable by similar means; especially by means which had been successful in answering these other questions, which in fact did turn out to be either empirical or a priori, even though the distinction between the two was not always consciously drawn. When some branch of human enquiry, say physics or biology, won notable successes by employing this or that new and fertile technique, an attempt was invariably made to apply analogous techniques to philosophical problems also, with results, fortunate and unfortunate, which are a permanent element in the history of human thought. Thus the unprecedented successes of the mathematical method in the seventeenth century left a mark on philosophy, not merely because mathematics had not clearly been discriminated from philosophy at this time, but because mathematical techniques – deduction from 'self-evident' axioms according to fixed rules, tests of internal consistency, a priori methods, standards of clarity and rigour proper to mathematics – were applied to philosophy also; with the result that this particular model dominates the philosophy as well as the natural science of the period. This led to notable successes and equally notable failures, as the over-enthusiastic and fanatical application of techniques rich in results in one field, when mechanically applied to another, not necessarily similar to the first, commonly does.

If the model that dominated the seventeenth century was mathematical, it is the mechanical model, more particularly that of the Newtonian system, that is everywhere imitated in the century that followed. Philosophical questions are in fact *sui generis*, and resemble questions of mechanics no more closely than those of mathematics (or of biology or psychology or history); nevertheless the effect upon philosophy of one model is very different from that of another; and it is the influence of this new model that links the otherwise often very different eighteenth-century philosophers.

The eighteenth century is perhaps the last period in the history of Western Europe when human omniscience was thought to be an attainable goal. The unparalleled progress of physics and mathematics in the previous century transformed the generally held view of the nature of the material world, and, still more, of the nature of true knowledge, to such a degree that this epoch still stands like a barrier between us and the ages which preceded it, and makes the philosophical ideas of the Middle Ages, and even the Renaissance, seem remote, fanciful and, at times, almost unintelligible. The application of mathematical techniques – and language – to the measurable properties of what the senses revealed became the sole true method of discovery and of exposition. Descartes and Spinoza, Leibniz and Hobbes all seek to give their reasoning a structure of a mathematical kind. What can be said must be stable in quasi-mathematical terms, for language less precise may turn out to conceal the fallacies and obscurities, the confused mass of superstitions and prejudices, which characterised the discredited theological or other forms of dogmatic doctrine about the universe which the new science had come to sweep away and supersede. This mood persists into the eighteenth century, Newton's influence being the strongest single factor. Newton had performed the unprecedented task of explaining the material world, that is of making it possible by means of relatively few fundamental laws of immense scope and power to determine, at least in principle, the properties and behaviour of every particle of every material body in the universe, and that with a degree of precision and simplicity undreamt of before. Order and clarity now reigned in the realm of physical science:

> Nature, and Nature's laws lay hid in night.
> God said, *Let Newton be!* and all was light.[1]

   Yet the ancient disciplines of metaphysics, logic, ethics, and all that related to the social life of men, still lay in chaos, governed by the confusions of thought and language of an earlier and unregenerate age. It was natural, and indeed almost inevitable, that those who had been liberated by the new sciences should seek to apply their methods and principles to a subject which was clearly in even more desperate need of order than the facts of the external world. Indeed this task was of crucial importance: for without a true and clear picture of the principal 'faculties' and operations of the human mind, one could not be certain how much credence to give to various types of thought or reasoning, nor how to determine the sources and limits of human knowledge, nor the relationships between its varieties. But unless this was known the claims of ignoramuses and charlatans could not be properly exposed; nor the new picture of the material world adequately related to other matters of interest to men – moral conduct, aesthetic principles, laws of history and of social and political life, the 'inner' workings of the passions and the imagination, and all the other issues of central interest to human beings. A science of nature had been created; a science of mind had yet to be made. The goal in both cases must remain the same: the formulation of general laws on the basis of observation ('inner' and 'outer') and, when necessary, experiment; and the deduction from such laws, when established, of specific conclusions. To every genuine question there were many false answers, and only one that was true; once discovered, it was final, it remained for ever true; all that was needed was a reliable method of discovery. A method which answered to this description had been employed by 'the incomparable Mr Newton';[2] his emulators in the realm of the human mind would reap a harvest no less rich if they followed similar precepts.

---

[1] loc. cit. (p. 30 above, note 1).

[2] John Locke, *An Essay concerning Human Understanding*, 'Epistle to the Reader'.

If the laws were correct, the observations upon which they were based authentic, and the inferences sound, then true and impregnable conclusions would provide knowledge of hitherto unexplored realms, and transform the present welter of ignorance and idle conjecture into a clear and coherent system of logically interrelated elements – the theoretical copy or analogue of the divine harmony of nature, concealed from the view by human ignorance or idleness or perversity. To comprehend it is, for a rational creature, tantamount to conforming to it in all one's beliefs and actions; for this alone can make men happy and rational and free.

It was essential to guarantee the efficacy of the instruments of investigation before its results could be trusted. This epistemological bias characterised European philosophy from Descartes' formulation of his method of doubt until well into the nineteenth century, and is still a strong tendency in it. The direct application of the results of this investigation of the varieties and scope of human knowledge to such traditional disciplines as politics, ethics, metaphysics and theology, with a view to ending their perplexities once and for all, is the programme which philosophers of the eighteenth century attempted to carry through. The principles which they attempted to apply were the new scientific canons of the seventeenth century; there was to be no a priori deduction from 'natural' principles, hallowed in the Middle Ages, without experimental evidence – principles such as that all bodies come to rest when no longer under the influence of any force, or that the 'natural' path sought after by heavenly bodies, in the quest for self-fulfilment, is necessarily circular. The laws of Kepler or Galileo contradicted these 'natural' principles, on the basis of observation (the vast mass of data, for instance, accumulated by the Danish astronomer Tycho Brahe) and experiment (of the kind conducted by Galileo himself).

This use of observation and experiment entailed the application of exact methods of measurement, and resulted in the linking together of many diverse phenomena under laws of great precision, generally formulated in mathematical terms. Consequently only the measurable aspects of reality were to be treated as real – those susceptible to equations connecting the variations in one aspect of a phenomenon with measurable variations in other phenomena. The whole notion of nature as compounded of irreducibly different qualities and unbridgeable 'natural' kinds was to be finally discarded. The Aristotelian category of final cause – the explanation of phenomena in terms of the 'natural' tendency of every object to fulfil its own inner end or purpose, which was also to be the answer to the question of why it existed, and what function it was attempting to fulfil (notions for which no experimental or observational evidence can in principle be discovered) – was abandoned as unscientific, and, indeed, in the case of inanimate entities without wills or purposes, as literally unintelligible. Laws formulating regular concomitances of phenomena – the observed order and conjunctions of things and events – were sufficient, without introducing impalpable entities and forces, to describe all that is describable, and predict all that is predictable, in the universe. Space, time, mass, force, momentum, rest – the terms of mechanics – are to take the place of final causes, substantial forms, divine purpose and other metaphysical notions. Indeed the apparatus of medieval ontology and theology were to be altogether abandoned in favour of a symbolism referring to those aspects of the universe which are given to the senses, or can be measured or inferred in some other way.

   This attitude is exceedingly clear in the works not only of Locke and Hume, who had a profound respect for natural science, but also in those of Berkeley, who was deeply concerned to deny its metaphysical presuppositions. To all of them the model was that of contemporary physics and mechanics. The world of matter, for Newton, and indeed for those pre-Newtonian physicists with whose works Locke was probably acquainted rather better, was to be described in terms of uniform particles, and the laws of its behaviour were the laws of the interaction of these particles. The British empiricist philosophers, whose work gradually came to dominate European thought, applied this conception to the mind. The mind was treated as if it were a box containing mental equivalents of the Newtonian particles. These were called 'ideas'. These 'ideas' are distinct and separate entities, 'simple', possessing no parts into which they can be split, that is, literally atomic, having their origin somewhere in the external world, dropping into the mind like so many grains of sand inside an hour-glass; there, in some way, they either continue in isolation, or are compounded to form complexes, in the way in which material objects in the outer world are compounded out of complexes of molecules or atoms. Locke attempts something like the history of the genesis of ideas in our minds and an account of their movement within it, their association and dissociation from each other, like a contemporary chemist analysing the ingredients and physical behaviour of a compound substance.

Thought, at least reflective thought, is for Locke a kind of inner eye corresponding to the outer physical eye which takes in the external world. When Locke defines knowledge as 'the perception of the connection and agreement or disagreement and repugnancy, of any of our ideas',[1] this 'perception' is conceived by him as something which inspects two ideas as if they were discriminable particles; the inner eye is then able to see whether they agree or not, and so whether the proposition asserting their connection is or is not true, much as the outer eye can inspect two coloured objects and see whether the colours match each other or not. When Berkeley criticises Locke's theory of abstract general ideas, what he is principally attacking is the notion that there can be an idea which is not an absolutely determinate image, since ideas are entities; and 'abstract ideas', as invoked by Locke in order to explain how general terms mean, seem to Berkeley a contradiction in terms, because if they are ideas, they must be concrete entities, and cannot also be abstract, that is, not determinate, not having any particular properties given to the senses or the imagination. Whether his attack upon Locke is fair or not, what is characteristic is the assumption common to both (and to Hume and many other contemporary empiricists, particularly in France) that the mind is a container within which ideas circulate like counters and form patterns as they would in a complicated slot-machine; three-dimensional Newtonian space has its counterpart in the inner 'space' of the mind over which the inner eye – the faculty of reflection – presides.

Philosophy, therefore, is to be converted into a natural science. The facts with which it is to deal are to be discovered by introspection. Like every other genuine human investigation it must begin with empirical observation. Hume echoes this: 'As the science of man is the only solid foundation for the other sciences, so, the only solid foundation we can give to this science itself must be laid on experience and observation.'[2] Philosophy is in reality a kind of scientific psychology; among the extreme followers of this doctrine, particularly in France, it becomes a kind of physiology –

[1] *An Essay concerning Human Understanding*, book 4, chapter 1, section 2.
[2] *A Treatise of Human Nature*, Introduction.

an early version of behaviourism or 'physicalism'. The French disciples of Locke and Hume – Condillac, Helvétius, La Mettrie – push this to extreme limits. Condillac undertakes to reconstruct every human experience – the most complex and sophisticated thoughts or 'movements of the soul', the most elaborate play of the imagination, the most subtle scientific speculation – out of 'simple' ideas, that is, sensations classifiable as being given to one or the other of our normal senses, each of which can, as it were, be pinpointed and assigned to its rightful place in the stream of sensations. The great popularisers of the age, whose writings reached educated readers in many lands beyond the borders of their native France, headed by Voltaire, Diderot, Holbach, Condorcet and their followers, whatever their other differences, were agreed upon the crucial importance of this sensationalist approach. There are 'organic' – anti-atomic – notions in the writings of Diderot as well as in those of Maupertuis or Bordeu, and some of these may have influenced Kant; but the dominant trend is in favour of analysing everything into ultimate, irreducible atomic constituents, whether physical or psychological.

Hume, who believes that the sciences of 'Mathematics, Natural Philosophy [that is, natural science], and Natural Religion, are in some measure dependent on the science of man',[1] believes this because the task of philosophy is to deal with the ultimate ingredients of all that there is. His theory of the mind is mechanistic, and conceived by analogy with Newton's theory of gravitational attraction, the association of ideas being called upon to perform the same function in the mind as gravitation does in the material world. This association of ideas is described by him as 'a kind of Attraction, which in the mental world will be found to have as extraordinary effects as in the natural, and to show itself in as many and as various forms'.[2] La Mettrie conceives the true philosopher as a kind of engineer who can take to pieces the apparatus that is the human mind; Voltaire describes him as an excellent anatomist, who (he is speaking in praise of Locke) can explain human reason as he can explain the springs of the human body. Scientific images abound in the philosophical treatises of the French *philosophes* and their disciples in other countries; nature, which was conceived as an organism by Butler at the beginning of

---

[1] loc. cit (p. 43 above, note 2).   [2] ibid., book 1, part 1, section 4.

the century, was compared to a watch by Paley half a century later. 'Natural morality' and 'natural religion' (common to all men, but more evident in the least corrupt – rural or primitive – societies) can be studied scientifically like the life of plants or animals. Diderot compares social life to a great workshop factory.

Berkeley, so far from finding this empiricism unpalatable because he is a Christian and a bishop, on the contrary finds it alone compatible with the spiritualism which impregnates all his beliefs. For him Locke is, if anything, not empiricist enough. And, in a sense, Berkeley is right; the science of the seventeenth century, which Locke admires and which he seems to apply to mental phenomena, was anything but strictly empiricist. On the contrary, the world of the senses is regarded by Galileo and Descartes as vague, deceptive and blurred, full of phenomena describable only in qualitative terms, that is, not admissible in a properly quantitative, scientific world-picture. The 'primary' qualities with which the sciences deal are not themselves directly given to the senses.

There are two domains: [the quantitative, precisely measurable domain of objects in space, possessing such properties as motion and rest, determinate shape, solidity, specific temperatures (which are the motions of particles) and so forth, is contrasted with the domain of colours, smells and tastes, degree of warmth and cold, loud and soft sounds and the rest, which are subjective, and therefore unreliable.] Locke, who starts from the principle that we have no knowledge except that which comes from the senses, finds it difficult to explain why the 'primary' qualities, which for him must, if he is to be consistent, depend as much on the evidence of the senses as the 'secondary' ones, should nevertheless be accorded the kind of primacy and authority which physical science seemed to give them. So he alternates between inconsistency and half-hearted attempts to represent the secondary qualities as in some way generated by the primary ones, which are not so much themselves sensible as somehow causally responsible for the data of the senses. He finds himself in similar difficulties with regard to material substance, which for the physicists was certainly something not directly given to the senses, nor anything that could be so given, and must therefore be unacceptable to strict empiricism.

Berkeley quite consistently rejects attempts at the 'appeasement' of physics, and rejects all efforts at compromise with its alleged demands. Indeed he looks at such dualism as incompatible with the out-and-out empiricism which he advocates. The contrast between subjective sensations and objective properties of matter is specious. The senses are the sole source of knowledge. The world consists of thoughts, feelings, sensations – 'ideas' in the minds of agents, of God and his creatures, men. Beyond that there is nothing, at least so far as the material world is concerned. He combines a consistent empiricism with regard to the material world with belief in the reality of spiritual substances – eternal souls or spirits – active beings, whose existence does not depend, as that of passive entities must, on being sensed, or being otherwise the content of someone's experience: substances of which we possess not 'ideas' but (as his predecessors in the seventeenth century had called this non-sensible awareness) 'notions', which may also embrace relations, since these are, apparently, not sensible either. His position in this regard – a peculiar union of Platonism and sensationalism – is not as inconsistent as it has too often been taken to be by his critics from Hume onwards.

For Berkeley the notion of external substances so cut off from possible sensible experience that no idea of them can in principle be formed is unintelligible. He is at once a complete spiritualist and a consistent sensationalist. His whole argument rests upon the view that, if we do not allow ourselves to be befuddled by scientific terminology which suggests the existence of imperceptible matter, while at the same time basing all our knowledge upon the evidence of what can be perceived and it alone, we shall arrive at the orthodox Christian position that the universe is spiritual in character. Whereas for Locke and Hume mathematics represents the most perfect form of knowledge – indeed the ideal of lucidity and impregnable certainty, in comparison with which all other claims to knowledge are defective – for Berkeley mathematics suggests that there are mythological entities which have no existence in the world. Geometrical figures for Berkeley are not ideal entities, free from the need that all real entities have to justify themselves by empirical observation, but are the contents of sensation no less than anything else. A line consists of a certain, in principle countable, number of *minima sensibilia* – and if it consists of an odd number of these, cannot be precisely bisected, whatever geometers may say. This eccentric view is interesting if only as evidence of what extremes empiricism and nominalism can reach.

Both Locke and Hume hold a more plausible view of mathematics, and although their accounts of mathematical reasoning are not altogether convincing, they realise no less clearly than Leibniz the difference between it and statements of empirical fact. Hume, in particular, is clear about the difference between statements of formal entailment, that is, those of logic and arithmetic or algebra (he is confused and hesitant about geometry), and those of a factual kind, that is, those asserting existence. Indeed, his major achievement rests precisely on the recognition that since such notions as necessity and identity, strictly interpreted, belong to the world of formal disciplines – what the rationalists had called 'truths of reason', known to be such because their contradictories are self-contradictory (as opposed to 'truths of fact', which cannot be tested by any purely formal process) – they have no place in the realm of statements about the world, the assumption that they have being largely responsible for the very existence of the false science of metaphysics.

Necessity and identity are relations not to be discovered either by observation of the external world, or by introspection, or by any combinations of the data of these 'faculties'. They are, therefore, not real relations uniting real entities, or discoverable in the real world. Knowledge must therefore be of two types: either it claims to be 'necessary', in which case it rests on formal criteria and can give no information about the world. Or it does claim to give information about the world, in which case it can be no more than probable, and is never infallible; it cannot have certainty, if what we mean by this is the kind of certainty achieved only by logic or by mathematics. This distinction between the two types of assertion, closely related to the distinction between 'synthetic' and 'analytic', 'a posteriori' and 'a priori', is the beginning of the great controversy which awakened Kant from his dogmatic slumber and transformed the history of modern philosophy.

The heroic attempt to make philosophy a natural science was brought to an end by the great break with the traditions both of rationalism and of empiricism as they had developed hitherto, inaugurated by Kant, whose philosophical views are the source of much of the thought of the nineteenth century. It was he who first grasped firmly the truth that the task of philosophy is – and has always been – not to seek answers to empirical questions of fact, which are answered by the special sciences, or at another level by ordinary common sense. Nor can it be a purely deductive discipline as used by the formal sciences such as logic or mathematics. He was the first great philosopher to realise that the principal questions of philosophy are neither those for which there is a clear method of solution by empirical investigation (for example, the question of the genesis of our ideas – the attempt to find out where they 'come from', which is a question for psychologists, physiologists, anthropologists and the like), nor those to be answered by deduction from self-evident or a priori axioms, as had been held by the schoolmen and rationalists; for what is self-evident – or a matter of faith and direct revelation – to one person may not be so to another. Kant rightly held that mere deduction cannot add to our knowledge either of things or of persons; and does not answer those questions, or solve those puzzles, which seem characteristically philosophical. The questions which he asked, and the methods which he employed (whether valid or not), were concerned rather with analysing our most general and pervasive concepts and categories. He distinguished the types of statements we make in the light of the kinds of evidence they require, and the relations to each other of the concepts which they presuppose.

Kant is particularly clear on an issue confusion about which lies at the heart of the major fallacies of eighteenth-century philosophy, namely that questions concerning types of judgements and kinds of categories involved in normal experiences are far from identical with questions about the 'sources' of our data or beliefs or attitudes. It is obvious that there must be differences of logical principle (and not merely of origin) between such propositions as 'Every event has a cause' or 'This sheet of paper cannot be both blue and brown in the same place at the same time', on the one hand, and such propositions as 'There are no snakes in Ireland' or 'I had a headache yesterday', on the other. If someone doubts whether every event has a cause, or whether Pythagoras' theorem is true, or whether this piece of paper is both brown and blue at the same time, it is useless to accumulate for his benefit more and more instances of, say, events in this or that relation to one another; or more and more right-angled triangles together with instruments for measuring the areas of the squares on the sides; or further sheets of paper, some entirely brown, others entirely blue, but none simultaneously and wholly both. These methods of confuting the doubter are useless, because the way to convince someone of the truth of such propositions is clearly quite different from the way in which we demonstrate the truth of factual propositions about the world, that is, by the production of empirical evidence of some kind. The question here is 'What is the correct sort of evidence or guarantee which one should produce for the truth of such and such a proposition?', and this is altogether different from such a question as 'How do I, or you (or men in general) come to learn the truth of such and such a proposition?' The answer to this last question is one of genetic psychology, and depends on many empirical accidents and vicissitudes of a man's life. It is characteristic of the great classical empiricists (even of Hume, who was so keenly aware of differences of logical type, and so triumphantly, and with such devastating results, proved that precisely because inductive argument could never be rendered deductive, therefore there was a sense in which certainty was impossible about matters of fact) that they confused these two questions, and supposed that a certain kind of answer to the latter question – the question of the genesis of knowledge or of ways of learning – automatically entailed a certain sort of answer to the first, namely the question of what was the correct procedure for establishing the truth of, and what concepts were involved in, a given proposition.

This confusion emerges in the way in which these philosophers tend to conflate these two distinct questions into one unclear enquiry, 'How can we know proposition X?', which is neither 'What is the right evidence for, or proof of, propositions like X?' nor yet 'Whence do we acquire the knowledge (or impression) of X?' One of the best examples of this muddle is to be found in the first book of Locke's *Essay*, where he tells us that children, for example, are not born with the knowledge of the law of non-contradiction, and seems to think that this proves something about the logical status of such propositions. The question of the sources of knowledge is one of fact, and the empiricists who, following Hobbes or Locke, argued that it was neither 'innate', that is, 'imprinted' on the mind before birth by God or nature, nor derived by 'intuition', that is, some channel other than and superior to the senses, were in effect saying that the answer to this question could be provided only by psychology, correctly conceived as an empirical science. It was the attempt to show that philosophy consisted in this empirical procedure (for if it is not to be based on observation, what value can it have?) that led to some of the most illuminating insights of eighteenth-century thought, as well as the major fallacy which vitiates it – the identification of philosophy with science.

Kant himself is by no means free from this kind of error; nevertheless, he did shift the centre of philosophical emphasis from the two questions 'What is deducible from what?' and 'What entities are there in the world, whether outside, or in, the mind?' to an examination of the most general concepts and categories in terms of which we think and reason – frames of reference or systems of relations like space, time, number, causality, material thinghood, of which we seem unable to divest ourselves save very partially, even in imagination, and which are not dealt with in the textbooks devoted to special sciences, because they are too universal and too pervasive, and, *prima facie* at any rate, do not fit into any classification, either empirical or formal. The history of philosophy has largely consisted in dealing with such questions, whose subject-matter is difficult to classify; in seeking to solve, or at least to elucidate, puzzles which haunt many men's minds in a way quite different from perplexities within the field of some special science, where the method of finding the answer, however difficult, is not itself a puzzle. These philosophical problems change from one age to another, representing no straight line of progress (or retrogression), as human thought and language change under the impact of the factors which determine the forms and the concepts in which men think, feel, communicate – factors which seem to pursue no regular pattern of a discernible kind.

These considerations were relatively remote from the minds of the great empirical philosophers of the eighteenth century. To them everything seemed far clearer than it can ever have done to any but a very few of their successors. What science had achieved in the sphere of the material world, it could surely achieve also in the sphere of the mind; and further, in the realm of social and political relations. The rational scheme on which Newton had so conclusively demonstrated the physical world to be constructed, and with which Locke and Hume and their French disciples seemed well on the way to explaining the inner worlds of thought and emotion, could be applied to the social sphere as well. Men were objects in nature no less than trees and stones; their interaction could be studied in the same way as that of atoms or plants. Once the laws governing human behaviour were discovered and incorporated in a science of rational sociology, analogous to physics or zoology, men's real wishes could be investigated and brought to light, and satisfied by the most efficient means compatible with the nature of the physical and mental facts. Nature was a cosmos: in it there could be no disharmonies; and since such questions as what to do, how to live, what would make men just or rational or happy, were all factual questions, the true answers to any one of them could not be incompatible with true answers to any of the others. The ideal of creating a wholly just, wholly virtuous, wholly satisfied society was therefore no longer Utopian.

Nor is this view confined to the natural scientists and their allies and spokesmen. It was held no less confidently by the rationalist followers of Leibniz and his disciple Wolff. They held that rational thought was a means of obtaining truth about the universe vastly superior to empirical methods. But they also believed, if anything even more strongly than their empiricist adversaries, that the truth was one single, harmonious body of knowledge; that all previous systems – religions, cosmologies, mythologies – were but so many different roads, some longer or wider, some more twisted and darker, to the same rational goal; that all the sciences and all the faiths, the most fanatical superstitions and the most savage customs, when 'cleansed' of their irrational elements by the advance of civilisation, can be harmonised in the final true philosophy which could solve all theoretical and practical problems, for all men, everywhere, for all time. This noble faith animated Lessing, who believed in reason, and Turgot, who believed in the sciences, Moses Mendelssohn, who believed in God, and Condorcet, who did not. Despite great differences of temperament and outlook and belief this was the common ground. Theists and atheists, believers in automatic progress and sceptical pessimists, hard-boiled French materialists and sentimental German poets and thinkers seemed united in the conviction that all problems were soluble by the discovery of objective answers, which once found – and why should they not be? – would be clear for all to see and valid eternally. It is true that dissident voices, first in Germany, then in England, were beginning to be raised in the middle of the century, maintaining that neither men nor their societies were analogous to inanimate objects or even to the zoological kingdom; and that the attempt to deal with them as if they were would necessarily lead to disaster. Johnson and Burke, Hamann and Herder (and to some degree even Montesquieu and Hume) began the revolt which was destined to grow in strength. But these remained isolated doubts.

A very great deal of good, undoubtedly, was done, suffering mitigated, injustice avoided or prevented, ignorance exposed, by the conscientious attempt to apply scientific methods to the regulation of human affairs. Dogmas were refuted, prejudices and superstitions were pilloried successfully. The growing conviction that appeals to mystery and darkness and authority to justify arbitrary behaviour were, all too often, so many unworthy alibis concealing self-interest or intellectual indolence or stupidity was often triumphantly vindicated. But the central dream, the demonstration that everything in the world moved by mechanical means, that all evils could be cured by appropriate technological steps, that there could exist engineers both of human souls and of human bodies, proved delusive. Nevertheless, it proved less misleading in the end than the attacks upon it in the nineteenth century by means of arguments equally fallacious, but with implications that were, both intellectually and politically, more sinister and oppressive. The intellectual power, honesty, lucidity, courage and disinterested love of the truth of the most gifted thinkers of the eighteenth century remain to this day without parallel. Their age is one of the best and most hopeful episodes in the life of mankind.

ONE OF THE BOLDEST INNOVATORS
IN THE HISTORY OF HUMAN THOUGHT

GIAMBATTISTA VICO died in 1744, and since then has remained a peculiar figure in the history of thought. Famous in the country of his birth, his name is scarcely known outside its frontiers. As for his ideas, they are seldom mentioned even among professional philosophers, at any rate in English-speaking countries. Yet he is one of the boldest innovators in the history of human thought. Such fame as he had was mainly due to two men: the historian Jules Michelet, who said of him near the end of his life, 'I had no master but Vico. His principle of living force, of *humanity creating itself*, made both my book and my teaching',[1] and the philosopher Benedetto Croce, who celebrated his genius tirelessly throughout his long and productive activity. Nevertheless, Vico was in his own time, and he remains in ours, at the periphery of the central philosophical tradition. He has not entered the canon; he remains among the apocrypha – a queer, isolated figure, of interest to specialists in the philosophy of history or in Italian thought and literature, or to the students of the early eighteenth century. Like Berlioz half a century ago among composers, or Piero della Francesca in the nineteenth century among painters, he is a master passionately admired by a small minority, but dismissed with a few sentences by the majority of writers on the subject.

Yet Vico's achievements are astonishing. He put forward audacious and important ideas about the nature of man and of human society; he attacked current notions of the nature of knowledge, of which he revealed, or at least identified, a central, hitherto undiscussed variety; he virtually invented the idea of culture; his theory of mathematics had to wait until our own

[1] Preface of 1869 to *L'Histoire de France*: vol. 4, p. 14, in Jules Michelet, *Oeuvres complètes*, ed. Paul Viallaneix (Paris, 1971–); quoted in M. H. Fisch's admirable introduction to *The Autobiography of Giambattista Vico*, trans. Max Harold Fisch and Thomas Goddard Bergin (Ithaca, New York, 1944), p. 79.

century to be recognised as revolutionary; he anticipated the aesthetics of romantics and historicists, and almost transformed the subject; he virtually invented comparative anthropology and philology, and inaugurated the new approach to history and the social sciences that this entailed; his notions of language, myth, law, symbolism, and the relation of social to cultural evolution, embodied insights of genius; he first drew that celebrated distinction between the natural sciences and humane studies that has remained a crucial issue ever since. Yet, unlike the philosophers of classical antiquity, unlike Descartes and Spinoza, Leibniz and Locke, Berkeley and Hume, Kant and Hegel, he has remained outside the central tradition. After being discovered by this or that champion of his thought – by Coleridge or Leopardi or Michelet – he fell into oblivion once again; rediscovered later in the last century, he was again forgotten save in the land of his birth.

Today, new interest in him is being taken, but it seems unlikely to last – Vico will surely be ignored once more, only to be disinterred again by thinkers made indignant by his lack of recognition. The principal reason for this destiny is probably the obscurity and chaotic nature of his writing. His thought is a tangled forest of seminal ideas, recondite allusions and quotations, sudden excursuses and divagations – rich, strange, confused, arresting, immensely suggestive, but unreadable. Too many novel ideas are jostling to find expression at the same time; he is trying to say too much about too much; the ideas conflict and obscure each other, and although this communicates a kind of turbulent vitality to all that he writes, it does not make for lucidity or elegance. The reader tends to be buffeted, bewildered and exhausted; no idea is properly presented or developed or organised into a coherent structure. It is a very punishing style. As Bizet said of Berlioz, he had genius without any talent. Yet much of what he has to say is of cardinal importance – original and convincing.

Vico's life somewhat resembled his writings: ill-organised, frustrated, without adequate recognition. His father was a poor bookseller in Naples, and he probably owed his considerable but unsystematic erudition in large part to the opportunities offered by the books and by conversations with his father's clients. An accident in his early youth made him a cripple and undermined his health. He was always poor, his life was one long struggle to keep himself and his family alive, he found it difficult to interest scholars in his work, although towards the end of his life his fame grew. He became professor of rhetoric at the University of Naples, but the post was ill-paid, and he was forced to supplement his income by constant hack-work for various notables upon whose favour he depended. He was, in short, a poverty-stricken, irritable, somewhat pathetic scholar, who wrote when and as he could, in a society which did not recognise his extraordinary gifts. And yet, despite his constant craving for recognition, he knew, when he had conceived the central ideas of the *New Science*, that the standard cliché of entering a land where no man's foot had trodden before was, in his case, genuinely valid: he knew he had made a discovery of genius, and this sustained him.

What was this discovery? The heart of it is this: that men were able to understand their own history in a fashion different from and, in Vico's view, superior to that in which they understood the works of nature; and, as a corollary of this, that to understand something, and not merely to be able to describe it, or analyse it into its component parts, was to understand how it came into being – its genesis, its growth – and that its essence consists in coming to be what it is; in short, that true understanding is always genetic, and, in the case of men and their works, always historical, not timeless, and not analytic.

Historical studies were by no means neglected towards the end of the seventeenth century. Indeed, learned antiquaries, both within and outside the Church, were laying the foundations of modern historical science. Nevertheless, historical study was viewed with suspicion by the real intellectual masters of his time, the mathematicians and the natural scientists whose achievements were the glory of the age. Descartes and his disciples dominated thought in Vico's youth, and Descartes had made it plain that true knowledge rests on clear and irrefutable axioms and the application of rules whereby conclusions may be rigorously drawn from such premises, so that a system can be constructed that is logically guaranteed in all its parts.

Only upon such adamantine foundations could a genuine structure of true knowledge be built. Where were the transformation rules, the demonstrative conclusions of history? What historical theorems had been proved beyond possible doubt? History might be like travel, an agreeable pastime, but the most minute researches into the ancient world did not yield new knowledge in the sense in which the magnificent progress of the natural sciences was clearly doing. In the sciences men build on the work of their predecessors: a later generation can see further or deeper than an earlier one, for it is lifted on its shoulders; but in the humanities – in recovering the knowledge of the past – we can at best know only what they knew. About nature we know far more than the ancients, but what, Descartes enquires, could the most erudite student of Rome discover that was not known to Cicero's servant girl? Is this progress? Moreover, the methods used by historians were anything but scientific, neither demonstrative nor experimental, and therefore unworthy of respect: their conclusions might be entertaining, but could not be important. No serious man capable of advancing knowledge would waste his time upon such enquiries.

There was another quarter also from which an attack upon history was made. Since the middle of the fifteenth century sceptics had pointed out that there was little reason to trust historians: they were apt to be subjective, biased, and, even when not actually venal or corrupt hacks, liable, out of vanity or patriotic pride or partisan spirit or sheer ignorance, to distort the truth. All history in the end rests on eye-witness testimony. If the historian was himself engaged in the affairs he was describing, he was inevitably partisan; if not, he would probably not have direct access to that vital information which only participants possessed and were hardly likely to divulge. So the historian must either be involved in the affairs he describes, and therefore partisan, or uninvolved and liable to be misled by those who had an interest in bending the truth in their own favour; or, alternatively, remained too far from the true sources of information to know enough. Hence the notorious fact that historians contradict each other freely, and that opinions alter from age to age and almost from historian to historian.

What then was the value of systematised gossip of this kind? If one attempted to get away from literary sources and use only surviving monuments, these did not provide enough evidence of the real life, the motives and purposes and acts of the human beings whom the historian was attempting to describe and explain. Monuments could be fitted into almost any theory; they were too bare, too uninformative.

Vico was at first impressed by this – not so much by the scepticism of the Pyrrhonists (as they were called) as by the frontal onslaught of the Cartesians. The success of the natural sciences, above all of mathematics, was too vast and arresting to be denied, and yet his own interests lay elsewhere. He was by temperament an antiquarian and a jurist steeped in the history of law, of institutions, especially of the Roman world; he was devout, intuitive, literary, imaginative, sensitive to nuances of style, outlook, expression – not to the structure of abstract systems or to the quantifiable properties of the external world. He belongs to the tradition of those who respond to the impalpable and unanalysable characteristics of experience, rather than to that which alone is measurable, definable, capable of fitting into a transparent, logically organised scientific system.

He raised the banner of revolt: he conceded that all that Descartes had said about mathematics was true, demonstrable, wholly clear and irrefutable; but this was so because mathematics conveyed no information about the world. Mathematics was a system created by the human mind, like a game whose moves are invented arbitrarily, so that they are wholly intelligible because they have been constructed for this very purpose. Mathematics was a human construction: it was not a transcript of reality. He boldly denied what had been believed since Pythagoras or Plato, that mathematical propositions embodied perfect, eternal truths, lifted high above the world of change, and corresponding to the most general characteristics – the bony structure, the permanent skeleton – of reality. The real world, unlike mathematics, was not transparent at all: it was opaque. [He went back to an ancient Christian truth according to which one could understand fully only what one had oneself created. If, like God, one created something out of nothing (for God knowing was creating), then one understood what one had made because one had made it – it was the product of one's free creative will. Only God understood the world wholly, for he alone created it. As for man, external nature could not be fully intelligible to him, because he had not created it; we understood geometry wholly because we made it; we would understand the material universe wholly if only we could make it, but we cannot. There was in the science of physics something that was impenetrable to us, namely matter itself, which we could know only, as it were, *ab extra*, not as God knew it, who had willed it to be – whose thought in a sense it was. We understand only what we have made: mathematics, works of art, legal systems, constitutions, which, because we have created them, we can know, as it were, from within.]

This, originally medieval, doctrine, developed by Hobbes in his own fashion, was used by Vico to draw a line between two types of knowledge; his fully fledged doctrine of this appeared in 1710. As

God knows men, so Shakespeare, say (though Vico uses no such example), knows what it is to be Hamlet because he made him, but does not know what it is to be a rock or a tree, because he did not make them. We can say what a tree looks like, what happens to it, that is, what it is for an external observer, but we cannot 'understand' it, because we cannot be a tree, and we cannot make one. Something in the world of nature must for ever remain opaque to us, for we cannot create matter. Descartes does indeed talk of knowledge by means of clear and distinct ideas; this works in the case of mathematics because mathematics is not 'in nature' but 'in us', and is indeed knowable, but offers no information about the world.

As for external matter, clearness and distinctness are not enough. 'When I suffer, for instance, I cannot recognise any form in my suffering; I am not aware of any boundaries of my mental anguish'; yet 'the idea of the suffering is vivid and bright beyond anything else'.[1] Am I to say that it is not real because it is not definable, measurable, analysable into uniform atomic constituents? Are qualities not real because they are not susceptible to Cartesian categories? We know more about mechanics than we know about physics, because there, as Hobbes had learned, we can manipulate the parts at will. We understand our own manipulations, for we do it ourselves; but external nature obeys laws that we have not made, that we can only record and describe but not understand, as only he who has made them with a purpose of his own can understand them. Hence mathematics, physics and natural sciences in general are not the vaunted paradigm of knowledge that they have been represented as being from the time of the Greeks to the Renaissance and after it.

But there is one province where I can know more than this, where I need not confine myself merely to recording uniformities – what happened next to what, after or before or simultaneously with what – but can ask a further question, 'Why did it happen?' or 'With what end in view?' If I explain my own conduct I do not merely describe it, but give my motive, my reason for acting, the plan of which this action forms an element. I convey the form of life in which it plays a part – something which, at any rate in theory, I can alter at will, adopt or discard, something for which I am responsible. There is clearly a sense in which I invent my own

---

[1] *De antiquissima italorum sapientia*, chapter 4, section 2 (near the end).

conduct, at least when I am acting consciously; and here I can ask not merely what my body is doing, but also *what I am at*, what my movements are intended for, or meant to achieve. This is precisely what I cannot do in the case of trees or rocks or indeed animals, into whose motives, if they have them, I cannot pretend to penetrate.

If I can introspect and explain my own conduct in terms of purpose – in terms of hopes, fears, wishes, decisions, doubts, love, hatred, self-interest, principle and the like – then I can do this also in the case of others, for in the very process of communication I assume them to be creatures like myself. And if I can do this for the present, I can do it also for my own past, through memory and imaginative re-creation; and do it also for those with whom I am linked, my family, my tribe, my city, my class, my profession, my nation, my Church, my civilisation, humanity at large. I do not know others merely by observing their bodily movements and inferring causes, as a biologist might. I understand them by immediate analogy, by the response they give to me, by the sheer phenomenon of interaction. Creatures similar to myself speak to me, and I understand them. In civilised times they use developed language, but men can speak to each other in other ways also – by means of gestures, by hieroglyphs, by song and dance; writing may well precede spoken words. They speak to each other, and they speak also to the unseen powers that they believe to be greater than themselves, the powers by which they believe themselves to be governed – the gods of earlier civilisations, the nymphs and the dryads of the Greeks and Romans, the true God of the Jews and Christians. To them they speak by acts of worship.

Men's institutions are moulded by such efforts to communicate, express themselves, create a common structure responding to their beliefs, their hopes, their desires, their fears, their fantasies. Because we are men we can enter into the experience of other men; we may make mistakes – such knowledge is not infallible. But the very possibility of such intercommunication, based as it is on the understanding of motives, outlooks, ways of life, rests in principle on something different from the knowledge that we have of the external world, which can never, in the end, be more than a recording of what occurs, or how, without knowledge of why it occurs, or indeed whether such a question makes sense at all. This kind of understanding is different, too, from the formal disciplines – mathematics, logic, the rules of games, which we can indeed know through and through, because we have made them ourselves, but which (unlike our knowledge of ourselves) do not give knowledge of reality, news of what is there. This is the kind of knowing that re-creates the past in our minds.

This was Vico's great move. He reached it in about 1720, when he was overwhelmed by the fascinating vista of rewriting the history of mankind in terms of the acts of men, based on insight into their monuments, the frozen relics of such acts; relying not upon the writings of historians, which may indeed be adequate or mendacious, but on what men have made in order to communicate with others, men or gods: artefacts, words, works of art, social institutions, which can be understood by other men because they are men, and because these communications are addressed by men to men.

When I read a book or hear a man speak I understand what he is saying, that is, I understand what he is at. Nature is a book only for God; but human institutions – myths, fables, structures of language, rites, poems, works of art, laws, customs – men have made these to express themselves with, and therefore other men can by imaginative sympathy grasp them. To know that one tree is taller than another, or that water extinguishes fire, or that Caesar conquered the Gauls, or how to count, or ride a horse, are very different kinds of knowledge from knowing what it is to love one's country, fear God, be jealous of a rival, resist a tyrant, pray, starve, exert authority, defend a principle, be a traitor, make a revolution.

Vico's ambition was to create a truly new science – a science based on an examination of what men have made, been, done, suffered, from an 'inside' point of view, that of a participant, not an observer, by means of a process which, he insisted, was possible, though at times exceedingly difficult – the 'entering' by means of *fantasia* – imagination – into the minds of men remote from one's own society in space or time. This can be achieved by letting their works speak directly to one, by seeking to understand how they saw the world, what they wanted to do in it and with it, how it appeared to them and how they tried to make themselves at home in it, understand it, mould it, dominate it, dominate each other, enter into new relationships, create, express themselves, act. Vico had read Lucretius in his youth. Lucretius was a pagan and, worse, an Epicurean atheist, and Vico therefore did not, being a timid member of a highly authoritarian and powerful Church, emphasise this; nevertheless he was deeply influenced by him, and in particular by his description of mankind as rising from brutal barbarism towards more civilised modes of living. It is only by the most appalling efforts, Vico tells us, that we can enter the imaginations of those gross, cruel and primitive men, who are very different from us; nevertheless they are men and, therefore, communicators, doers; and if we try hard enough, we can, at any rate to some degree, reconstruct their world. As they approach our own times, they become easier to understand by 'empathetic' insight.

The central principle is still that men can truly understand only that which they have made; they understand best what they have made themselves, but they can understand also what others have made, because creation is collective, most of all in primitive times. Hence myths, so far from being false stories about reality spread by wicked priests, impostors seeking to bamboozle the foolish masses, or artificial embellishment created by poets to entertain and delight, or by philosophers to put their truths in more attractive guise, are, in fact, ways of conceiving and ordering the world natural to early man, the concepts and categories that govern his vision. When the Roman poet says that everything is full of Jove, what can he possibly mean? On the one hand, Jove is a bearded thunderer, the father of the gods; yet he is also the sky. It means nothing to us to say that the thunder is at the same time the illimitable sky; but it must have meant something to those primitive men who articulated the vision of their society, and the task is to transpose oneself into a condition where one can begin to have some inkling of what the world must have looked like to those who expressed themselves in this fashion – by means of what Vico calls 'credible impossibilities'[1] – to whom such metaphors, images, similes were a natural way of description and expression.

To the Greeks Poseidon is both a God wielding a trident and all the seas of the world, Cybele is both an enormous woman and the whole earth, Heracles both a single hero and yet multiple too. There is an Argive and an Athenian and a Theban Heracles; he is many and also one. The fact that this is unfamiliar, indeed unintelligible, to us now does not mean that it was always so. It must (Vico believes) be possible to enter into the consciousness of those remote savages, to see the world as they saw it, and then, and only then, will their poetry, their myths, their institutions, their

[1] *New Science*, paragraph 384.

rites, their entire society, whence we ourselves originate, become intelligible to us.

To understand is to enter into the outlook of those who speak to others, and whom we too can overhear. By tracing the history of words we can trace the altered attitude towards, the sense of, the things that the words denote, the part that they played in the lives of those whom we seek to comprehend. Hence the crucial importance of the history of languages. Vico's etymologies are sometimes wildly fanciful, but the idea is new and fertile; the growth of a language is not merely evidence for, it is part of the very essence of, the growth of consciousness of which the language is an expression, with which it is one. So too with the history of myth and art and law and religion. The history of mankind is the history of the activities of men building their worlds, and the histories of their constituent stages are the histories of successive attitudes towards these worlds, of the collective lives in which men play one, and then another, part. Art is not mere embellishment – it is a voice speaking, an effort to embody a vision in a concrete material form.

Vico believes that all nations are destined to pass through the same cycles of culture: from savagery to barbarism and stern oligarchy, followed by plutocracy, democracy, freedom of speech, scepticism, decadence; from piety, severity, discipline through growing permissiveness and luxury to collapse. This is followed either by the conquest of the soft and degenerate peoples by some more vigorous society still at an earlier phase of its own development, or by a return to a firmer morality reimposed by a powerful ruler bent on the regeneration of his society (Augustus, for example; Vico in the main thinks of Rome when he thinks about the past); or by total disintegration, and return to the caves; after which the entire cycle begins again.[1]

The Jews alone are exempt from this, for to them the true word of God was vouchsafed, and they could pursue a conscious path, instead of an evolution which God (or Providence) imposed upon

---

[1] One of Vico's most brilliant formulations is of what he calls 'the second barbarism' – the condition into which a society falls when mounting luxury, materialism, egoism have destroyed the social bonds to which he thinks religious authority indispensable. When this has taken place, men, though they still throng together, 'live like wild beasts in a deep solitude of spirit and will, scarcely any two being able to agree', base savages 'under soft words and embraces' (*New Science*, paragraph 1106). Modern critics of the dehumanising effects of 'post-industrial society' could hardly better this description of 'alienated' man.

all other men without necessarily revealing his purposes to them. It is only because we lack historical imagination that the poetry of the ancients and their myths seem mere childish errors to us. We shall never understand the magnificent poetry of primitive times, the Homeric poems, for example, if we do not understand the society of which this was the natural vision and expression. Homer for Vico was not a single author who created his poem arbitrarily out of his head as a later poet might have done at some other time; he was the entire Greek people celebrating its heroic forms of life, as Dante did at the corresponding stage of the second cycle – the second Middle Age of mankind.

The notion of a predetermined order of civilisations each of which has its own quality, its own central style, its own life, all the aspects of which are intertwined by a unitary structure, so that to certain kinds of economic organisation there must always correspond certain types of linguistic usage, of visual art, of religious belief and forms, certain types of poetry or prose – in fact the notion of a culture unified by some central pattern that determines all the activities of its members – this new idea is one of Vico's most original and pregnant conceptions. Armed with it, he argued, for example, that the accepted tradition according to which the Romans derived their earliest laws – the Twelve Tables – from Solon's Athens was patently absurd. Such transmission was historically impossible. He based this on the fact that the kind of Latin idiom characteristic of Rome at that time – the language of the Twelve Tables – together with what we know of early Roman customs as embodied in legends (which always have some 'ground of truth', that is, sense of reality, in them) – these forms of life and the language which is their vehicle are totally incompatible with the culture of Solonian Athens as, in its turn, expressed by its language, laws, habits, literary monuments, and are not translatable from or into it. The cultural chasm is too wide.

This art of historical periodisation and attribution, whereby one is enabled to say not merely that a given poem or vase or type of warfare not only did not belong to some given age or culture, but could not have belonged to it, because it does not fit in with other manifestations of the age – the kind of knowledge of the structure of a civilisation on which the histories of art, technology, economic activity (to take only a few instances) today are based – was virtually invented by Vico. The fact that no one outside Italy read him with any understanding (and, for that matter, not many in

Italy) is a sad and curious fact. Vico's immediate influence may
have been limited to the Neapolitan jurists; but his originality is
not thereby diminished.

That historical understanding is different from the way in which
we know or have beliefs about the external universe, from scientific
method, whether deductive, or hypothetico-deductive, or inductive; from metaphysical 'intuitions' or conceptual analysis (however these may be defined); and from the methods of the formal
sciences, logic, mathematics, game theory, heraldry and the like –
this thesis, whatever its degree of validity, is one of Vico's claims to
immortality. So is the notion that nature is not static, but a flow:
that human nature is not a permanent kernel, identifiable as such in
all men at all times, as maintained by the advocates of natural law,
but a constant process of growth, *nascimento*, a coming to be,
whence *natura* is derived; that all that occurs in the history of
mankind can take place only at its appropriate place in the great
cyclical pattern.

Hence Polybius' lament, some nineteen centuries before, that
men might have avoided their errors and follies if only philosophers (and not priests) had presided over their beginnings is
absurd. Vico answers Polybius and the rationalists by saying that
philosophy not merely does not, but cannot, occur except at an
advanced stage of culture. The order of development is unalterable:
magic must precede rational thought. Men see the world in the
various ways that they do; these ways depend on the stage reached:
to each stage its own mode of vision and expression. Thus the
beauty and power of the Homeric poems belong uniquely to the
barbarian society, governed by cruel, ambitious and avaricious
oligarchs, from which they sprang, and cannot be re-created in an
age of legal disputations, philosophy, prose, bereft of those vivid
and spontaneous metaphors and images which conveyed the vision
natural to an earlier, far less sophisticated and self-conscious
culture.

If myths are one door through which the movements of men's
minds can be traced, their vision of the universe 'entered into',
metaphors are not, as they are in modern times, a conscious,
artificial, baroque embellishment attacked by those French critics
of Vico's time who contrasted such luxuriance unfavourably with
the classical plainness and clarity of the great writers of the Grand
Siècle. Metaphor, simile, at the times in which they begin, are a
natural mode of expression. If the poets of the heroic age spoke of

blood boiling in their hearts, it was because the condition of rage literally seemed to them to resemble the physical condition of inner boiling more closely than anything else in the world with which they were familiar. [When men of this 'age of heroes' speak of mouths of rivers, lips of vases, necks of land, veins of mineral, the bowels of the earth (or of the heavens as smiling, of the waves as murmuring, of willows as weeping), they do it not to heighten language, or to be consciously poetical, or to convey mysterious, esoteric truths, but as a natural and spontaneous expression of how the world felt to them.]

[margin, handwritten:] language + personal experience

Animism and anthropomorphism are types of collective consciousness which belong to, and pass away with, their own type of social organisation; the poetry that springs from it, and is the voice of a particular stage of civilisation, has a power and a sublimity that will never recur in the history of the world until the same type of development is again reached in the ever cyclical movement of human history. To expect primitive men to describe their universe in what we should call literal terms is to lack all sense of how humanity develops, and therefore of what men are, for men *are* their coming to be, rise, apogee, decline. What seem conscious metaphors to us are our ancestors' natural mode of expressing what they saw, felt, heard, feared – all that they were bound up with. All art must be understood in this way, as a form of natural reaction and expression. It is, for that reason, a direct door to the past.

The very notion of one perfect way of knowing what is true or right, the idea of natural law as being something that any man can, in principle, get to know at any time, anywhere, as implied by Aristotle and maintained by the Stoics long ago, and by Grotius in Vico's century, struck him as wholly untenable. Primitives do not, and cannot, live their lives according to unvarying, timeless principles, for then there would be no growth, no historical change, only eternal repetition, as in the lives of animals. Man is a self-transforming creature, the satisfaction of each set of needs alters his character and breeds new needs and forms of life: he *is* a perpetual growing, directed by Providence working through his passions, through his very vices. There is no fixed, unalterable 'core' common to all men at all times; everything in human life and history can be understood only as a function of a process. This process can be known because it obeys an intelligible pattern of which he, Vico, has discovered the eternal principles, a pattern in which spiritual, economic and social factors are interwoven.

Like other innovators of genius, possessed by a new vision, Vico tends to overstate his case. Euclid and even Thucydides were the children of their age, but their words can be understood (if not fully understood) even by those who do not see them in their proper cultural context. Nevertheless Vico's ideas are transforming. He is the true father of historicism, of the sociology of culture, of the notion of the validity of each form of art or culture for its own time, and, consequently, the earliest opponent of what Wyndham Lewis once called 'the demon of progress in the arts'.[1] Above all, he distinguished the notion of what it is to understand a joke, a poem, a character, an outlook, a system of values, an entire civilisation, from mathematical and scientific knowledge, practical skills and ordinary knowledge of facts. Yet he is most famous for the least original and plausible of all his doctrines, the cyclical theory of history. The ill luck that dogged him during his life pursued him after death.

The great lights of his time largely ignored him. A handful of Italian scholars did what they could; disciples – Duni, Cesarotti, Filangieri – tried to spread his fame. But the most celebrated thinkers of his time remained largely unaware of his work. Even if an editor of a learned journal, and one or two minor German scholars, took some notice of his writings (he circulated them tirelessly to the luminaries of his time), there is no evidence that Montesquieu, for example, read him. (The assertions of one or two later commentators that he echoed him seem without foundation.)

Italian jurists and critics derived a good deal from him and maintained that some French writers did too. But there is no evidence that either Voltaire or Fontenelle, either Christian von Wolff or Hume had ever heard of him. Yet he anticipated some of the most brilliant achievements of German classical scholarship of the next century. 'If Pythagoras recalled that in a previous life he had fought beneath the walls of Troy,' Michelet wrote in 1831, 'these illustrious Germans might have remembered that they had all formerly lived in Vico. All the giants of criticism are already contained, with room to spare, in the little pandemonium of the *New Science*.'[2] Neither the great Homeric scholar F. A. Wolf, nor the equally eminent Roman historian B. G. Niebuhr, showed much pleasure when this fact was brought to their reluctant notice.

[1] In a book of this title (London, 1954).
[2] Preface to *Histoire romaine*: vol. 2, pp. 340–1, in *Oeuvres complètes* (see p. 53 above, note 1); quoted by Fisch, op. cit. (ibid.), p. 78.

Coleridge and Thomas Arnold, Marx and Dilthey, Yeats and Joyce (*Finnegans Wake*, for example, is full of Vichian echoes and allusions) recognised his genius. But he remains unread outside his native land save by specialists in the history of literature or ideas. The philosophers and the historians of philosophy, with rare exceptions, ignore him still. Evidently it is the fate of his writings, like that of human culture in his own theory of *corsi* and *ricorsi*, to be forgotten, then to rise again, achieve brief glory, then again fall into oblivion, till the next cycle, and so on for ever.

RUSSIAN INTELLECTUAL HISTORY

WHAT IS intellectual history? It is not a clear and self-explanatory concept. Such terms as 'political history', 'economic history' and 'social history', however vague their frontiers, however much they may overlap with one another, are not in this sense obscure. They denote accounts of what certain more or less definable groups of human beings have done and suffered, of the interaction between their members, of the deeds and destinies of those individuals who have been influential in altering the lives of their fellows in certain specific ways, of the interplay between them and external nature or other groups of human beings, of the development of their institutions – legislative, judicial, administrative, religious, economic, artistic – and so on. Similarly, the idea of a history of the arts and sciences, however many difficulties it presents in practice, is easily grasped in principle: the concept of a work of art or of a scientific discovery or invention, and of the circumstances in which it is achieved, is relatively clear. But what is intellectual history? A history of ideas? What ideas and conceived by whom? Not ideas in any one well-demarcated province; accounts of mathematical, philosophical, scientific, aesthetic, technological and economic ideas all belong to histories of their respective 'technical' disciplines. Yet it is clear that the mere juxtaposition or combination of these histories does not itself make a general history of ideas.

Leaving this problem undiscussed, let us, for the sake of argument, concede that it is possible to ask what ideas, and perhaps, more vaguely, what attitudes, were prevalent in a given society at a given time; moreover, that it is possible and indeed tempting to speculate about the influence of this or that body of ideas on a particular turn in the history of the society in question; in addition, that it may reasonably be argued that a particular school of thought exaggerates, or underestimates, the part that is played by particular ideas, or of ideas in general – that Idealists or

Marxists or Positivists were right or mistaken when they supposed that a revolution or a war would not have occurred, or taken the form that it took, had it not been for certain beliefs or ways of thought in the mind of this or that individual, this or that group. Historians, philosophers and sociologists quarrel about whether such ideas or attitudes are themselves by-products of some non-mental process – geographical or economic or biological – or, on the contrary, are independent forces, not to be fully explained in terms of anything other than themselves. What is the subject of such speculations and disagreements? If not the specific ideas that belong to specific disciplines, then what? General ideas, we shall be told. What are these? This is much more difficult to answer. In the end, no more than an approximation can be attempted here.

By 'general ideas' we refer in effect to beliefs, attitudes and mental and emotional habits, some of which are vague and undefined, others of which have become crystallised into religious, legal or political systems, moral doctrines, social outlooks, psychological dispositions and so forth. One of the qualities common to such systems and their constituent elements is that, unlike a good many scientific and common-sense propositions, it does not seem possible to test their validity or truth by means of precisely definable, agreed criteria, or even to show them to be acceptable or unacceptable by means of widely accepted methods. The most that can be said of them is that they are to be found in that intermediate realm in which we expect to find opinions, general intellectual and moral principles, scales of value and value judgements, mental dispositions and individual and social attitudes – everything that is loosely collected under such descriptions as 'intellectual background', 'climate of opinion', 'social mores' and 'general outlook'; that which is often referred to in ordinary language (this is part of our Marxist inheritance) as ideology. It is this ill-defined but rich realm and its vicissitudes that histories of ideas or 'intellectual histories' supposedly describe, analyse and explain.

The existence of such histories is itself a symptom and a product of that growth of human self-consciousness which has generated distinctions between, on the one hand, this realm – home of ideologies, outlooks, attitudes, myths, rationalisations and the like – and, on the other, the better-ordered kingdoms populated by the concepts and propositions of the more developed exact sciences and disciplines. The history of ideas, as a branch of knowledge, was born in Italy and grew in Germany (and to a lesser extent in France

and England) in the eighteenth century. In due course interest in it
spread both east and west. In no country was there a greater degree
of historical self-awareness, or was greater or more intense
attention paid to ideological issues, than in Russia in the nineteenth
and twentieth centuries.

It is in Russian writings that such titles as 'the history of social
thought' (*obshchestvennaya mysl'*) or 'the history of the intelligentsia' are most often found. Other countries have produced
historians of culture or of civilisation; Russia is the home of the
history of general opinions, of the beliefs and general intellectual
outlook of educated persons affected by the progress of the arts
and sciences and by political, economic and social phenomena, but
not necessarily involved in professional concern with them – of the
outlook of amateurs, not experts. There are many historical causes
of this: the isolation of educated persons in tsarist Russia at the
beginning of the nineteenth century; the conflict of the Western
character of humane studies with Russian reality; the coincidence
of the emergence of Russia as a world power with the rise of
romantic ideas, particularly in Germany; the decay of religion
among the educated and the search for a moral and spiritual
substitute; the repression by the government of free political and
social activity and, as a result, the forcible canalisation of the quest
for self-expression and individuality – especially in its acute,
rebellious forms – into the realm of thought, which, for this reason,
became the opium of the civilised, their only substitute, pale as it
was, for action. This is not the place for the discussion of this large
subject. Whatever the reasons, there is no doubt that ideas were
taken more seriously, and played a greater and more peculiar role,
in Russian history than anywhere else. And yet there is a paradox
here, for few of these ideas were born on Russian soil.

At this stage it is relevant to repeat the second question raised
above: Whose thoughts are the proper subject of intellectual
history? It is perhaps an idle enquiry, and one that rests on a vulgar
misconception of both thought and action, to seek to identify the
exact origin or authorship of a belief or an ideal that has played a
part in human history. Who invented the idea of democracy? Or
the rights of man? Or duty or honour or individual objectivity, or
progress, or any of the other concepts and categories that have
dominated the Western world? Nevertheless, some attributions can
be made. The fundamental concepts of Western political theory
evolved in Greece, not in India or Judaea; so did those of

mathematics and the natural sciences: the Stoics first discussed causality in the modern sense, and they and the Epicureans first argued about the solution to the problem of freedom of the will. A clear distinction between individual and collective responsibility may be found in Jeremiah before we encounter it elsewhere; the contrast between love and justice as governing relations between human beings is not (despite the *Antigone*) of Greek origin, whereas that of impersonal natural law is; and so on. New beginnings – ideas that transform thought and action – do occur. Radical innovations are rightly attributed to Plato and Aristotle, Epicurus and Euclid, the authors of the Book of Isaiah and the Gospels, of the Roman Digest and the Code Napoléon, to Descartes, Kant, Marx, Darwin and Freud. No doubt these men had forerunners, and the seeds of their doctrines may be found elsewhere, but it is their formulations, however arrived at, that have made the critical difference and have affected thought, feeling and practice in a decisive fashion. Such identifications are still more certain within specific provinces of thought, even outside the natural sciences: Spinoza is the true father of higher criticism, Montesquieu of the comparative method in history, Saint-Simon of technocracy, and so on.

What part has been played in this advance by the Russians? They have contributed their full share of genius in mathematics and the natural sciences. Their poetical achievement is of unique magnificence; their novelists of the nineteenth century tower above all others; musical talent continues to flower to this day on Russian soil – since the beginning of the nineteenth century Russia has in no sense been a cultural backwater. But in the realm of general ideas her most striking characteristic is not inventiveness but a unique degree of responsiveness to the ideas of others. This Russian trait has proved to be a major factor in the modern world. That objective truth exists, that it can be discovered, and that life, individual and social, can be lived in its light – this belief is more characteristic of the Russians than of anyone else in the modern world. To take ideas with complete seriousness itself transforms them; this is a crucial corollary of the central insight of both Marx and Freud into the unity of thought and practice. No matter where an idea may have been born, writers, artists, critics, the educated minority in the capitals, and, at their hands, a growing number of sincere and idealistic semi-educated Russians elsewhere, sought to discover the truth in its light and to shape their lives accordingly. A capacity for rigorous reasoning from premises believed to be true even if they led to unpalatable conclusions, intellectual enthusiasm, integrity, courage, and the rational conviction that only if a man understands the truth and lives by it can he rise to his full stature and be happy, creative, wise and virtuous – these convictions, inherited from the age of reason, were never abandoned by the vanguard of Russian society. It is this faith that, for good or ill, has enabled it to move mountains. Others have invented ideas or come upon them, delighted in them, paid serious attention to them or played with them, conceived them as expressions of their own creative, self-assertive personalities or regarded them with scientific detachment as part of their professional task, while their private and inner lives were, at times, lived in a different province and at another level. But the Russian intelligentsia, or at least those of its members who set their stamp on Russian mental development in the nineteenth century (and on the Russian Revolution in the twentieth), went much further: it surrendered itself to what it believed to be true with a lifelong singleness of purpose seldom known outside the religious life in the West. The intelligentsia did not embrace the whole of educated Russian society – far from it – but it constituted its most active element. Nor did it always fully live up to its professions (no educated Russian needs reminding that two of the most passionate and effective enemies of serfdom – Nekrasov and Turgenev – did not, in fact, liberate their own serfs). But its words inspired others to acts of heroism and martyrdom.

Above all, it preached and practised the notion of the unbreakable unity of men's nature. The idea of professionalism – the division of what one does as an expert from one's activity as a human being, the separation of public *métier* from private life, the notion of man as an actor who plays now this role, now that – has always been weaker in Russia than in the West. Differentiation of functions, specialisation, a tidy social system in which every man has his place and his calling, has never been a central Russian idea in theory or practice. Even in the early eighteenth century, Feofan Prokopovich was not merely a bishop, a clerical administrator, and a theologian, but also a social and political reformer and an educator. As for Lomonosov, what realm of Russian spiritual development did he regard as alien to him? Poet, physicist, grammarian, educator, composer, administrator and universal sage, the 'Russian Leonardo' stands worthily at the head of that extraordinary procession of many-sided personalities who are characteristic of Russian civilisation. No doubt in a country without a true tradition of scholastic learning, where – despite occasional heresies and the penetration of Western ideas among the immediate neighbours of Roman Catholic Poland – there occurred no Renaissance and no Reformation, a small élite of educated persons was obliged to do everything for its benighted brothers. Novikov was not a man of great intellectual power, but he became all that he could be; he left none of his intellectual, artistic, or social gifts – such as they were – undeveloped. In what other country did eminent professors of chemistry or serious experts in ballistics become renowned composers? Where else did (and do) artists see themselves not as purveyors of objects, no matter how beautiful, but as heralds and prophets, solely because they take it upon themselves to speak in public? In Russia (and where else to a comparable degree?) this act alone has been conceived of as imposing on the élite the task – indeed, the sacred duty – to say only what is true, or only what they truly believe and are prepared to express and defend with their lives, so that any effort to escape this, any deception or self-indulgence, is viewed as being not merely aesthetically false, but morally treasonable.

Most of the central figures of the intelligentsia display this characteristic in some degree. While Shcherbatov was no more earnest and admonitory than contemporary European, and in particular German, historians, Novikov was a martyr to the public interest. Fonvizin was a traveller, an essayist, and above all a writer of satirical comedies whose primary purpose was, if anything, even more patriotic and didactic than that of his peers in the West. The famous historian Karamzin was consumed with concern for the future of his country, to which the past, which he recorded with such love, labour and literary talent, was but the noble opening. He set the tone for Russian conservatism much as Burke did for its English prototype. While the central notions of both these founders may have had their obvious origins in France and Germany and the ancient world (with tributaries in the case of Karamzin from Byzantium and the Orthodox Church), the emphasis in each case was not on a true account of the facts for their own sake, but on the application of such truths to the present or the immediate future. It was this moral and social concern that gave their ideas dominant influence over their own generation and the entire nineteenth century. Pnin is an even better example of this universalising tendency. He was a far smaller figure than, say,

Humboldt, but his aims were no less wide: his entire life was dedicated to translating the ideas of the Enlightenment for use at home; they emerged, as one would expect, drastically transformed.

As for Chaadaev, the originality of the notorious 'Philosophical Letter', characteristically enough, consisted not in the presentation of new ideas but in the denunciation of his country for its cultural inferiority to the West, for lacking anything authentic or original of its own. Chaadaev's attack, with its deification of Western traditions, ideas and civilisation, was the key to later Russian 'social thought'. Its importance was enormous. It set the tone, it struck the dominant notes which were echoed by every major Russian writer up to and beyond the Revolution. Everything is there: the proclamation that the Russian past is blank or filled with chaos, that the only true culture is in the Roman West, and that the Great Schism robbed Russia of her birthright and left her barbarous, an abortion of the creative process, a caution to other peoples, a Caliban among nations. Here, too, is the extraordinary tendency toward self-preoccupation which characterises Russian writing even more than that of the Germans, from whom this tendency mainly stems. Other writers, in England, France, even Germany, write about life, love, nature and human relations at large; Russian writing, even when it is most deeply in debt to Goethe or Schiller or Dickens or Stendhal, is about Russia, the Russian past, the Russian present, Russian prospects, the Russian character, Russian vices and Russian virtues. All the 'accursed questions' (as Heine was perhaps the first to call them) turn in Russian into the notorious *proklyatye voprosy*[1] – questions about the destinies (*sud'by*) of Russia: Where do we come from? Whither are we bound? Why are we as we are? Should we teach the West or learn from it? Is our 'broad' Slav nature higher in the spiritual scale than that of the 'Europeans' – a source of salvation for all mankind – or merely a form of infantilism and barbarism destined to be superseded or destroyed? The problem of the 'superfluous man'[2] is

---

[1] This Russian phrase seems to have been coined in 1858 by Mikhail L. Mikhailov when he used it to render 'die verdammten Fragen' in his translation of Heine's poem 'Zum Lazarus' (1853/4): see 'Stikhotvoreniya Geine', *Sovremennik* 1858 No 3, p. 125; and vol. 3 p. 225, in *Heinrich Heines sämtliche Werke* (see p. ix above, note 1). Ed.

[2] The concept of the 'superfluous man' was given its familiar name by Turgenev in *Dnevnik lishnego cheloveka* ('Diary of a superfluous man'): see entry for 23 March 1850. Ed.

here already; it is not an accident that Chaadaev was an intimate friend of the creator of *Eugene Onegin*. No less characteristic of this mental condition is Chaadaev's contrary speculation that was also destined to have a career in subsequent writing, in which he wondered whether the Russians, who have arrived so late at the feast of the nations and are still young, barbarous and untried, do not thereby derive advantages, perhaps overwhelming ones, over older or more civilised societies. Fresh and strong, the Russians might profit by the inventions and discoveries of the others without having to go through the torments that have attended their mentors' struggles for life and civilisation. Might there not be a vast positive gain in being late in the field? Herzen and Chernyshevsky, Marxists and anti-Marxists, were to repeat this with mounting optimism. But the most central and far-reaching question was still that posed by Chaadaev. He asked: Who are we and what should be our path? Have we unique treasures (as the Slavophils maintained) preserved for us by our Church – the only truly Christian one – which Catholics and Protestants have each in their own way lost or destroyed? Is that which the West despises as coarse and primitive in fact a source of life – the only pure source in the decaying post-Christian world? Or, on the contrary, is the West at least partially right: if we are ever to say our own word and play our part and show the world what kind of people we are, must we not learn from the Westerners, acquire their skills, study in their schools, emulate their arts and sciences, and perhaps the darker sides of their lives also? The lines of battle in the century that followed remained where Chaadaev drew them: the weapons were ideas which, whatever their origins, in Russia became matters of the deepest concern – often of life and death – as they never were in England or France or, to such a degree, in Romantic Germany. Kireevsky, Khomiakov and Aksakov gave one answer, Belinsky and Dobrolyubov another, Kavelin yet a third.

Ideas travelled from the West and, transmuted by Russian logic and Russian passion, acquired an influence which would have astonished some of their authors. The Russian intelligentsia was bred on Western doctrines, movements and events: French eighteenth-century scepticism, scientific materialism and positivism; German historicism, romanticism and idealism; the principles and dogmas of the French Revolution and of its aftermath; the new rational organisation created by Napoleon; European revolutions in the early years of the nineteenth century, for which centralised

France acted as a model; the Utopias of Saint-Simon, Fourier, Owen, Cabet, Leroux; the counter-attacks of Maistre, Bonald, Schelling; the destruction of metaphysics by Comte, Feuerbach, Strauss; the social doctrines of Sismondi, Mill, Spencer and the Darwinians. All had their fervent disciples in Russia. Dostoevsky was exiled for reading the celebrated philippic by Belinsky, which, in its turn, was an expression of the democratic radicalism that, everywhere in the civilised world, called for revolt in the name of reason, justice and human freedom. This was the creed in the name of which, not many weeks after Belinsky's death, revolutions broke out in all the great capitals of the European continent. The intellectual preoccupations of Western thinkers – the relations of mind to body, of scientific to moral truth, of the individual to society, the patterns of history, the goals toward which humanity should (or is compelled to) march, the issue of freedom and determinism, of culture and the masses, of the primacy of economic versus political factors – these issues were matters of deep concern to the best minds of Europe. Yet even though they were not without influence on practice, they remained for the majority matters of theory. But for the Russian radicals and their conservative opponents they were questions of desperate urgency, causes for which men were prepared to risk their prospects and their lives, as they later fought (and died) for or against populism or Marxism, or in the name of one of the variants of these creeds against another. The reader of Turgenev's *Fathers and Children* – and to some extent *On the Eve* and *Virgin Soil* too – finds himself in the world which Chernyshevsky and Dobrolyubov, Kavelin and Annenkov described and, by and large, condemned. Nothing like it existed in the West; the total and unquestioning, at times fanatical, intellectual and moral dedication of the intelligentsia, its purity of character and unswerving pursuit of the truth, and the horror with which any lapse from integrity – collaboration with the enemy, whether State or Church or other obscurantist powers – was regarded by it, are probably unique in human history. Unless this is grasped, the later history of Russia, not merely intellectual but social, economic and political, cannot be adequately understood.

The history of the development of these psychological character-istics is another story. Suffice it to say that the seeds of Marxism here fell on the most fertile soil imaginable; and their growth was fostered by a mood of stern renunciation of the world and passionate social faith not known in Europe since the Jacobins, perhaps since the Puritans.

Yet to identify this attitude with educated Russian opinion in general would be a serious distortion of the facts. For this attitude was not characteristic of any Russian born before the nineteenth century – Russian art and thought in the early decades of the nineteenth century had far more in common with contemporary movements in the West than is often supposed. When Mérimée translated Pushkin's prose, or when Pozzo di Borgo described Chaadaev as being 'un Russe parfaitement comme il faut', these discoveries may have been a source of surprise in the West, but they should not have been so. For society in Petersburg and Moscow (the world described in *War and Peace*) was highly civilised by any Western standard, and Russian literature and art of the early part of the century were for the most part its direct expression. On the contrary, Bazarov in Turgenev's *Fathers and Children* is, if not a caricature, a stylised and exaggerated portrait of the 'men of the '60s', and Pisarev, who proudly acknowledged his kinship with Bazarov, preached a crude and violent form of positivism that became less characteristic toward the end of the century. Chernyshevsky, Pisarev, Tkachev and Nechaev represented peaks of passionate and narrow dogmatism which, together with Dostoevsky's obsessed and equally uncharacteristic vision, and Chekhov's studies in futility, contributed to the notorious synthetic image of the 'Slav soul' that has in the West so often been mistaken for reality.

During the two reigns that preceded the Revolution the leaders of the Russian intelligentsia, both radical and moderate, Marxist and anti-Marxist, and the writers and artists who belonged to their world, lacked neither breadth of knowledge nor balanced imagination, nor critical judgement, nor – although they have often been accused of it – sober common sense. Anyone who doubts this proposition should tear himself away from Chernyshevsky's *What is to be done?* or Pisarev's *The Destruction of Aesthetics* and turn to the arts and letters, and still more the social and political literature, of the years preceding and immediately succeeding the abortive Revolution of 1905. This 'Silver Age' of Russian culture – in the realms of science (including the social sciences) and the humanities as well as that of pure art – is part and parcel of a great European advance, and not the peculiar achievement of a remote, barbarous, exotic or unbalanced civilisation.

A later generation had become more sceptical. The Russian intelligentsia had grown disillusioned, a notorious chasm divided the educated from the uneducated, deprived the educated of 'organic' connection with the society which they criticised and sought to guide, and rendered them incapable of influencing events. The swan song of the old intelligentsia takes the form of a correspondence between a famous and aging critic and his friend and contemporary, a greatly gifted, civilised and influential symbolist poet, about the crumbling of the world in which both were brought up. The critic, Mikhail Gershenzon, a Jew, confesses to being crushed by the enormous burden of the unforgotten, unburied past – the weight of tradition too heavy to be borne by those who are, for good or ill, steeped in Hebraic as well as Western culture with its obsessive historical sense. The poet, Vyacheslav Ivanov, who speaks as a 'Hellene' and an heir of Byzantium, seeks a synthesis of pagan classicism and Christianity, of Dionysus and Christ, through which the individual, if not the masses, can be transformed and saved. This is the final, fascinating and tragic document of a declining civilisation, overwhelmed by a cataclysm partly of its own making, consciously averting its eyes from the 'new shores' towards which the post-revolutionary society was to drive full steam ahead. It is the social and political outlook of this civilisation, and the impact on it of the West in the two centuries that preceded the epoch-making (for once this term preserves its literal meaning) collision in our own day of two worlds, that the writings of the intelligentsia call up from the half-forgotten past.

THE MAN WHO BECAME A MYTH

WHEN Ivan Aksakov in 1856 described his tours of the provincial centres of European Russia, he wrote:

> The name of Belinsky is known to every thinking young man, everyone who is hungry for a breath of fresh air in the reeking bog of our provincial life . . . If you need an honest man capable of showing compassion for the oppressed in their piteous misfortune, or an honest judge, not afraid of a fight, go and look in the provinces among Belinsky's followers.[1]

Obviously we are dealing with a major phenomenon of some kind – someone upon whom idealistic young Russians of the 1830s or 1840s, exasperated by the social, intellectual and moral condition of Russia, looked as their natural leader. The reminiscences of the intellectuals of the period – Turgenev, Herzen, Annenkov, Dostoevsky – agree in stressing this aspect of him, the 'conscience' of the Russian intelligentsia, the inspired and fearless publicist, the ideal of *révoltés* young men, the man who almost alone in Russia had the character and the eloquence to proclaim clearly and harshly what many felt, but either could not or would not openly say.

Vissarion Belinsky's name became the greatest Russian myth in the nineteenth century, detestable to the supporters of autocracy and the Orthodox Church. For the same reason he became the idealised ancestor of the liberal and the revolutionary movements of the nineteenth century, and in a very real sense he is one of the founders of the movement culminating in 1917 in the overthrow of the social order, that order which towards the end of his life he hated and denounced. Every radical Russian writer since the day of Belinsky's death claimed to be descended from him; the left-wing authors of the 1860s – the revolutionary propagandists Nekrasov

---

[1] *Ivan Sergeevich Aksakov v ego pis'makh* (Moscow, 1888–96), vol. 3, pp. 290–1.

and Chernyshevsky, Pisarev and Dobrolyubov – and the socialists who followed them, Lavrov, Plekhanov, Lenin and his followers, formally recognised him as one of the earliest and, with Herzen, the greatest of the heroes of the heroic social struggles of the 1840s.

Clearly, then, he was, to say the least, an arresting figure in the history of Russian social evolution. Herzen has revealed his genius in his incomparable memoirs, translated into several European languages: but Belinsky remains sealed in his original Russian, and so is still relatively unknown in the West.[1] And yet he is the true father and the perfect master of systematic social criticism of literature, of which so much was to be heard later in the century; the best and most formidable enemy of the aesthetic, the religious and the irrationalist attitudes to history and to art. Throughout the nineteenth and well into the twentieth century his views were the great central battlefield between rival schools of Russian critics, between the impressionists and the realists, the spiritualists and materialists, the aesthetes and the socialists, between radically incompatible views of art and of society and indeed of life. In the Soviet Union the fight is over, the victors have silenced the defeated and Belinsky has been canonised as a founding father of the new form of life. But the issue in the West is open still. This alone makes him infinitely worthy of study.

His life is a gloomy and outwardly an uneventful story. He was born in poverty in 1810 or possibly 1811, in the city of Chembar in the government of Penza in Central Russia. His father was a naval doctor who later settled down to a small practice and to drink. He grew up a thin, consumptive, over-serious, pinched little boy who soon attracted the attention of his schoolmasters by his single-minded devotion to literature and embarrassingly violent passion for the truth. He went to Moscow as a poor endowed scholar, had his share of all the troubles and misfortunes of impoverished students of humble birth in what was still the home of the gentry and nobility – the University of Moscow – and was expelled for reasons which are still obscure, but probably connected with the

---

[1] This was written in 1947. Since then some of Belinsky's work has been translated into other languages. The following three volumes contain translations into English: V. G. Belinsky, *Selected Philosophical Works* (Moscow, 1948; reissued 1956); Ralph E. Matlaw (ed.), *Belinsky, Chernyshevsky, and Dobrolyubov: Selected Criticism* (New York, 1962; repr., Bloomington and London, 1976); W. J. Leatherbarrow and D. C. Offord (trans. and ed.), *A Documentary History of Russian Thought from the Enlightenment to Marxism* (Ann Arbor, 1987). Ed.

writing of a bad and only mildly subversive play denouncing serfdom. He was taken up by a professor of fine arts of radical views and encouraged to write literary criticism. From 1835 onwards Belinsky poured out a steady stream of articles, critical notices and reviews in various periodicals. They preached a new gospel and split educated Russian opinion for ever into rival camps. Belinsky wrote to keep alive, and consequently wrote too much. Much of his writing was composed in haste, a good deal is turgid and uninspired – mere hack-work. But his best work, despite all hostile criticism, is today regarded in Russia as classical and immortal.

Belinsky looked like a peasant, and moved like one in an awkward, nervous and abrupt fashion; before strangers he was painfully shy, and often sullen. But with his intimates, the young radicals Turgenev, Botkin, Ivan Aksakov, Bakunin, Granovsky, he was full of life and gusto. In the heat of a literary discussion his eyes would shine, his pupils dilate, and he would walk from corner to corner, talking loudly, rapidly and with violent intensity, coughing and waving his arms. In society he was unbelievably clumsy and frightened, and once upset a bottle of wine over the court uniform of Zhukovsky. He disappeared in the general *mêlée*, ran all the way to his lodging, and went to bed in a state of nervous collapse for three days. Herzen in his memoirs declares that Belinsky was at his best in argument with an opponent:

> Unless there was a controversy, unless he was irritated, he did not talk well; but when he felt wounded, when his dearest convictions were affected, the muscles of his cheeks would begin to tremble, his voice would break: ah, one should have seen him then: he would fling himself on his opponent like a leopard and tear him to pieces, he would render him ridiculous, absurd, pathetic. And in the course of this he would develop his own thought with astonishing power and poetry.[1]

Belinsky lived a life of abnormal intensity, punctuated by acute crises, intellectual and moral, which destroyed him physically. The subject which he had chosen was literature, and although he was most acutely sensitive to purely literary quality, to the sounds and the rhythms of words, to images, poetical thought and the aesthetic

---

[1] *My Past and Thoughts*, part 4, chapter 25: SS [see p. 10 above, note 1] ix 31.

emotions directed towards them, they were not the central factor of his life. This factor was the influence of ideas, not merely in the intellectual or rational sense in which ideas are judgements or theories, but in that sense which is more familiar, but more difficult to express, in which ideas embody emotions and instincts and types of behaviour as well as thoughts. Ideas in this sense perpetually excited Belinsky and kept him in a state sometimes amounting to a kind of moral frenzy. The problems which tormented him were concerned with the relation of the individual to himself, to other individuals, and to society, but particularly with the imaginative work of the artist. The problem for Belinsky is always a moral problem. Ideas to him were not merely interesting or delightful or even intellectually important. Ideas were above all true or false, and if false then evil, and to be exorcised. All books embody ideas, even when least appearing to do so, and it is for these the critic must seek to probe.

To illustrate this I shall give a curious example: Belinsky printed a short routine review of a new Russian translation of *The Vicar of Wakefield*, and this obscure piece makes his attitude very clear.[1] Belinsky does not like Goldsmith's masterpiece because he thinks that, in the character of the Vicar, Goldsmith represents apathy, placid stupidity and incompetence as ultimately superior to the qualities of the fighter, the reformer, the aggressive champion of ideas. The Vicar is represented as a simple soul, a good man, full of Christian resignation, and this natural goodness, it is implied, is somehow antipathetic and superior to cleverness, intellect, action. This to Belinsky is a deep and damnable heresy. All books embody points of view, rest on underlying assumptions, social, psychological and aesthetic, and the basis on which the Vicar rests is philistine and false. It is a glorification of persons who are not engaged in the struggle of life, who stand on the edge, uncommitted, pure and untarnished, who enter only to be deceived and taken in, and so incur material defeat, but also spiritual and moral victory. It is not far from this to the notorious Russian ideal, the holy fool,

[1] At the time this essay was written (1947) it was generally assumed by Belinsky scholars that this (unsigned) review, published in *Sovremennik* in November 1847 (1847 vol. 6.1, part 3 ['Russkaya literatura'], 77–86), was by Belinsky. It has since emerged, however, that it was in fact written by A. D. Galakhov, who mentions it in 'Moe sotrudnichestvo v zhurnalakh', *Istoricheskii vestnik* 26 (1886), 312–35, at p. 323. Since Galakhov's attitude echoes Belinsky's closely, and may indeed have been influenced by it, I have retained this useful illustration of their views. Ed.

Dostoevsky's idiot, Tolstoy's Platon Karataev. But to Belinsky it is simply a paean to the faith in 'muddling through' of the average bourgeois Russian, the pathetic Oblomov of Goncharov's famous novel. It is a mere excuse for idleness, a dishonest representation of cowardice as a deeper wisdom, of failure and compromise as a profound understanding of life. One may say that this is exaggeration, and is putting too ludicrous a burden on the shoulders of the poor Vicar. But it is a striking application of the new principle of social criticism to literature. Characters are judged no longer by whether they are good or bad, virtuous or vicious intrinsically in themselves, but by their relation to their society.

Books and ideas to Belinsky were crucial events, matters of life and death, salvation and damnation, and he therefore reacted to them with the most devastating violence. Belinsky was a moralist, secular and anti-clerical through and through. Religion was to him a detestable insult to reason, theologians were charlatans, the Church a conspiracy. He believed that objective truth was discoverable in nature by the sciences, in society by history, and in the hearts of men by moral sense. If you want to understand what life is really like, and therefore what can and should be made of it, you must distinguish what is eternal and desperately important from the ephemeral, however attractive.

To do this you must sink beneath the mere flow of life, what Virginia Woolf called the 'semi-transparent envelope'[1] which encloses our existence from birth to death; you must examine the structure of the ocean bed and how the winds blow and how the tides flow, not as an end in itself, but in order to master the elements and to steer your craft, it may be against infinitely great odds, with unending suffering and heroism; but the goal is truth and social justice, which is the only goal worth seeking. To linger on the surface, to spend yourself in increasingly elaborate descriptions of the surface and of your sensations, was either moral idiocy or calculated immorality, which would in the end destroy the man who espouses it. Only whole truth was beautiful, it could never be hideous or destructive or trivial and it did not live in the outer appearance, in the mere flux of life. The truth lay beneath and was revealed only to those who cared for it alone, and was therefore

---

[1] [Virginia Woolf], 'Modern Novels', *The Times Literary Supplement*, 10 April 1919, p. 189, col. 4. This anonymously published article was revised and reprinted by Woolf as 'Modern Fiction' in her collection entitled *The Common Reader* (London, 1925).

not for the neutral, the indifferent, but for the morally committed, for those who were prepared to sacrifice all in order to establish truth and liberate themselves and others from illusions, conventions and self-deceptions. This was the creed – enunciated for the first time – of the Russian intelligentsia, of the moral and political opposition to autocracy, the Orthodox Church and nationalism, the triple support of the regime.

If anything seemed new or important to Belinsky, or even true, he would fly into ecstasies and proclaim his discovery to the world in ill-written, impassioned sentences, as if to wait might be fatal because the attention of the vacillating public might be distracted. Moreover one must herald the truth tumultuously, for to speak in an even voice would perhaps not indicate its crucial importance. And in this way Belinsky, in his exuberance, did discover and over-praise a handful of worthless writers and critics whose names are today justly forgotten. But in the course of this he did also reveal – and for the first time – the full glory of the great sun of Russian literature, Alexander Pushkin, and he discovered and assessed at their true worth Lermontov, Gogol, Turgenev and Dostoevsky, not to mention such writers of the second rank as Goncharov or Grigorovich or Koltzov. Of course Pushkin had been recognised as a writer of genius before Belinsky had begun writing, but it was Belinsky who revealed Pushkin's importance, not merely as a poet of magnificent genius, but as in the literal sense the creator of Russian literature proper, of its language, its direction and its place in the national life. Pushkin is represented as at once the invader of hitherto remote foreign territory, and the integrator of the deepest and most national elements of the Russian past, a poet who justly saw himself as a herald and prophet who by his art had made Russian society conscious of itself as a spiritual and political entity, with its appalling anachronistic inner conflicts and its queer, anomalous position among other nations.

Russian criticism is never confined to literature, but integrates it with that of morals, of politics, of institutions, of every aspect of spiritual activity, and in this sphere Pushkin occupies a wholly unique and central position. This unique domination of one author over the imagination of a vast nation, over the notion of itself which it carries in its own breast, is a fact to which there is scarcely a parallel; neither Dante nor Shakespeare, neither Homer nor Virgil, nor Goethe, transformed the national consciousness of their people to a comparable degree.

It was Belinsky who first saw in Pushkin the Russian sun, the central star in whose radiance Russian thought and feeling grew so rapidly. Pushkin himself, who was a gay, elegant, fastidious, frivolous man, thought this most odd, and spoke of Belinsky as 'a queer character who for some strange reason seems to adore me'. He was a little frightened of him, thought him unpresentable, and successfully avoided a personal meeting.

It is really in terms of Pushkin's art and Pushkin's personality that Belinsky, whether he realised it or not, tried to define his own ideas of what a creative artist is and should be. Belinsky as a critic did not belong to those whose main purpose and skill consists in a critical or historical analysis of artistic phenomena. He detested detail and had no bent for scrupulous scholarship; he read widely but very unsystematically; and he read and read and absorbed inexhaustibly, in a feverish, frantic way (his friends called him 'Bessarione Furioso') until the last possible moment and then he wrote in a kind of fury for nights and days. His unique quality as a literary critic, the quality which he possesses to a degree scarcely equalled by anyone in the West, is the astonishing freshness and passion with which he reacts to any and every literary impression. It is this that distinguishes him from other accomplished critics: his vision is wholly direct, there is nothing between him and the object.

The central question for all Russians concerned about the condition of their country was social, and perhaps the most decisive single influence on the life and work of Belinsky was his social origin. He was born in poverty and bred in the atmosphere, at once bleak and coarse, of an obscure country town in a backward province. Moscow did, to some degree, soften and civilise him, but there remained a core of crudeness, and a self-conscious, rough, sometimes aggressive tone in his writing. This tone now enters Russian literature, never to leave it. Belinsky spoke in this sort of accent because this kind of raised dramatic tone, this harshness, was as natural to him as to Beethoven. Belinsky's followers adopted his manner because they were the party of the *enragés*, and this was the traditional accent of anger and revolt, the earnest of violence to come, the rough voice of the insulted and the oppressed peasant masses proclaiming to the entire world the approaching end of their suffering at the hands of the discredited old order.

Belinsky was the first and the most powerful of the 'new men', the radicals and revolutionaries who shook and in the end destroyed the classical aristocratic tradition in Russian literature. The literary *élite*, the friends of Pushkin, despite radical ideas obtained abroad after the Napoleonic wars, despite Decembrist tendencies, was on the whole conservative, if not in conviction, yet in social habits and temper, connected with the court and the army, and deeply patriotic. Belinsky, to whom this seemed a retrograde outlook, was convinced that Russia had more to learn from the West than to teach it, that the Slavophil movement was romantic illusion, at times blind nationalistic megalomania, that Western scientific progress offered the only hope of lifting Russia from her backward state. And yet this same prophet of material civilisation, who intellectually was so ardent a Westerner, was emotionally more deeply and unhappily Russian than any of his contemporaries, spoke no foreign languages, could not breathe freely in any environment save that of Russia, and felt miserable and persecution-ridden abroad. He found Western habits worthy of respect and emulation, but to him personally quite insufferable. When abroad he began to sigh most bitterly for home and after a month away was almost insane with nostalgia. In this sense he represents in his person the uncompromising elements of a Slav temperament and way of life to a far sharper degree than any of his contemporaries, even Dostoevsky.

This deep inner clash between intellectual conviction and emotional – sometimes almost physical – predilection is a very characteristically Russian disease. As the nineteenth century developed, and as the struggle between social classes became sharper and more articulate, this psychological conflict which tormented Belinsky emerges more clearly: the revolutionaries, whether they are social democrats, or social revolutionaries, or communists, unless they are noblemen or university professors – that is, almost professionally members of an international society – may make their bow with great conviction and sincerity to the West in the sense that they believe in its civilisation, above all its sciences, its techniques, its political thought and practice, but when they are forced to emigrate they find life abroad more agonising than other exiles. Belinsky can no more be thought of as a voluntary émigré than Dr Johnson or William Cobbett.

To some degree this peculiar amalgam of love and hate is intrinsic to contemporary Russian feeling about Europe: on the one hand intellectual respect, envy, admiration, desire to emulate and excel; on the other emotional hostility and suspicion and contempt, a sense of being clumsy, *de trop*, of being outsiders; leading as a result to an alternation between excessive self-prostration before, and aggressive flouting of, Western values. No recent visitor to the Soviet Union can have failed to remark this phenomenon: a combination of intellectual inadequacy and emotional superiority, a sense of the West as enviably self-restrained, clever, efficient and successful; also cramped, cold, mean, calculating and fenced in, incapable of large views or generous emotion, incapable of feeling which at times rises too high and overflows its banks, unable to abandon everything and sacrifice itself in response to some unique historical challenge; incapable of ever attaining a rich flowering of life. This attitude is the most constant element in Belinsky's most personal and most characteristic writings: if it is not the most valuable element in him, it is the most Russian: Russian history past and present is not intelligible without it, today more palpably than ever.

Belinsky established the relation of literature to life in a manner which even writers not sympathetic to his point of view, such as Leskov and Goncharov and Turgenev, all of whom in some sense pursued the ideal of art, were forced to recognise; they might reject his doctrines, but they were conditioned by the power of his invisible presence into at least having to settle accounts with him. If they did not follow him they felt compelled to explain themselves on this matter. Thus, for example, Turgenev, pulled one way by Flaubert, another by the awful apparition of his dead friend, vainly tried to placate both and so spent much of his life in trying to persuade himself and his Russian public that his position was not morally indefensible and involved no betrayals or evasions. This practice of trying to determine one's proper place in the moral and the social universe continued in Russian literature until the revolt of the aesthetes and the symbolists under Ivanov and Bal'mont, Annensky and Blok; but this movement, splendid as its fruits were, did not last long, and the Soviet Revolution has attempted to revive, albeit in a crude and unrecognisably utilitarian form, the canons of Belinsky and the social criterion of art.

A REVOLUTIONARY
WITHOUT FANATICISM

ALEXANDER IVANOVICH HERZEN was born in his father's house in Moscow on 6 April 1812, some six months before Napoleon occupied the city; he died in Paris on 21 January 1870, during the last days of the Second Empire. His father, Ivan Alekseevich Yakovlev, came of an ancient, wealthy and aristocratic Moscow family. During his travels abroad he met Luisa Haag, the daughter of a minor official in Württemberg, and returned to Moscow with her. He established her as mistress of his household, but, perhaps for reasons of social disparity, did not marry her. Her son Alexander did not inherit his father's name, and was called Herzen almost as if to mark the circumstances of his birth.

He seems to have been treated in every other respect as his father's true son and heir: he received the normal education of a well-born Russian of those days, and after a succession of private tutors, among whom he remembered best a French émigré with crypto-Jacobin views and a Russian student of mildly radical leanings, he entered Moscow University in 1829, and attended lectures on philosophy, literature and the natural sciences, or what went under that name in Moscow at that time.

Like other young men in Europe in the new dawn of radical thought, he admired the writings of French socialists and German Idealist philosophers, and defended their views with fervour and wit in the Moscow literary salons. His contemporaries liked (or disliked) him for his gaiety and charm, his passionate and uncompromising character, his overflowing imagination and wide culture, his sensitiveness, his rapid, darting, bold and (as one of his friends called it) 'predatory' intellect, his dialectical skill, above all his singular combination of generous moral idealism and a biting, intolerant, often highly destructive, ironical humour.

Herzen found himself politically suspect comparatively early in his university career, probably for discussing and supporting left-wing social views, and his subsequent career in government service was broken by two periods of exile, in each case for entertaining 'dangerous' ideas. Both in exile and in Moscow and St Petersburg he wrote, and occasionally published, essays, short stories and novels, imbued with that spirit of violent protest against the political and social environment of his time which in varying degrees characterised all the *révolté* young intellectuals in Russia during the reign of Nicholas I, and in particular his friends Turgenev, Bakunin, Stankevich, Granovsky, Belinsky, Ogarev and other members of the remarkable group of young radicals who created the traditions of the Russian intelligentsia.

Herzen's early essays are typical of the preoccupations of the time: they deal with historical and philosophical topics – the 'new' French sociological school of historians (he actually translated Augustin Thierry's Merovingian tales), the nationalism of the Slavophils, distinctions in subject and method between the various arts and sciences. There are semi-Hegelian disquisitions on the true vocation of man in the nineteenth century and on the relations of nature to history; fragments of autobiography; an elegant and amusing account of the difference between the spirit of Petersburg and that of Moscow; and finally a lengthy dissertation on the competing dangers of dilettantism and pedantry.

The last of these essays is perhaps the most acute and the best written. Herzen draws an entertaining and very telling contrast between impressionable and easily excited but superficial amateurs who view facts through a telescope and do not see the trees for the wood, as against the microscopic pedantry of professional scholars, happy victims of the worst German academic models. He enjoys himself equally at the expense of both these failures of perspective, but, on the whole, is severer towards the amateurs who shrink before the awful prospect of losing their own precious, unique individuality in preoccupation with scholarship, than to the purblind specialists who cling timorously to their own narrow field.

As for Herzen's novels and stories, they are typical radical denunciations of conventional morality and social oppression, written under the influence of Schiller, the French romantics, George Sand and the passionate 'literature of protest' of the period. His best novel, *Who is to Blame?*, deals with a situation common enough at that time – of a rich and unhappy young Russian landowner (the 'superfluous man')[1] vainly struggling against his environment – a figure to become celebrated later in the novels of Herzen's contemporaries, Goncharov, Dostoevsky, Tolstoy, but especially Turgenev – the prototype of many a Russian Hamlet, too idealistic and too honest to accept the squalor and the lies of conventional society, too weak and too civilised to work effectively for their destruction, and consequently displaced from his proper function and doomed to poison his own life and the lives of others by neurotic behaviour induced by the vices of a society that sins against the moral ideals which the author holds dear, a society either irremediably corrupt, or still capable of regeneration, according to the author's social or religious beliefs.

On his father's death in the spring of 1846, Herzen, now financially secure, asked himself what career he was to pursue. He was ambitious and knew this; he wished to make his mark in the world, to build himself a monument. His inability to be a model government official had shown him plainly that there was no room in Russia for a high-spirited, gifted, violently liberty-loving, romantically inclined aristocratic young man who wished to enter the field of public activity. In the winter of 1847, taking with him his wife, his mother and his entire household, he left for Paris. He never saw Russia again.

After slowly crossing Germany and France the travellers reached the French capital. In Paris Herzen plunged headlong into the great ferment of ideas and emotions in which the political émigrés, gathered there from every European country, lived their agitated lives. The arresting quality of his mind and personality made an impression even in that extraordinary assembly of talent and genius; he was, with Bakunin, almost the first denizen of the barbarous and frightening Russian Empire to be recognized as almost an equal by the political thinkers of the fabled West – as a serious social critic and thinker, and not, like other cultured Russian travellers, as a gifted and agreeable visitor from an exotic land, or an indolent and curious passer-by. A new revolution was clearly gathering in Europe and Herzen was caught in its mounting tide.

During 1848–9 he travelled in Switzerland, Savoy and Italy, and his descriptions of the stirring events which he witnessed in Rome and Paris during the *annus mirabilis* are masterpieces of acute observation and literary talent. He does not conceal his sympathies:

[1] See p. 74 above, note 2.

he detests kings and priests, soldiers and policemen, bankers, bourgeois politicians, authors of appeals to good sense and order; he idealises the *blouses bleues* – the workers of Paris – and pays a glowing tribute to the generous and simple-hearted plebeian masses in Rome; he is for republicans, revolutionaries, the triumvirs of Rome, Garibaldi, for the leader of the Roman populace, known as Cicerovacchio, for Saffi and Mazzini. He speaks with affection and irony about his friend Bakunin, the greatest of Russian political agitators, invaluable on the first day of a revolution, disastrous on the second; he admires and likes Proudhon, Michelet, the Swiss radical James Fazy, Karl Vogt; his most intimate friends are the revolutionary German poet, Wagner's friend, Georg Herwegh, and Herwegh's wife.

By a bitter irony of circumstance the relationship between himself, his wife (and first cousin) Natalie and Herwegh began more and more to resemble the plot of his own *Who is to Blame?*, in which a fascinating stranger falls in love with the happily married wife of a man who trusts him, and duly destroys himself and his friends. Herzen perceived this analogy himself and rejected it with indignation. His 'superfluous' hero Bel'tov was at least capable of moral agony and heroic martyrdom, whereas Herwegh now seemed to him a contemptible philistine and scoundrel, married to an equally repulsive wife. Herzen set down the details of the entire episode with a self-revealing candour and painful precision, oddly unexpected in so proud and sensitive a man. Natalie, left by her lover, returned to her husband, to die in his arms a year later.

Blow followed blow. Herzen's mother and one of his sons were drowned in a tempest off Genoa. The revolution in Europe collapsed ignominiously in one country after another. In a state of acute personal and political misery, Herzen left France and settled in the free but, to him, bleak and chilly atmosphere of England. He lived in and near London intermittently until the middle 1860s. In London he established his free printing press, and in the 1850s began to publish two periodicals in Russian, *The Pole Star* and *The Bell* (the first issues appeared in 1855 and 1857 respectively), which marked the birth of systematic revolutionary agitation – and conspiracy – by Russian exiles directed against the tsarist regime.

Herzen's London house – or houses, for he moved from one to another constantly – became a place of pilgrimage for the radical exiles of many lands, particularly Poles, with whom he was one of the few Russians to remain on warm terms all his life, and Italians, to whom he early lost his heart. His attitude to Frenchmen was more reserved: the self-importance, the rhetoric, the monomania of the *ci-devant* tribunes of the people and their entourage offered too much material for his highly developed sense of the ridiculous. He found the mystical Hungarian worship of Kossuth more bizarre than awe-inspiring; the Germans, in particular Karl Marx and his friends, he found personally unbearable.

As for the English, he met few among them. He piously called on the aged and senile Owen; he corresponded with Carlyle; he respected Mill. He was helped by Joseph Cowan and other radicals. But, on the whole, little attention was paid to him in England, and he responded with mingled admiration and dislike for his hosts. His warmest friendships remained those of his early years, with his Russian friends and contemporaries – first and foremost with the poet Ogarev, with whom he set up house in London in the 1850s, and with Bakunin, who had escaped from his Siberian exile, and whom, in the 1860s, he viewed, as before, with a mixture of irritation and indulgence. He delighted in the stream of Russian visitors who came to see him – writers and journalists, liberal aristocrats with a taste for taking political risks, old Slavophil opponents, vehement young radicals who thought him a useless relic of a previous epoch, dissident Orthodox priests, university professors, old acquaintances of all sorts, whom his growing prestige drew towards what had in fact become the official centre of the opposition to the Russian government.

Herzen became a European celebrity, and *The Bell*, which specialised in exposing specific abuses in Russia and in naming names, in the heyday of its fame – the late 1850s and early 1860s – exercised a unique influence even in official circles in St Petersburg. After the suppression of the Polish Rebellion in 1863 its influence – it had supported the Poles in the face of almost universal patriotic indignation in Russia – began to fall precipitately. After lingering in a desultory manner in London, where he lived intermittently and not too happily with Ogarev's gifted and neurasthenic wife, Herzen travelled in Italy and Switzerland, and died in Paris on 21 January 1870. He is buried in Nice and his statue stands above his tomb.

Early in his London period he began his celebrated autobiography or biographical memoirs – *My Past and Thoughts* – on which his fame as a writer ultimately rests. This work is a literary and political masterpiece worthy to stand beside the great Russian novels of the nineteenth century. The book has no formal design but consists of a succession of episodes connected by a loose chronological sequence, in the course of which Herzen records private and public experiences, draws vignettes of personalities and predicaments, offers analyses of present and future social and political conditions, both in Europe and Russia, together with scattered personal observations, fragments of a diary, epigrams, historical and psychological sketches, travel notes, accounts of the impact made upon him or of the role played by political or historical ideas; vivid and exact descriptions of his feelings, of incidents in his life, encounters, conversations, confessions, entertaining and memorable sketches of the characteristics and eccentricities of various groups of émigrés in London and elsewhere, of episodes in their lives, and of their reactions to one another and to their English hosts – this vast and apparently heterogeneous amalgam held together by a gift for narrative and descriptive writing which, in its own kind, has never been excelled. *My Past and Thoughts* is an autobiography of genius, and remains preeminent even in the nineteenth century, which was exceedingly rich in this genre. It has been translated into several languages, but it is only in the author's native land that it is recognised as a major classic, comparable in quality and scope with *War and Peace*.

Besides this famous work, Herzen, during more than twenty years of uninterrupted activity as a publicist – the voice of free Russia abroad, calling for revolution – poured out a mass of articles, letters, essays, proclamations, the best of which are original masterpieces both of journalism and of art. He was one of the most perspicacious observers of the European scene in the nineteenth century – in this respect only Marx and Tocqueville are comparable to him – and the *Letters from France and Italy* (he called an earlier version *Letters from Avenue Marigny*), which he sent in instalments to his friends in Moscow, to be printed in the radical Russian journal *The Contemporary*, contain the best general analyses of the political and social scene of the West just before and during the revolutions of 1848–9. He continued to observe, record and analyse public and private life in France, in England, in Russia, in articles and improvisations, all his life. Unsystematic, brilliantly entertaining and permanently valuable, these fragments are scattered in the thirty volumes of the great Soviet edition of his works, and still form a unique account of the public life of Europe in the middle years of the last century.

More important than most of these historical sketches is the long essay which Herzen entitled *From the Other Shore*. This is an attempt to assess the consequences, and point the moral, of the final failure of the European revolutions of 1848. As a piece of writing this essay exhibits, at any rate in the original, that combination of acuteness, irony, imagination, moral distinction, fiery, often poetical, eloquence, and penetrating intellectual force coupled with an elegance of style and poignant feeling which forms the peculiar quality of Herzen's personality as a writer. It is designed as a post-mortem on the liberal and democratic doctrines – and phraseology – which had suffered shipwreck in the failure of the revolution, and contains ethical and political ideas which are of interest not simply as scattered *pensées* but as an expression of a moral and social philosophy of considerable originality, possessing affinities with views fully articulated only in our own time.

From the Other Shore deals with the débâcle of 1848 neither in the detached and ironical mood of Tocqueville's celebrated memoir, nor as an application of a specific theory of society to contemporary events, like the two justly celebrated essays on the same theme by Karl Marx. Herzen wrote neither to justify individuals and parties, nor to demonstrate a particular philosophy of history. But he resembled Marx and Tocqueville in that he, too, sought to describe the situation, to examine the views and ambitions and desires, of the various parties and individuals and classes, and their social and historical roots; to consider the manner and the causes of the betrayal of the revolution by its principal supporters; to expose the emptiness and the confusions of the social and political programmes themselves – and to trace this to specific fears, muddles and evasions on the part of those high-minded but craven liberals who at the same time undermine the old order and cling to it, light the fuse and try to stop the explosion.

Herzen's essay attempts neither social nor economic analysis, but is, in the main, a frontal attack upon the doctrine at that time preached by almost every left-wing orator in Europe (with the notable exception of Proudhon, the German anarchist Max Stirner and a handful of other anarchists to whom no one listened), about the sacred human duty of offering up oneself – or others – upon the altar of some great moral or political cause, some absolute principle or abstract noun capable of stirring strong emotion, such as Nationality, or Democracy, or Equality, or Humanity, or Progress.

For Herzen (influenced perhaps by the views of Stirner) these are merely modern versions of ancient religions which demanded human sacrifice, faiths which spring from some irrational belief (rooted in theology or metaphysics) in the existence of vast and menacing powers, once the objects of blind religious worship, then, with the decay of primitive faith, degraded to becoming terms of political rhetoric. The dogmas of such religions declare that mere invocation of certain formulae, certain symbols, renders what would normally be regarded as crimes or lunacies – murder, torture, the humiliation of defenceless human bodies – not only permissible, but often laudable.

Against this Herzen advances his own positive beliefs: that man is, within narrow but discernible limits, free; that he is neither the impotent plaything of natural forces, nor a trivial unit in a uniform mass of historical raw material intended by some unknown deity for consumption by the great historical process – the Hegelian 'slaughter-bench'[1] of history – and consequently doomed to a kind of creative self-immolation, that thereby the march of the spirit might be rendered more glorious. This was the image at the heart of much historical romanticism as interpreted both by the reactionary right and by the revolutionary left; and indeed has formed the content of much subsequent German thought and art, with its recurrent emphasis upon the supreme value of the death and transfiguration, if need be, of entire peoples and civilisations, in wars and revolutions and other forms of terrible, but rationally directed, historically inevitable, and thereby sanctified, cataclysm.

Herzen rejected this as a sadistic mythology possessing no moral justification, founded on no empirical evidence. He believed that morality was neither a fixed nor an evolutionary objective code, a set of immutable commandments which rational human beings were merely required to discern and obey, whether these commands were ordained by a personal deity or were found in 'nature' or in some intelligible 'logic of history'. He maintained that men create their own morality; that, animated by that egoism without which there is no vitality and no creative activity, the individual is responsible for his own choices, and cannot plead the

---

[1] Georg Wilhelm Friedrich Hegel, *Sämtliche Werke*, ed. Hermann Glockner (Stuttgart, 1927–51), vol. 11, p. 49.

alibi of either nature or history for failing even to try to bring about that which he considers, for whatever reason, to be good, or just, or delightful, or beautiful, or true.

This denial on his part that it was, in principle, possible to formulate general and eternal moral rules, a denial made without a trace of Byronic self-dramatisation or Nietzschean hyperbole, is a doctrine that is not often encountered in the nineteenth century; indeed, in its full extent, not until well into the twentieth, where it forms a bridge between empiricists endowed with moral imagination and historically conscious existentialists who have something genuinely intelligible to say. It hits both right and left: against romantic historians, against the Hegel of the *Philosophy of Right*, and to some degree against Kant, against utilitarians and against supermen, against Tolstoy and against the religion of art, against 'scientific' and 'evolutionary' ethics, against all the Churches. It is empirical and naturalistic, recognises values that are absolute for those who hold them, as well as change, and is overawed neither by determinism nor by dogmatic socialism. And it is exceptionally independent.

Herzen attacked with particular force those who appealed to general principles to justify savage cruelties and defended the slaughter of thousands today by the promise that millions would thereby be made happy in some invisible future, condoning unheard-of miseries and injustices in the name of some overwhelming but remote felicity. This attitude Herzen regards as a pernicious delusion, perhaps a deliberate deception; for the distant ends may not be realised, while the agonies and sufferings and crimes justified by appeals to them in the present remain only too real; and since we know so little of the future, and possess no means of accurate prediction, to affirm the opposite and seek to condone the effects of our brutal acts by holding out such hollow promises is either lunacy or fraud. We cannot tell whether the millions will ever achieve the happy condition we have so confidently guaranteed to them; but what we do know is that thousands will perish, unheard, today. Distant ends are for Herzen not ends at all, but a monstrous delusion – ends must be closer at hand, 'the labourer's daily wage, or pleasure in the work performed'.[1]

Inhabitants of the twentieth century scarcely need to be reminded of the tyranny of the great altruistic systems; of liberators who crush, of 'the arithmetical pantheism of universal

---

[1] *From the Other Shore*: SS [see p. 10 above, note 1] vi 34.

suffrage' and 'superstitious faith in republics'[1] on the one hand, or the brutal arrogance of minorities on the other. Herzen, however, was writing over a century ago, in a time of mounting democratic eloquence, when the enemy was cold-hearted individualism, or clerical and dynastic despotism, and against them there rose the vast, visionary Utopias of socialists and Catholics, Hegelians of the left and positivists, and many another among the great metaphysical and religious system-builders of the nineteenth century.

This was the dominant current, and Herzen resisted it both intellectually and emotionally, because it seemed to him to threaten individual liberty and human rights. As a thinker in the Western tradition (and, despite his paeans to the Russian peasant, Herzen's populism, like Tolstoy's, derives from Rousseau rather than from native soil), he is enlightened and sceptical. He belongs to the tradition of Erasmus and Montaigne, Bayle and Fontenelle, Voltaire and Constant, Humboldt and the English philosophic radicals, of all those who protest against despotism wherever they find it, not merely in the oppression of priests or kings or dictators, but in the dehumanising effect of those vast cosmologies which minimise the role of the individual, curb his freedom, repress his desire for self-expression, and order him to humble himself before the great laws and institutions of the universe, immovable, omnipotent and everlasting, in whose sight free human choice is but a pathetic illusion.

All such systems seemed to Herzen equally spurious. In *From the Other Shore* he attacks the meanness and enviousness of the bourgeoisie which crushes everything original, independent or open, as he attacks clerical or military reaction, or the hatred of freedom and the barbarous brutality of the masses. He has a sense of impending doom no less vivid than Marx or Burckhardt, but whereas in the writings of both Marx and other Hegelian visionaries there is an unmistakable note of triumph in the very thought of vast and destructive powers unchained against the bad old world, Herzen is free from any desire to prostrate himself before the mere spectacle of irresistible power, however just or in the service of reason; he is free from contempt for or hatred of weakness as such, and from the romantic pessimism which is at the heart of the nihilism and Fascism that were to come. If communism – the revolt of the masses – is ever allowed to sweep across Europe,

[1] *My Past and Thoughts*: SS xi 70.

it will be 'dreadful, bloody, unjust, swift',[1] and, in the name of the blood and tears of the oppressed, will mow down all that civilised men hold dear.

But, unlike the apocalyptic prophets of his time, Herzen thinks this cataclysm neither inevitable nor glorious. When he warns his friends against the 'Phrygian cap'[2] or the red flag of the masses as being no less murderous than the 'bloodstained sword'[3] of the ruling class, he does so not out of romantic despair, but with a positive purpose, because he thinks that knowledge, reason, will-power, courage can avert the danger, and alter the course of mankind. It may, of course, be too late; Europe – the West – may well be going under; must Russia, too, be submerged in the tidal wave?

The clearest exposition of Herzen's hopes and fears for his own country is contained in the open letter addressed to the celebrated French historian Jules Michelet. A friend of the great poet Mickiewicz, the greatest of all the victims of Russian oppression, and of his fellow exiles from partitioned Poland – 'the martyr of Europe' – Michelet had written passionately denouncing the Russians as barbarous brutes unfit to associate with European nations. Herzen replied temperately, with genuine sympathy for the Poles, and expounded, in answer to Michelet, some of those optimistic, and indeed Utopian, notions on which, as he grew progressively more pessimistic about the prospects of the Western world, he had fixed his hopes.

He saw salvation in the communal organisation of the Russian peasant, and wrote eloquent pages about their generous and spontaneous Russian character, uncontaminated by the corroding doubts and moral squalor of the Western world in decline. He had somehow persuaded himself that the uncorrupted Russian peasantry, with its natural socialism, would of itself suffice to solve the 'greatest social problem' of the century – how to reconcile the claims of individual liberty with the demands of an inevitably more and more centralised authority, how to preserve personal life without 'atomising' society, the central dilemma which the Western world had thus far failed to solve.[4] Collectivised production together with the preservation of the rights and freedoms of individual persons – rights and freedoms in which neither Marx

[1] *From the Other Shore*: SS vi 104.
[2] ibid: SS vi 46.
[3] *Letters from France and Italy*, fourteenth letter: SS v 211.
[4] ibid., fourth letter: SS v 62; cf. SS xii 112.

nor Cabet nor Louis Blanc, in his view, had shown the least interest – that is the answer with which the Russian peasant will astonish the world.

True, the peasant commune had not been sufficient to save Russia from the nightmare of Byzantium, or the Tartar yoke, or the big stick of German officialdom, or the tsar's knout; but, armed with Western scientific techniques, the unbroken Russian *moujik* would yet teach the world a great lesson in social organisation. Russian populism, whether sentimental or realistic, owes more to the ungrounded optimism with which Herzen comforted himself than to any other single source.

Herzen struck impartially in all directions, and so was duly condemned by both sides: by the Russian right wing as a subverter of Church and State; by the left, particularly by the new young revolutionaries in Russia, as a self-indulgent sceptic, too rich, too civilised, too elegant, too much a gentleman, too comfortably established in the West to understand the harsh realities of the Russian situation, and dangerous too, because prone to sound a note of disillusion, even of cynicism, and so to weaken the sinews of the revolution – liable to become ironical and, worse still, entertaining, at a time when serious men must decide to commit themselves to one side or the other without so much fastidious regard to their private consciences and hyper-civilised needs and scruples.

Herzen replied to 'the youth of the '60s' that organised hooliganism and nihilism solved nothing; and in one of his last writings drew his own vignette of the 'new men'. The new generation would say to the old: 'You are hypocrites, we will be cynics; you spoke like moralists, we shall talk like scoundrels; you were civil to your superiors, rude to your inferiors; we shall be rude to everyone; you bow without feeling respect, we shall shove and jostle and offer no apologies . . .'.[1]

On the whole, it is Herzen's totalitarian opponents both of the right and of the left that have triumphed. And it is a singular curiosity of history (of a kind which Herzen himself delighted to describe with incomparable malice and wit) that, on the strength of laudatory references to him by Lenin, this enemy of authority, who was, perhaps, the most devastating, as he certainly was the most understanding, opponent of the many out-and-out communisms of his day – the enemy of all dogma, who declared that *salus populi* was as vicious a cry as *lèse-majesté*,[2] that no ideal at which

---

[1] *My Past and Thoughts*: SS xi 351.
[2] *From the Other Shore*: SS vi 46.

one was forbidden to smile was worth anything at all – it is a strange irony that Herzen, who had no love for Marx and the 'Marxids' (as he called them), either personally or politically, should find himself canonised in his native country today[1] as one of the sacrosanct founders of the new way of life.

The 'nihilists' of the 1860s and the socialist writers of a later date who attack him for his liberal inclinations are a good deal more honest and consistent. Their suspicions turned out to be valid enough. For Herzen does like the style and colour of free human beings; best of all he likes fire, originality, aesthetic feeling, even when it is found in oligarchies and aristocracies. He has no affinity with the mass of the oppressed as such, only indignation and a desire for justice. The qualities that he loves best are those which they too seldom possess – imagination, spontaneity, humanity, civilised feelings, natural generosity, courage, wide horizons, instinctive knowledge of what individual freedom is, and hatred of all forms of slavery, arbitrary rule, human humiliation and degradation.

He extols these virtues wherever he finds them, even in the camp of the oppressors; and rejects political formulae and generalisations, however deeply sanctified by the martyrdom of fighters for a cause which he called his own. He declares over and over again that words and ideas offer no substitute for experience, that life teems with exceptions and upsets the best-made rules and systems. But in his case this attitude led not to detachment or quietism – to the tolerant conservatism of Hume or Bagehot – but was allied to an impatient, passionate, rebellious temperament, which made him the rarest of characters, a revolutionary without fanaticism, a man ready for violent change, never in the name of abstract principles, but only of actual misery and injustice, of concrete conditions so bad that men were morally not permitted – and knew that they were not permitted – to let them exist.

Starting from this kind of clear-sighted empiricism, influenced by the imaginative sweep of Hegel but sceptical of his metaphysical dogmas, Herzen gave expression to theses original enough to be rediscovered only in our own time: that the great traditional problems which perennially agitate men's minds have no general solutions; that all genuine questions are of necessity specific, soluble only in specific contexts; that general problems,

---

[1] 1956.

such as 'What is *the* end (or *the* meaning) of life?' or 'What makes all events in nature occur as they do?' or 'What is *the* pattern of human history?' are not answerable in principle, not because they are too difficult for our finite intellects, but because the questions themselves are misconceived, because ends, patterns, meanings, causes differ with the situation and outlook and needs of the questioner, and can be correctly and clearly formulated only if these are made part of the question. It is Herzen's grasp of this fact that makes him a forerunner of much twentieth-century thought, and marks him as one of the few men who preserved a free critical intellect in a time of rising ideological tyrannies.

Herzen never forgot, as some of his most inspired fellow revolutionaries often did, that actual human beings, and specific problems, can be lost sight of in the midst of statistical generalisations. In his discussion of what men live by, there occurs the smallest proportion of abstraction and generalisation, and the highest proportion of vivid, three-dimensional, 'rounded' perception of actual character, authentic human beings with real needs, seeking attainable human ends, set in circumstances which can be visualised. And in the course of his analyses he uses the Russian language with a virtuosity to which no translation is ever likely to do complete justice. It was not for nothing that Tolstoy admired his writing and Dostoevsky recognised him as a poet.[1]

Essayist, agitator, publicist, revolutionary, philosopher, novelist, author of at least one work of genius, Herzen achieved a position in the history not merely of Russian literature but of Russia itself (as his friend, the critic Belinsky, had prophesied when they were both still in their early thirties) that is today unique and secure. But he deserves to be read beyond the borders of Russia, if only for his moral and political opinions. Many of his predictions were falsified by events, and his practical remedies, since they were not, and

---

[1] In his *Diary of a Writer* Dostoevsky expresses his deep admiration for *From the Other Shore* and tells the story of how he personally congratulated Herzen on it, saying that what had particularly impressed him was the fact that the author's opponent in the dialogue was not a man of straw, but a formidable controversialist who managed to drive Herzen into awkward corners – 'Ah, but, of course, that is the whole point,' Herzen replied. F. M. Dostoevsky, *Polnoe sobranie sochinenii v tridtsati tomakh* (Leningrad, 1972–90), vol. 21, p. 8. It may just be worth adding that the views of the interlocutor were founded on the real opinions of one of Herzen's Russian friends of this period.

perhaps could not have been, applied, can be written off as Utopian. But his central insights remain as fresh and arresting today as when they were first uttered by him more than a hundred years ago, and their relevance to our times seems even greater than to his own.

POSTSCRIPT 1979

Since this was written, almost a quarter of a century ago, nothing, it seems to me, has happened to lessen the relevance to our own times of Herzen's analysis of the shipwreck of liberal illusions in 1848–9. He was not a liberal or a constitutionalist, but a radical and a revolutionary: he rejected the cautious gradualism of his erstwhile friends Granovsky and Turgenev. But, unlike Marx, Herzen did not believe that men's theory and practice are unalterably conditioned by their relations to the forms of production at work in their societies. He believed that ideas in men's heads (not themselves determined by some historical libretto) could be decisive in generating great social changes, both good and evil; and the recent history of the oscillation between right-wing tyrannies and left-wing dictatorships (as well as the rise of governments which contain the worst elements of both) does not disprove this.

For those who, like Herzen, believe that faith in impersonal forces or causes, justifying acts which would be accounted monstrous on any normal reckoning, is fatal to all that men live by, and that the free play of the mind is indispensable to the existence of a tolerable human society, *From the Other Shore* remains one of the sharpest and most vivid statements of what is at stake for people who are not prepared to sacrifice their right to doubt and differ for the sake of obedience and security. Brave and civilised men like Sakharov or Mihailov, or the humane Spanish and Portuguese socialists, are today the true heirs of Herzen. Perhaps the old adage that heresies cannot be crushed by brute force is, despite all the tragic examples to the contrary, not after all quite the pious fallacy that John Stuart Mill once gloomily pronounced it to be.

THE ROLE OF THE INTELLIGENTSIA

THE WORD 'intelligentsia', like the concept, is of Russian origin and was invented some time in the 1860s or 1870s. It did not mean simply educated persons. It certainly did not mean merely intellectuals as such. Russian society in the nineteenth century was, to use a contemporary term, underdeveloped. It was a backward society, consisting to a vast extent of a mass of illiterate, semi-starved peasants, a certain number of bureaucrats holding them down with various degrees of efficiency, and a small class of persons who had received sufficient education either to be officials, administrators or clerks, or to form that minimum number of lawyers, doctors, land surveyors and teachers without which even so backward a mass as the Russians could scarcely be expected to get on. There was a very oligarchical, not to say despotic, regime at the top, and a Church with no central tradition of scholasticism or rational argument – with many saints and martyrs and visionaries but with none of the intellectual discipline which formed the Church of Rome; knowledge and learning were scarce. The small minority of persons who had access to the civilisation of the West and freely read foreign languages felt relatively cut off from the mass of the people; they felt they were almost foreigners in their own land – what is nowadays called 'alienated' from society. Those among them with sensitive consciences were acutely aware of a natural obligation to help their fellows who were less happy or less advanced than themselves.

These people gradually became a group, who held that to speak in public, to write, to lecture imposed on them a direct and peculiar moral obligation. If you lived in Paris in the '30s or '40s of the nineteenth century, you lived in a world in which a great many ideas circulated and collided: faiths, ideologies, theories, movements clashed with each other and created a general 'climate of opinion'. But no given ideology, no given set of concepts, so dominated that society as to create a fanatical ascendancy. In a country like Russia, cut off from the West in the first place by the great medieval religious schism, a country into which few ideas from outside were allowed to penetrate, in which literacy was very low, almost any idea which came in from the West – provided that it possessed any degree of initial attractiveness – fell upon marvellously rich and virgin soil, and was taken up with a passion hardly imaginable in the West. If there is a large vacuum, and a very fresh and untutored people, many of them eager for light, then almost any idea – no matter how fanciful or obsolete – is likely to find some ready response somewhere. This was the position in Russia in the second quarter of the nineteenth century. Hence the immense addiction to theories and doctrines – not merely as something of intellectual interest, not merely as something to while away an idle hour, but to some a source of salvation, something which, if believed in and acted upon, might lead people to a better life, like that which some of them fondly imagined was being led in the West.

These young men were pro-Western if only because they groaned under a yoke which prevented them from obtaining that minimum degree of normal education which, it was imagined, was becoming more and more open to the inhabitants of the West. Consequently they idealised the West. Like the enlightened thinkers of an earlier day in France and Germany, they believed that only by the critical use of reason could the reign of superstition, prejudice, tradition, dogma, blind obedience, arbitrary rules and servility be arrested. They believed in modern science and in human progress. They discovered that certain Western thinkers – in particular after the failure of the French Revolution – had turned away from reason and science back to non-rational sources, religious and aesthetic, dogmatic and intuitive. Some of the Russians were influenced by this too, but most of those who drank of Western sources in the end regarded this as a false path: a betrayal of the present to the past. Burke and Maistre made relatively little headway among them. The Russian intelligentsia – because it was small and consumed by a sense of moral responsibility for its brothers who lived in darkness – grew to be a dedicated order bound by a sense of solidarity and kinship. Isolated and divided by the tangled forest of a society impenetrable to rational organisation, they called out to each other in order to preserve contact. They were citizens of a State within the State, soldiers in an army dedicated to progress, surrounded on all sides by reaction.

This is the kind of phenomenon which, it seems to me, tends to occur in large, socially and economically backward communities, run by an incompetent government and an ignorant and oppressive Church. In this sense, there can be said to have been an intelligentsia in Spain in the nineteenth century; perhaps in the Balkans and in certain countries of Latin America and Asia. It did not happen to such an extent even in France, where the notion of the intelligentsia as such, as an independent social formation, did not arise. Still less was it the case in England. I am not concerned – nor competent – to examine the social and economic roots of this phenomenon: I wish only to say something about its most obvious characteristics.

If you were a French or even an English writer in the nineteenth century, you might very well have taken the view that you were a purveyor like any other kind of purveyor. This was the attitude of some of the French writers who believed in art for art's sake, who believed that their business was simply to write in language which was as lucid or as expressive or as beautiful as they could make it, and who saw themselves simply as craftsmen, as persons who produce an object and wish to be judged by the object alone. If a man makes a silver bowl, provided the silver bowl is beautiful, that is all that can be expected of him. His private life, convictions, behaviour were none of the public's – or the critics' – business. This point of view was rejected with ferocity by the Russians of whom I speak. The idea that a man plays roles – that if he is a goldsmith you should judge him *qua* goldsmith, and that his private life has nothing to do with it, that if he is a writer you judge him solely by the merit of his novel or poem – was rejected by the best-known Russian men of letters, because they believed that man was one, that any form of compartmentalisation was a maiming of human beings and a distortion of the truth. This fundamental point of difference is what distinguishes the general attitude of most of those whom we consider typical Russian writers from a good many writers in the West. And it is central to the Russian concept of the intelligentsia.

I do not mean to say that all important Russian writers thought this. Those who were born in the eighteenth century – Pushkin and his contemporaries – for the most part cannot be regarded as belonging to the intelligentsia. Writers like Gogol and Tolstoy –

different as they were – rejected the very idea of it. Their view of human beings was quite different from, say, that of Belinsky or the young Herzen, or, in some moods, Turgenev. They did not believe in reason, in science, in the West; they looked with contempt upon those deluded imitators of 'Europe' who did not understand the inner life of man, which had nothing to do with progress or science or reason. This is also to a great extent true of Chekhov, even, at times, of Gorky. Turgenev stood betwixt and between. Sometimes he inclined to one side, sometimes to the other. He oscillated comfortably between qualified support and critical irony. The real members of the intelligentsia were the political pamphleteers, the civic-minded poets, the forerunners of the Russian Revolution – mainly journalists and political thinkers who quite consciously used literature, sometimes very poor examples of it, as vehicles for social protest.

Given that this is the central concept of the intelligentsia, let me now move to the West. Northrop Frye, in a suggestive contribu-tion to a recent collection of lectures,[1] makes an important point. He says that, broadly speaking, the tendency of Western thinkers has been to take science as the paradigm; and because science is objective and factual and means freedom from personal or subjective influences, and in particular from value-judgements, there has been a tendency among intellectuals to prize and overprize objectivity and scientific method, even to the point where such objectivity becomes detachment – detachment of the kind which is normally ascribed to those engaged in the natural sciences, which makes an atomic physicist shrug off enquiries about his social responsibility with a certain degree of irritation; he says that he is simply engaged in the discovery of the truth; the application of his discoveries is no more his business than that of any other citizen of the State, however it is governed. People engaged in psychological or physiological research are sometimes equally reluctant to admit their responsibility, though their experiments may lead to all kinds of astonishing transformations of human beings, and may give to certain individuals dangerous powers of conditioning people, of altering their responses. This is called the detachment or objectivity of science; and Frye thinks that it can go too far, that scientists engaged upon work which has

---

[1] 'The Knowledge of Good and Evil', in Northrop Frye and others, *The Morality of Scholarship* (Ithaca, New York, 1967).

obvious social implications cannot simply opt out of responsibility in these matters, although he does not, in the end, tell us how much responsibility these persons bear, or what they should do about it. He also says that social concern, such as I have attributed to the Russian intelligentsia, can go too far.

Such social concern can easily, in moments of crisis, become a kind of hysteria, as it does in the case of those who seek to protect our societies against real or imagined perversion, and this is responsible for all kinds of censorships, intellectual crusades, attempts to organise writers or artists to defend their nation, against Communism or against Fascism or against atheism or against religion. The organisation of artists and writers can become a danger. The attempt to cling to some existing order and to rationalise the defence of this order as some kind of intellectual duty – if I do not misinterpret Frye – becomes a form of intolerance, a suppression of freedom of speech and of freedom itself. Between these two poles the unfortunate dealers in ideas and other forms of human communication are compelled to live and find some kind of acceptable equilibrium.

These are the dangers of the West. But in the land in which the intelligentsia was born, it was founded, broadly speaking, on the idea of a permanent rational opposition to a status quo which was regarded as in constant danger of becoming ossified, a block to human thought and human progress. This is the historic role of the intelligentsia as seen by itself, then and now. It does not just mean intellectuals or artists as such; and it certainly does not mean educated persons as such. The educated can be reactionary, just as the uneducated can. So can intellectuals. So can artists. We know this very well in our day. It is a melancholy phenomenon which happens on both sides of the Iron Curtain. Nor does it mean sheer opposition to the Establishment as such. Protesters and marchers, people who oppose the use of atomic energy for destructive purposes, or the Vietnam war, no matter how sympathetic their moral position, or admirable their sense of social responsibility, are not members of the intelligentsia simply because they are protesting against the behaviour of their government. These persons do not necessarily believe in the power of reason or the beneficent role of science, still less in the inevitability, or even the desirability, of human progress, conceived in secular and rational terms. Some of them may appeal to irrational faiths, or wish to escape from industrial society into some simpler, but wholly Utopian, world.

Sheer protest, whether justified or unjustified, does not qualify one to be a member of the intelligentsia as such. What does do so is a combination of belief in reason and progress with a profound moral concern for society. And this, of course, is much more likely to occur in countries where the opposition is deepest and blackest; and least likely to occur in loose, democratic, relatively open societies, where those persons who might be made indignant in the more reactionary societies are apt to bend their energies to ordinary pursuits – to being a doctor, lawyer, professor of literature – without any oppressive sense that in doing so they are somehow failing in their duty, that in not taking part in some kind of collective civic indignation they are indulging private desires and deserting their civic post. The *intelligentsia militans* – and this is what the original intelligentsia was, and it is part of its essence – is generated by truly oppressive regimes. There are, no doubt, many despotisms: but to look on England, of all countries, as despotically ruled seems perverse. There are many other things wrong, socially and economically; but a country in which the government needs to make up to a wide electorate, however it does this, and is in danger of being turned out, is, whatever else it may be, not a despotism. To say, therefore, that British society stands in need of this kind of ferocious, unsurrendering, well-organised revolutionary intelligentsia seems to me an exaggeration. Others may think quite differently.

To the old nineteenth-century intelligentsia the very notion of a class of persons involved in intellectual pursuits – such as professors, doctors, engineers, experts, writers, who in other respects live ordinary bourgeois lives, and hold conventional views, and who play golf or even cricket – this notion would have been absolutely horrifying. If a man was a professor in late nineteenth-century Russia, then the mere fact of his involvement with ideas made him an implacable opponent of the regime in which he lived; if it did not, he was, in the eyes of the militant, a traitor, a man who had sold out, a coward or a ninny.

No doubt it is the duty of those who deal in ideas to be rational and to suit the action to the word, to live integrated lives, not to divorce their thoughts from their actions (the kind of thing of which Goethe was accused by Russian critics), not to say to themselves that to be a professor or an artist is a profession like that of a blacksmith or an accountant, which does not impose special social responsibilities. But it does not follow that awareness of one's intellectual responsibilities must in any modern Western society turn one into a permanent subversive, into someone systematically opposed to the status quo, on the grounds that those who are comfortable in it, and those whose lives it penetrates, are automatically enemies of progress and of mankind. And that is why one cannot, if the valuable use of the term is not to be hopelessly diluted, really speak of an English intelligentsia. One can speak of English intellectuals; one can speak of persons who like ideas and those who do not; of levels of education; of progressives and reactionaries, rationalists and sceptics; one can talk about the duties of literacy. But if you said to someone who was educated, and fascinated by, or at least at home with, ideas (for example, to some politically inactive first-generation Bloomsbury figure, or a follower of, say, André Gide in France), that for him not to be politically rebellious was a moral abandonment of his social post, an acceptance of cowardly ideological illusions, he could answer: 'This is true only on certain assumptions.' For example, on Marxist assumptions, which entail that one necessarily belongs to one's class, which is engaged in class warfare; either to the class which is fighting or to the class which is fighting back; either to the class which is progressive or to the class which needs to be destroyed. But if you do not accept these assumptions, then such obligations do not necessarily follow. It is one thing to be critical, to take part voluntarily in controversy; it is another thing to assume that, since there are very few such people, they constitute a kind of standing *force de frappe*: ready to fight and die in a resistance which never lets up, always at the barricades.

The two things are not identical. In Russia they were, for the particular historical reasons which I have tried to indicate. Something of the sort was and is also true in certain other countries; it is true of some of the children of East European immigrants in America or Israel; it may be true in much of Asia and Africa today; but there is a complacency about the direct and automatic application of this notion in essentially less repressive forms of government. America is at present possessed by discussion and doubts on this very subject, and is in a peculiar position. Huge, dark forces have arisen – and are being justly resisted there. But for whatever reasons, the enemies of enlightenment do not seem to me to be so powerful and so sinister in England today, and neither hippies nor militant students, neither war-resisters nor Americanophobes, whatever view one may take of their acts or goals, resemble the old intelligentsia in its heyday, save to the degree to which it stood (and stands) for human decency against cruelty, hypocrisy, injustice and inequality. The same is true of every progressive movement in history – yet early Christianity was not the revolt of an intelligentsia, nor is Buddhism. This is not a pedantic, verbal point. Central notions, even labels, which have played a part in human history have some claim to have their integrity respected.

LIBERTY

WHAT IS political liberty? In the ancient world, particularly among the Greeks, to be free was to be able to participate in the government of one's city. The laws were valid only if one had had the right to take part in making and unmaking them. To be free was not to be forced to obey laws made by others *for* one, but not *by* one. This kind of democracy entailed that government and laws could penetrate into every province of life. Man was not free, nor did he claim freedom, from such supervision. All democrats claimed was that every man was equally liable to criticism, investigation, and if need be arraignment before the laws, or other arrangements, in the establishing and maintaining of which all the citizens had the right to participate.

In the modern world, a new idea – most clearly formulated by Benjamin Constant – makes itself felt, namely that there is a province of life – private life – with which it is thought undesirable, save in exceptional circumstances, for public authority to interfere. The central question posed by the ancient world is 'Who shall govern me?' Some said a monarch, some said the best, or the richest, or the bravest, or the majority, or the law courts, or the unanimous vote of all. In the modern world, an equally important question is 'How much government should there be?' The ancient world assumed that life was one, and that laws and the government covered the whole of it – there was no reason to protect any corner of it from such supervision. In the modern world, whether historically because of struggles of the Churches against intervention by the secular State, or of the State against the Church, or as a result of the growth of private enterprise, industry, commerce, and its desire for protection against State interference, or for whatever reason, we proceed on the assumption that there is a frontier between public and private life; and that, however small the private sphere may be, within it I can do as I please – live as I like, believe what I want, say what I please – provided this does not interfere with the similar rights of others, or undermine the order which makes this kind of arrangement possible. This is the classical liberal view, in whole or part expressed in various declarations of the rights of man in America and France, and in the writings of men like Locke, Voltaire, Tom Paine, Constant and John Stuart Mill. When we speak of civil liberties or civilised values, this is part of what is meant.

The assumption that men need protection against each other and against the government is something which has never been fully accepted in any part of the world, and what I have called the ancient Greek or classical point of view comes back in the form of arguments such as this: 'You say that an individual has the right to choose the kind of life he prefers. But does this apply to everyone? If the individual is ignorant, immature, uneducated, mentally crippled, denied adequate opportunities of health and development, he will not know how to choose. Such a person will never truly know what it is he really wants. If there are people who understand what human nature is and what it craves, and if they do for others, perhaps by some measure of control, what these others would be doing for themselves if they were wiser, better informed, maturer, more developed, are they curtailing their freedom? They are interfering with people as they are, but only in order to enable them to do what they would do if they knew enough, or were always at their best, instead of yielding to irrational motives, or behaving childishly, or allowing the animal side of their nature the upper hand. Is this then interference at all? If parents or teachers compel unwilling children to go to school or to work hard, in the name of what those children must really want, even though they may not know it, since that is what all men as such must want because they are human, then are they curtailing the liberty of the children? Surely not. Teachers and parents are bringing out their submerged or real selves, and catering to their needs, as against the transient demands of the more superficial self which greater maturity will slough off like a skin.'

[If you substitute for parents a Church or a Party or a State, you get a theory on which much modern authority is based. We are told that to obey these institutions is but to obey ourselves, and therefore no slavery, for these institutions embody ourselves at our best and wisest, and self-restraint is not restraint, self-control is not slavery.]

The battle between these two views, in all kinds of versions, has been one of the cardinal political issues of modern times. One side says that to put the bottle beyond the dipsomaniac's reach is not to curtail his liberties; if he is prevented from drinking, even by force, he will be healthier and therefore better capable of playing his part as man and citizen, will be more himself, and therefore freer, than if he reaches the bottle and destroys his health and sanity. The fact that he does not know this is merely a symptom of his disease, or ignorance of his own true wishes. The other side does not deny that anti-social behaviour must be restrained, or that there is a case for preventing men from harming themselves or from harming the welfare of their children or of others, but denies that such a restraint, though justified, is liberty. Liberty may have to be curtailed to make room for other good things, security or peace or health; or liberty today may have to be curtailed to make possible wider liberty tomorrow; but to curtail freedom is not to provide it, and compulsion, no matter how well justified, is compulsion and not liberty. Freedom, such people say, is only one value among many, and if it is an obstacle to the securing of other equally important ends, or interferes with other people's opportunities of reaching these ends, it must make way.

To this the other side replies that this presupposes a division of life into private and public – it assumes that men may wish in their private lives to do what others may not like, and therefore need protection from these others – but that this view of human nature rests on a fundamental mistake. The human being is one, and in the ideal society, when everyone's faculties are developed, nobody will ever want to do anything that others may resent or wish to stop. The proper purpose of reformers and revolutionaries is to knock down walls between men, bring everything into the open, make men live together without partitions, so that what one wants, all want. The desire to be left alone, to be allowed to do what one wishes without needing to account for it to some tribunal – one's family or one's employers, or one's party, or one's government, or indeed the whole of one's society – this desire is a symptom of maladjustment. To ask for freedom from society is to ask for freedom from oneself. This must be cured by altering property relations as socialists desire to do, or by eliminating critical reason as some religious sects and, for that matter, Communist and Fascist regimes seek to do.

In one view – which might be called organic – all separateness is bad, and the notion of human rights which must not be trampled on is that of dams – walls demanded by human beings to separate them from one another, needed perhaps in a bad society, but with no place in a justly organised world in which all human streams flow into one undivided human river. On the second or liberal view, human rights, and the idea of a private sphere in which I am free from scrutiny, is indispensable to that minimum of independence which everyone needs if he is to develop, each on his own lines; for variety is of the essence of the human race, not a passing condition. Proponents of this view think that destruction of such rights in order to build one universal self-directing human society – of everyone marching towards the same rational ends – destroys that area for individual choice, however small, without which life does not seem worth living.

In a crude and, some have maintained, a distorted form, totalitarian and authoritarian regimes have stood for one of these views: while liberal democracies incline to the other. And, of course, varieties and combinations of these views, and compromises between them, are possible. They are the two cardinal ideas that have faced one another and dominated the world since, say, the Renaissance.

THE PHILOSOPHY OF KARL MARX

KARL MARX was not primarily a philosopher. His fame rests on a prodigious effort to discover and formulate the laws that govern the behaviour of men in society, and on the creation of a movement designed to transform the lives of men in conformity with these laws. He was a sociologist, economist and active revolutionary into whose purview philosophy entered not as a separate study but as an element in his general theory of man. Nevertheless, he began as a philosopher and his philosophical position, despite considerable gaps and incoherences, can be pieced together from his early writings, which were, for the most part, not published in his lifetime. The Marxist philosophy of our own day is an amalgam compounded out of published and unpublished sketches by Marx himself, the metaphysical works of his collaborator Engels (who spoke of 'the dialectics of materialism'), and the subsequent glosses upon these and the development of them by later commentators. The term 'dialectical materialism', by which the philosophical doctrines binding on orthodox Communists are known, was invented by the Russian socialist Georgy Plekhanov.

One of the principal reasons for Marx's lack of interest in philosophy as a specific field of study was doubtless his belief, derived, like much else in his system, from Hegel, that ideas could not be profitably studied in isolation, since they were an inseparable part of the activity of individuals and groups, and were literally unintelligible unless seen as an aspect of the total activity of men. Theory must not be viewed as something distinct from practice. The real opinions, motives and concepts of men are embodied in their acts and in their unreflective behaviour as well as in their explicit beliefs. Moreover to insulate any one activity, even for the purpose of scientific inspection, and consider it without regard to its place in the historical evolution of the total human activity to which it belongs, is to misunderstand and misinterpret it. Such a tendency to 'abstraction' is itself a symptom of a particular delusion, socially and historically conditioned, which Marx undertook to explain and dispel. To understand Marx's philosophical theory it is therefore necessary to grasp his view of what men are and how they come to act as they do.

Like the leading French materialist radicals of the eighteenth century, to whom he owed much, Marx believed, in the first place, that man was an object in nature, a three-dimensional lump of flesh, blood and bone to whom the laws of nature discovered by the sciences applied no less fully than to other material objects. Like these materialists, he denied the existence of an immaterial soul, of spiritual substances of any type, and therefore of God, and regarded theology and metaphysics as tissues of falsehood, usurping the place of the natural sciences, which alone could provide true solutions to all questions of fact, among them the laws governing the evolution of individuals and societies.

For Marx men differed from objects in nature principally because they were able to invent tools. Man was endowed with a unique capacity not only for using but for creating instruments to provide for his basic needs – for food, shelter, clothing, procreation, security and the like. These inventions then altered man's relations to external nature and transformed him and his societies, thereby stimulating him to make further inventions to satisfy the new needs and tastes brought about by the changes which, alone among the animals, he brought about in his own nature and world. For Marx technological capacities are man's fundamental nature: they are responsible for that awareness of the processes of living and conscious direction of them which is called history. Men are made what they are and differ from each other, not through some fixed inner principles of their natures – for there are none such – but by means of the work that they cannot avoid doing if they are to satisfy their needs. Their social organisation is determined by the ways in which they labour and create in order to preserve or improve their lives.

For the eighteenth-century materialists the history of mankind was to a large degree the story of avoidable human error, of the follies and illusions which clouded men's minds before scientific method, founded on empirical observation and accurate reasoning, revealed both the right questions to ask and the right ways of seeking for the answers; a long night of ignorance and superstition illuminated by occasional flashes of genius, which the leaders of

men – kings or priests or soldiers – largely exploited for the
purpose of keeping mankind in subjection to themselves.

For Marx the story is less simple. Like the fathers of sociology,
Hegel and Saint-Simon, he did not believe in timeless truths about
individuals or societies, holding universally, any one of which was
in principle capable of being discovered by anyone at any time and
in any circumstances. He held that any technological advance in
human development carried with it its own intellectual and moral
horizons. Men's ideas were not born in isolation from the rest of
their activities: ideas were – and could not but be – weapons in the
pursuit of the goals of men or social groups, exactly like other tools
or inventions or ways of behaviour, such as armies, or gunpowder,
or agriculture, or slavery, or the feudal system. Man-made
technology determines ideas and forms of life, and not the other
way about: needs determine ideas, not ideas needs. The windmill
created the feudal regime and the spinning-wheel the industrial
one: this epigram is a characteristically Marxist formulation of the
basic factors of human history. The windmill, for Marx, creates a
certain type of social organisation, and this in its turn gives rise to
opinions and attitudes and ways of life likely to promote, maintain
and resist attack upon that particular society – that is to say, that
particular type of distribution of power and authority among men
– whether the men in question realise it or not.

For Marx the mental life of men, which takes concrete form in
moral, philosophical, political, juridical, religious, artistic works
and institutions, can be understood only as part of the whole life of
society, the goals of which are determined primarily by the
techniques which it employs to satisfy its needs. Inventions and
discoveries transform the needs – and the forms of life – which
gave rise to them, and create new desires, new inventions, new
orders of society. But the key to the understanding of social life
will always consist in determining the forms taken by the struggle
for survival or for the satisfaction of basic wants or for the power
which can satisfy these wants in a given time and place. This is the
dominant factor in any society; to grasp its character is to be able
to explain – and predict – the particular development of ideas,
attitudes, moral and social rules, ways of filling hours of leisure,
and, most important of all, the structure of power and authority in
a given society, to which the outlook of men necessarily adapts
itself.

This is a technological theory of the development of social life; it is historical through and through, in that it claims to be able to account for the entire physical and mental life of men by determining their specific place on the single evolutionary path along which all life necessarily moves, which, whether men know this or not, determines all their ideas, wishes, hopes, fears and forms of self-expression at a given stage. Consequently to call anything a timeless truth about men or society must be in principle absurd. For there is nothing timeless in the lives of man: all truths consist in some relationship between men's thoughts and the objects about which they think, and since both objects and thoughts do not stand still but alter with changing historical conditions, things will look different to those who are hemmed in by a given society and press against its walls – in whose interest it is to alter or destroy it – as compared with the way in which that society will look and feel to those who are in a high degree of harmony with it, and therefore, either instinctively or consciously, opposed to change.

There is, for example, no social or moral truth which will be equally valid for both classes; thoughts, beliefs, moral feelings are for Marx forms of action, and their validity – or truth – will, like that of propaganda, depend upon the interests of the group to which the beholder belongs. All that can be judged objectively is their relative effectiveness. Those elements in a given culture survive which contribute to, and are therefore transmuted and absorbed by, its successor – the next stage in the struggle for material progress. Like the rationalist philosophers of the seventeenth and eighteenth centuries, Marx believed that human liberty consists in the systematic mastery of whatever resists human needs, whether in external nature or in his own wild and self-destructive passions. Freedom is planned control of available resources; the more rational the method of control, the ampler the resources, the larger the number of persons exercising such control – the greater the freedom.

This vision has obvious affinities with the philosophy of Hegel, which influenced Marx decisively. Like Hegel, Marx believed that history was the key to understanding man and his attributes: for there was a discernible pattern and intelligible goal in the development of human capacities. Certain types of activity, whether intellectual or practical, could not occur until and unless the appropriate faculties had become sufficiently developed; this itself stimulated into existence new faculties and activities, neither possible nor conceivable at an earlier stage. Hence, for Marx, as for Hegel, to scrutinise theories, philosophies, creeds in isolation, in order to determine their truth or falsehood, was to be guilty of 'vicious abstraction' – to leave out the contexts in which alone these thoughts could have occurred or made sense – and made it impossible to give adequate answers to the questions. Truth and falsehood, depth and shallowness, for Marx, necessarily relate to the social worlds to which the ideas in question organically belong.

Thus the notion, for example, of individual freedom, or of private property, and the ideas connected with them, such as economic justice and individual rights, can literally have no meaning in, let us say, certain types of primitive societies where the idea of ownership does not exist; and the doctrines embodying these historically evolving notions cannot, therefore, express timeless truths or eternal values, the very idea of which turns out to be a chimera. This applies to all concepts save perhaps that of the historical process itself. For Hegel, this objective order in human development was part of the growing self-awareness of concrete social development. For him, reality was the story of the growth of self-mastery and the mastery of nature by human society through technological progress; and, as part of the story, of the development of successive beliefs, outlooks, cultures, attitudes, which, even if at times they acquire a momentum and decisive influence of their own, are but the 'reflections' of this material advance in 'men's heads', each leaving to its successor only what was effective in it, that is, only that which helped in the creation by men of a life – necessarily social – which would respond effectively to their material needs.

What form did this development take? Hegel had taught that human progress took place in the form of a discontinuous 'dialectical' spiral, characterised by sudden leaps from one stage to another. For Hegel every stage in the path historically traversed by human beings takes the form of a tension between some dominant attitude – embodied in appropriate actions and institutions – and its opposite, something that struggles against it from within; leading to a conflict between opposed principles or forces, into which human consciousness and human activity inexorably splits itself. It is this continuous duel between conflicting trends at every level of human thought and feeling and behaviour that is responsible for change and progress. Whenever the mounting tension reaches a critical point, there is a collision, an explosion, humanity (or some section of it – a Church or nation, or culture) takes a leap on to a new shelf. The contending forces mutually destroy each other, but generate something new – a novel state of consciousness or form of life, which in its turn struggles with its own inner contradiction towards a new crisis, and so on in an upward spiral, indefinitely.

The notion that conflict and crisis are the sole cause of progress is as old as Heraclitus, but Marx translated the Hegelian categories of the spirit and his logical apparatus (sometimes with logically absurd consequences) into sociological ones. For him, historical development consists of conflict generated in the first place by material needs and technological inventions, and it occurs not in men's minds but in society – between groups of men at war with one another. For Marx, a class is a body of persons unified by some objective social interest: an objective interest being the need to achieve or acquire that which renders those who have it more free, that is, better able to master their own lives in order to achieve the rational satisfaction of their own needs. For Marx, the history of mankind is a history of the struggles of classes. His philosophy of history is the source of all his philosophical beliefs.

Ever since, according to him, primitive communism, with which (if not in his, then in his collaborator Engels's view) the life of man began on earth, was ended by those technological inventions which placed those who controlled them in a position to extort labour and other forms of service from those who did not, the life of men has been dominated by the efforts of those who have cornered the means of production to preserve their power and exploit other men in their own interests. This takes the form of treating the exploited as cattle – that is, of appropriating the difference between what it costs to keep them active and capable of production, and the value of their products. This Marx calls 'surplus value', out of which all capital is formed, and to secure which the class struggle is waged.

In the course of this great coercive hold over one section of society by another, the masters become, willy-nilly, engaged in social and economic activity aimed at the perpetuation and increase of their power. This very activity cannot but breed technical methods which alter the social structure and add – however little the masters may have intended this – to the skills and powers of the exploited. These last, trained in their own arts by their masters, in their turn overthrow them, only to be threatened with the same fate themselves when their own exploitation of the class below them duly reaches the (technologically conditioned) stage of crisis, explosion and the 'dialectical' leap on to a new level.

Ideas are weapons which the master class generates and uses in the course of its struggle for power. The function of such ideas, in virtue of their very origin, must always begin by militating in favour of the dominant class. Those among the exploited who accept these ideas – and the institutions in which they are embodied – uncritically accept something which militates against their own interests and in favour of that of their masters. They may be unaware of this, and accept these ideas and institutions as if they were eternally valid – guaranteed by religion, or metaphysics, or the order of nature, which is regarded as eternal, unalterable and just, and so they treat what in fact are products of changing human interests, human skills, the human struggle for power as if they were something ordained by an eternal divinity or some objective standard of truth or goodness or beauty, which is the same for all men, at all times, in all places.

Such standards do not exist for Marx. Everything is valid only in its own place and time, and intelligible only in terms of the social structure which requires it. As for the illusion that there exist universal human values, or that institutions created by the masters may be right for, or beneficial to, the oppressed – that is to him a form of 'alienation' (another Hegelian category), an inevitable concomitant of the painful progress of mankind.

'Alienation' is a phenomenon which occurs when something created to minister to human needs acquires an institutional life of its own, an independent existence, and presents itself to men not as an artificial weapon forged by them in pursuit of some need which may, indeed, have vanished long ago, but as an objective entity with power and authority, like some inexorable law of nature or of an all-powerful God. For Marx, the moral and religious values of what he calls the capitalist system of his own time, which dominate the whole of society, from the powerful and rich to the humblest and poorest, are precisely such forms of alienation: values and institutions whose sole purpose (although this may have been forgotten) is to prop up the power of a given economically dominant class have come to be regarded by the whole of a society as being independently valid for all men; with the result that, in an ossified and canonised form, institutions designed to forward the interest of the masters destroy the lives not only of the oppressed, but to some degree of the oppressors too.

This is no less true of moral and political systems; indeed of everything which, designed as it inevitably must be to forward the interests of one passing class, unconsciously twists the lives of its victims, so that men are exposed no longer merely to the ravages of uncontrolled nature, but become Frankensteins at the mercy of monsters of their own making – institutions, habits, beliefs whose origins are forgotten and whose functions are no longer understood. Men treat commodities as if they possessed a life and value of their own; the producer is cut off from the product he creates, and from the tools themselves, which acquire a delusive independent status, often against the interest of their creators.

At the same time, merely to grasp and see through this predicament will not conjure it away. The ideas which are to destroy these survivals must themselves, to be effective, like all influential ideas, be part and parcel of a self-liberating and therefore practical revolutionary activity, which cannot occur until the victims have reached a certain stage of social, and, only by this means, intellectual and moral organisation. 'Alienation', that is, the destruction of human solidarity by the existence of institutions originally designed to promote it, is, according to Marx, inevitable so long as the lives of men are dominated by class war – the inescapable form of the human struggle towards the mastery of nature and of their own irrational passions. Only when the last class in the ladder of classes, the proletariat, the men who possess nothing and are therefore bought and sold as a commodity, triumphs over its oppressors, as in the pattern of history it inevitably will – only then will the historical dialectic reach its final resolution. The class war will cease; and the ideas and institutions which have been used by one set of men against the freedom of another will be replaced by institutions and ideas useful to all mankind.

If everything that matters in human life is conditioned by the class to which a man belongs, and by the position of that class in the class war, then it follows that a man's ideas, however powerful their influence, must be determined by his social and economic status, and not the other way about. Marx therefore calls ideas an element in the superstructure, which is determined by the basic 'structure', that is, the economic constitution of a given human group, itself determined by what instruments of production are in use, and who controls them. Such superstructures Marx calls ideologies.

Sometimes he speaks of them as if they were networks of fictions, designed to rationalise – give false but comforting explanations of – facts from which a given class or sub-class recoils instinctively, because they point to its own inevitable destruction at the hands of its opponents, the class which they exploit. Thus he speaks of the ideas of bourgeois society as a conscious or unconscious rationalisation of its interests – what it wants the world to be if it is to survive in it – disguised as universal ideals. Since it will, in fact, not survive, these rationalisations are fallacious and delusive. Yet Marx does not (as Engels does) assert that chemistry, for instance, or mathematics is invalid because it is bred in, and used by, members of the governing class of its own time. He is prepared to say that social conditions may be unpropitious for the appearance of this or that physical or mathematical discovery or invention, which must wait for the historically appropriate moment (for example, the discovery of the steam engine in ancient Alexandria, or the submarine of Leonardo da Vinci); that the progress of science is intimately bound up with the progress of technology and its accompanying social institutions; but not that a given chemical formula or mathematical theorem actually distorts the lives of men who belong to a class opposed to that of its inventors, as historical or ethical or legal ideas certainly appear to him to do. His followers attempted to expose specific scientific theories, as well as certain logical and philosophical doctrines, as class-conditioned delusions, or deliberate deceptions. But Marx stopped short of this conclusion. Moreover, he seemed to believe that, even though the objective conditions making for their effective application to society had conspicuously not yet been realised, his own doctrines were, nevertheless, relatively free from the inescapable distortion and bias which he denounced so bitterly in the ideas of his opponents.

This ambivalence also characterises his moral and political ideas. Sometimes he speaks as if moral judgements, and indeed all value judgements, whether explicit, or implicit in behaviour and ways of life, are never anything but open or disguised weapons in the struggle for power or survival. If this is the case, then the ethics of a given class – say the 'bourgeoisie' – need no examination, for they are merely a form of camouflage which will vanish with the inevitable destruction of that which they protect. It follows that no attempt at reaching rational agreement by discussion between self-conscious members of different classes about moral (or for that matter any) issues can ever be of use, since the members of a class condemned by history have, in principle, been rendered incapable of understanding the world in which they live, by a kind of defensive mechanism which creates for them a fool's paradise, and prevents them from perceiving the ruin to which they are inexorably condemned by history.

At other times, however, Marx speaks of values as if they were not distinguishable from facts at all. Mankind is marching in a single direction, class conquers class, until there are no classes left to vanquish, and men are free from the distortion to which the class struggle had condemned them, and can at last take up the task of organising their lives together in a rational manner. No rational being wishes to be frustrated or destroyed. A rational man is one who understands the laws and factors at work in his society. To ask for the impossible is irrational; to believe in it is to be deluded by a Utopia. To say of a course of conduct, therefore, that it is good, or right, is identical with saying that it promotes, rather than hampers, the advance of humanity towards the classless society, which is nothing but reason in action. To say that, although X should happen, Y will, is ultimately meaningless, for 'should' means 'justified by reason', and therefore bound to be realised if history is indeed the march of reason in the form of the class war, as Marx supposed. Hence 'good', 'realistic', 'successful', 'free', 'scientific', 'effective', 'objective', 'socially determined' all coincide in meaning and 'evil', 'folly', 'failure', 'subjectivism' – which describe efforts to swim against the stream of history – are also equivalent expressions. Don Quixote is not merely ridiculous, but wicked: to be finally defeated and to be vicious are identical. Justice, mercy, freedom – universal human values to which non-Marxist socialists appealed – are for him lying figments. The only true appeal is to the movement of history – to that which is in tune with the needs of the class which embodies the most advanced section of mankind. If a given act promotes the interests of this class, it is good and, which is to say the same thing, will succeed; if it hampers them, it is bad, an illusion, likely to lead to failure and the 'alienation' of the actor from the marching army whose interests determine all true values.

The view of ideals as mere rationalising illusions ('ideologies') and the view of ideals as determined by this kind of cosmic utilitarianism are never fully reconciled in the writings either of Marx or of his successors. So, too, his political concepts are never wholly clear: thus, he defines the State sometimes as the committee of the ruling class for the purpose of coercing those below, sometimes as leading a distinct life of its own by aiming at something which it cannot, given the logic of history, ever be – namely an impartial arbiter between the classes. In either case the State must disappear: for, with the victory of the proletariat, there will be no one left to coerce. Rational men will not disagree about ends: disagreements will be only technological – about means, capable of being settled by argument between experts without the employment of force. Hence the instrument of coercion – the State – will wither away. Similarly Marx sometimes speaks as if the revolution is as inevitable as the class war – it is an objective, automatic certainty. At other times the overthrow of the social system depends on conscious and timely efforts by the workers and their leaders, which depend on deliberate human choice. Again there are times when Marx speaks as if each stage of the class struggle represents an advance on its predecessor, and is therefore a 'better' condition, since it is nearer the ultimate goal – the only sense of 'good' he can consistently recognise. Yet he seems to accord independent value to cultural achievements of whatever stage of progress; thus he accords a higher worth to the works of Aeschylus, Dante and Shakespeare than to the art of the bourgeoisie. At other times he speaks as if no value could be attached to any of the stages in the evolutionary ladder until the final cataclysm, when classes and their despotism disappear for ever. Nor have later thinkers succeeded in dispelling these and other obscurities in his moral and political doctrines.

THE FATHER OF RUSSIAN MARXISM

THE PRINCIPAL founder of organised socialism in Russia, Georgy Valentinovich Plekhanov, was born in 1856 near the city of Tambov in central Russia. His father was a prosperous country gentleman, his mother was distantly related to the critic Belinsky. He received the normal education of young men of his class, first at a military academy for sons of the gentry, then at the Mining Institute in St Petersburg. The 1870s – the period immediately following the emancipation of the serfs in Russia in 1861, and the disenchantment and peasant disorders that followed – mark the highest point of social idealism among the Russian gentry. Young men of good birth, consumed with a sense of personal guilt and responsibility for the ignorance, misery, backwardness and lack of elementary justice in which the great mass of the peasants of Russia (that is to say, the vast majority of its population) were living, gave up their position and their prospects, and went in great numbers to the villages. Some worked as doctors, schoolmasters, agricultural experts, even farm labourers; other, more resolute, spirits tried to rouse the peasants by direct propaganda – to indignation, and ultimately to an armed rising.

This generous and passionate mood, with its promise of danger, secrecy and self-sacrifice in a great human cause, reached its highest peak in the universities and schools. There is a story that Plekhanov, then a schoolboy of sixteen, forced his widowed mother to sell land to her peasants at a price lower than that offered by a neighbouring landowner, threatening that if she refused he would set the landowner's ricks on fire and give himself up publicly to the police. At the Mining Institute he joined a revolutionary group of students, and in 1876, after delivering a fiery address before an illegal demonstration of students and workers in Kazan' Square in St Petersburg, was forced to escape abroad to avoid arrest. His die was cast. His life was henceforth dedicated to the cause of the Russian revolution.

Like other young men of his time he was, in the mid-1870s, a populist. That is to say, he believed that the tsarist regime was corrupt, stupid and oppressive beyond the hope of reform and that only a violent upheaval could bring justice and freedom. The enemy was neither a class nor a specific group of individuals, but the State. Emancipation from it could be attained by a people only by its own efforts, and not conferred upon it by the action of individuals or minorities, however enlightened and well disposed. The greatest evils were coercion and exploitation of a majority by a minority. They could be ended only by a rising of the people, culminating in the creation of a federation of free, self-governing groups of productive individuals – peasants, artisans, members of the liberal professions, merchants, manufacturers – a socialism not unlike that advocated by Proudhon in France, and later by the Guild of Socialists in England.

The Russian populists believed that this programme was not easily realisable in the West, for there the Industrial Revolution had destroyed the basis for socialism by atomising society into a chaos of self-seeking individuals engaged in cut-throat competition. Some of them maintained that, so far as the West was concerned, Marx and his followers might well prove right in their predictions that the mere process of expanding industrialisation would, in due course, weld the factory workers into vast, homogeneous units in the perpetually growing monopolistic combines, and so, willy-nilly, create a monolithic and disciplined proletarian army designed by 'history itself' to revolt, and so set all men free. But in Russia no comparable industrial revolution had occurred. There an unbroken community of peasants, closely connected with city workers who were themselves still barely urbanised peasants, existed as a natural basis for a socialist society. The populists maintained that her very backwardness offered Russia a greater opportunity of building the new, just, free society on a co-operative basis than any that existed in the bitterly individualistic West.

Plekhanov believed all this, but with a difference. The majority of the populists were half-educated, emotionally exalted, confused, heroically uncalculating idealists, who threw themselves into the sacred movement with everything they possessed. To such people the very idea of prudence or patience suggested something mean, cowardly and insincere. Plekhanov was no less dedicated to the cause of the revolution, but he genuinely believed in reason, scientific knowledge, patience and careful preparation, and his brain remained cool and clear under all circumstances. His socialism was neither a poetic dream, nor a religious or metaphysical vision, nor a rationalisation of personal resentment or defeats, but a belief in the possibility of a social organisation at once rational and just. It was to be based on solid knowledge of history and natural science. It was to be created democratically; that is to say, not until the majority of a given society was sufficiently enlightened to understand what alone would make it free, happy and equal – then only, and not before.

The majority of the populists felt that this process of education might take too long. They came more and more to believe in terrorism as the only method open to a revolutionary minority of toppling the wicked regime, after which, they were convinced, the new, free, morally pure world would of itself rise from the ashes of the old. Plekhanov denounced this as a fairy-tale from the beginning to the end of his life. He believed that only understanding of the permanent laws that govern social and individual life can permanently transform it; until the majority of a given society attained to this, stupid and wicked governments were inevitable: bullets and bombs were ineffective against ignorance and barbarism on both sides. He broke with his comrades over this issue, and took no part in the conspiratorial activities which culminated in the assassination of Tsar Alexander II in 1881.

In the 1870s the populist programme seemed to him practicable in Russia because it was still a largely pre-industrial society. In the 1880s he abandoned this diagnosis. Under the influence of the writings of Marx and Engels, and of his own analysis of what was occurring in Russian economic life, he changed his views. He now believed, and believed for the rest of his life, that although Russian development was retarded compared with that of the West, it would follow the same inevitable stages towards increasing industrialisation. He believed that history was a science whose laws could be discovered; that these laws were laws of the development of man's productive faculties; unless men understood these laws they would fall foul of them, and their efforts to improve their lot would remain frustrated and, indeed, self-destructive.

In short, Plekhanov had become a Marxist. Whereas in the 1870s he had believed that the laws followed by Russian social and economic development were peculiar and *sui generis*, by the early

1880s he had convinced himself that they were not. He declared that the Russian village economy was dissolving. The possibility of preserving the village commune, in which the populists had placed their deepest faith, was a dream. What the peasants desired was not communal but private ownership; in other words, to become capitalists themselves. A capitalistic phase in Russia was not avoidable, although it might be shortened, and indeed continuously sabotaged, by the creation, on the admired German model, of a powerful Social Democratic Party, founded upon the support of the growing masses of industrial workers in the big cities. They, they alone, would free Russia. Yet, he added, if socialism were imposed by force it would lead to a political deformation like that of the Chinese or Peruvian empires: a renewed tsarist despotism with a Communist lining. The revolution must be democratic or it would not be a true revolution. Therefore the key lay in tactics based on scientific training, and a programme of the widest possible education. Nothing was to be strictly irrelevant to such knowledge: not merely economics or sociology, but philosophy in the widest sense, the history of the whole field of human endeavour, that understanding of what human beings were and are and can be which can be derived only from the understanding of the arts as well as the sciences – that and nothing less is Plekhanov's full and somewhat Utopian ideal of the education of the perfect revolutionary.

But before a revolutionary can educate others, he must educate himself. Possessed by this characteristically Russian belief, Plekhanov set to work. Forced into exile, living in penury in Switzerland, he made himself the foremost Marxist scholar of his time. Within ten years he became the leading authority, and that not among Russian Marxists alone, on the civilisation and social history of Russia, on the theoretical foundations of Marxism, on the ideas of the Western precursors of socialism, but above all on European civilisation and thought in the eighteenth century. He understood the methods and ideals of the writers of the Enlightenment, particularly in France, as very few understood or mastered them before him. They were, of all schools of thought, the most sympathetic to him. The devoted effort of the French *philosophes* to reduce all problems to scientific terms; their belief in reason, observation, experiment; their clear formulation of central principles and applications of them to concrete historical situations; their war against clericalism, obscurantism and irrationalism; their search for the truth, sometimes narrow and pedestrian but always fearless, confident and fanatically honest; the lucid and often beautiful prose in which the best French intellectuals expressed themselves – all this he admired and delighted in. Civilised, sensitive and fastidious, Plekhanov towered head and shoulders above his fellow Russian socialists as a human being, as a scholar and as a writer.

Marxist writings are not among the clearest or most readable in the literature of socialism. It was not only Keynes who found himself physically unable to plod through *Das Kapital*; and if Lenin had not radically altered our world, I doubt whether his works would be as minutely studied as they necessarily are. Plekhanov has been badly served by his foreign translators: but if you read him in his native language you recognise at once – it is a feeling which those who have known it will be able to identify instantly – that you are in the presence of someone of first-rate quality. At its best his style is direct, limpid, rapid and ironical. The knowledge is vast, exact and lightly carried; the reasoning is clear and forceful; and the final deadly blows are delivered with an impeccable elegance and precision.

Plekhanov, more or less single-handedly, educated an entire generation of Russian Marxists and left-wing intellectuals, as Lenin handsomely admitted. He was a man of exceptional literary talent, an original historian of movements and ideas, who voluntarily submitted himself to the discipline of Marxism and remained uncrushed by it, at once dogmatic and independent, fanatically loyal to his master and yet with a clear voice of his own, a scholar and a critic in his own right. It is idle to pretend that the *obiter dicta* on art or history or literature of Lenin or Stalin, or even better-educated men such as Engels or Trotsky or Bukharin, are of much intrinsic value: they are interesting only because the men who uttered them interest us on other grounds. Plekhanov's essays are remarkable intellectual achievements in themselves. His studies of French materialists, of the early socialists, of Russian novelists, of the relationship of social and economic conditions and artistic activity, always first-hand and of the purest water, have transformed the history of these subjects, not least by the opposition, often legitimate enough, which his unbending Marxist orthodoxy has provoked. Naturally this distinction, not merely of manner but of personality, was occasionally found irksome by his fellow revolutionaries. They complained of his aloofness, his buttoned-up, disdainful manner, his professorial airs, his impatience, his mordant irony in dealing with unusually ignorant or uncouth members of the party.

Indeed, he did not suffer fools gladly. Both intellectually and personally he dominated his milieu. Brilliant, contemptuous, self-critical, touchy, liable to constant discouragement, often ill, forced to struggle painfully for daily existence in a cause which he held dear, he infuriated the pretentious, the confused and the sentimental with his acid comments. It was not altogether surprising that in the end he could not stomach Lenin, in whom he had early detected an almost monomaniacal lust for power and a total lack of scruple. He detested Trotsky far more; some among Trotsky's admirers believe that this was caused by jealousy. I know of no evidence for this. A simpler explanation is that Trotsky, man of genius as he was, seems to have possessed no likeable characteristics.

Presently, in 1903, there came the great doctrinal break: Lenin believed in the organisation of the Russian revolutionary Social Democratic Party by an élite of dedicated professional revolutionaries, against whose decisions there could, whatever they might order, for reasons of discipline be no appeal. Plekhanov had no more faith in the untutored masses than Lenin, and like him believed in efficiency, order and discipline. He believed, too, that all must yield to the needs of the revolution, but he never tired of quoting Engels's thesis that nothing could be more tragic for revolutionary socialists than to find themselves in power prematurely, that is, before the majority of the proletariat had become conscious of their historic role – or, worse still, before the proletariat had become the majority of the population. After the Bolsheviks broke off from the Mensheviks, Plekhanov came slowly to realise that what Lenin contemplated without qualms was precisely this kind of premature seizure of power, not by the majority of the people, but on their behalf by a self-appointed group of conspirators. This was to him pure Bonapartism, an irresponsible *putsch* of the kind advocated by such violent social incendiaries as Bakunin or Blanqui, a suppression of the interests of the working class, and therefore of democracy, by a handful of demagogues. Indeed, he declared as early as 1905 that the ultimate goal of Lenin's tactics was his own personal dictatorship.

Yet he began by supporting Lenin, because he stood for activism and organisation and was exceptionally dedicated, tough-minded and ruthless. He was totally opposed to Lenin only when he had finally convinced himself, by about 1911, that the Bolshevik leaders were not merely power-seekers but brutally cynical about means, recklessly and exultantly dishonest in their tactics, and with a 'dialectical' conception of democracy which turned it into its opposite. He violently condemned the abortive Moscow rising organised by the Bolsheviks in 1905 as a criminally premature resort to arms. A far greater crisis arose in 1914 when international socialism broke over the issue of participation in the War. The Bolsheviks under Lenin, and the left wing of the Menshevik Social Democrats led by Martov, declared that the War was a fight between the two rival imperialisms in which the working class had no stake; that the failure to organise a general strike in all belligerent countries, which would have stopped the War or paralysed it very early, was a betrayal on the part of those socialist leaders who had aligned themselves with the pro-war parties in their respective countries. They therefore boycotted the War and called on all socialists to do likewise. Plekhanov thought this suicidal folly. He argued that the triumph of Prussian and Austrian militarism was incomparably more dangerous to socialism and to the Russian proletarian revolution than the victory of the Western democracies engaged in self-defence. Thereupon he was indignantly branded by his opponents as a traitor to international socialism. (A not dissimilar situation arose in the United States and other neutral countries in 1939, when Communists and other anti-imperialists pronounced the war against Hitler to be a clash of rival capitalist systems, and declared themselves hostile to both sides and therefore isolationist and neutral.)

In 1917, after the February Revolution, Plekhanov returned to Petrograd to a great but short-lived personal triumph. He gave critical but fervent support to Kerensky and the provisional government, and engaged in a long and bitter duel with Lenin, whom he accused of conspiring to foist the yoke of the tiny Bolshevik Party upon the necks of the Russian people; thereby sinning against Marxist democracy, provoking a civil war, and with it the danger of counter-revolution; and was duly denounced by the Bolsheviks and their fellow-travellers as a compromiser, a reactionary, a chauvinist, a Westerner out of contact with the Russian masses, a bourgeois traitor to the working class. He argued that socialism could be established in Russia by the votes of the majority only in conditions of an expanding economy, requiring some degree of collaboration with other left-wing and liberal parties; and, as a prerequisite, the defeat of German autocracy. He was famous and revered, but scarcely anyone listened to him. The views were too moderate, the accent too civilised.

The October Revolution had cast its shadow long before. When it came, he denounced it with all the biting eloquence at his command. His chronic consumption had grown worse in the cold and hungry Petrograd of 1917, and he took to his bed. He expected to be arrested or assassinated, and on the second day of the Revolution a party of soldiers and sailors forced their way into his bedroom, ransacked his papers, threatened to shoot him, and finally wandered off with vague insults and menaces. Someone complained to Lenin. He seemed genuinely shocked. Plekhanov was the greatest figure in Russian socialism, and the dictator himself recognised a deeper debt to him, intellectually and politically, than to any other living man. An order was issued that the personal property of citizen Plekhanov was to be protected in the future. But he was fatally ill, and died on 30 May 1918 in a sanatorium in Finland, denouncing to the very end Lenin's betrayal of all they had both fought for, and his unchaining of violence and hooliganism in the land. His funeral turned into a vast, orderly and moving demonstration of his oldest friends, the Petersburg factory-workers.

In the last article by him to be published in Russia he recalled sardonically that the leader of the Austrian socialists, Victor Adler, used to say to him reproachfully 'Lenin is *your* child', and that he used to answer, 'But not a legitimate one.'[1] Attitudes towards him in his native land have remained ambivalent. The Soviet fashion to this day[2] is to say that he was virtually infallible until, say, 1903, and after that, having diverged from Lenin, lost all virtue. The centenary celebrations of his birth in the Soviet Union are being conducted in the same spirit of uncertain admiration. The dethroning of Stalin has led to some patronising praise of Plekhanov as on the whole the most formidable enemy of the cult of personality. His writings are again cautiously discussed, not least those among them which have acquired a peculiarly poignant meaning in this day and hour. For events have borne out his gloomiest prophecies on a scale undreamt of even on the rain-swept day when his body was carried to its grave.

---

[1] See G. V. Plekhanov, 'Buki az–ba' (1918), reprinted in *God na rodine* (Paris, 1921), vol. 2, pp. 257–68, at p. 268.

[2] This talk was broadcast in December 1956, shortly after the Hungarian Uprising.

REALISM IN POLITICS

'REALISM' normally means the correct perception of the characteristics of events or facts or persons without the distortions produced by feelings like hope or fear or love or hate, or by a disposition to idealise or depreciate or anything else that interferes with accurate observation (or action founded on it) as a result of emotional pressure of some kind. It has a further, more sinister, sense when people say that they ('fear that they') are 'realists' – usually to explain away some unusually mean or brutal decision.

This disagreeable sense of the word probably derives largely from Hegel and his followers, both conservative and radical, who were fond of contrasting their own unflinching vision of 'reality' – the ruin and cruel destruction caused by the 'inexorable' collisions of the 'objective' forces which composed the history of mankind – with the contemptible evasion of the facts by the foolish or the weak or the purblind, who shrank from 'reality' and lived in a fool's paradise. In the more apocalyptic versions of this German creed there were, on one side, the poor creatures who had deceived themselves into thinking that all was peace and happiness and benevolent progress, and that their own kindly and provincial modes of life would go on for ever, when, in fact, some terrible historical upheaval was round the corner, and they and their peaceful inhabitants were doomed to the most violent destruction; on the other, the 'realists' who saw the grisly but tremendous truth, and realised that the more savage aspects of existence were the more important – nearer the 'essence' of the historical process, not to be covered over by the feeble rationalisations of men who cannot face the truth.

The view that what is cruel and disagreeable is more likely to be true or 'real' than its opposite is a form of sardonic (or savage) pessimism as romantic and as little supported by the evidence of empirical observation as the optimistic humanitarianism of the Age

of Reason; and the great political movements which derive from
either – Fascism and Communism (for all the pretensions of the
latter to 'objective' scientific methods) – have on the whole failed
to establish their claims to be more successful in interpreting or
modifying the facts than many *ad hoc*, unsystematic assessments.

But there is a grain of truth in the 'unpleasant' attitude. It
consists in the rejection by it of the hopeful views of the eighteenth
century, when many ardent and intelligent thinkers were convinced that the vices, follies and miseries of mankind were due
almost entirely to ignorance and idleness; that the lives of men, as
of every object in nature, conformed to certain regularities of
behaviour which could be codified in laws; and that these laws
could in principle be made as precise and all-embracing as those
which Newton and his fellow physicists had established so
triumphantly in the realm of inanimate nature. It followed that
when these laws were discovered – as perhaps they had already
been – men could be administered as competently and successfully
by those versed in the natural science of government as the best
among them had for so long hoped without knowing how to
achieve this. After all, it was argued, human desires could be
ascertained as clearly as the processes which governed the lives of
plants or molecules; and they could now be satisfied by means at
last available to human beings, on a far more generous scale, with
fewer obstacles, than the ignorance and indolence and 'interested
error'[1] of the past had made possible. Statecraft was a science like
engineering or agriculture; it was something with methods of its
own founded upon the rational study of human nature, the fruit of
observation, logic and experiment. This science was not a mystery;
it could be learnt, taught to others, applied by experts, improved
and expanded to an unlimited degree, to the lasting benefit of
humanity.

This optimistic (and, because it was deterministic, somewhat
inconsistent) doctrine was discredited less by the arguments of its
opponents – theologians, political reactionaries, anti-rationalist
romantics – than by the failure of the French Revolution, which
somewhat undermined the prestige of the philosophy of the
Enlightenment (at any rate on the continent of Europe), much as

---

[1] The origin of this phrase is probably to be found in remarks made by
Holbach, who writes, for example, of 'erreurs utiles' in *Système de la nature*, part
2, chapter 12, and of 'hommes fortement intéressés à l'erreur' in *Le Bon Sens*,
§ 82. Ed. [See now also p. xv above.]

the Russian Revolution and its illegitimate offspring, Fascism, undermined the beliefs of Victorian liberals. Nevertheless the conviction that history does obey laws, that the acts of human beings are calculable, that it is possible to develop a natural science of human behaviour, is a perennial human obsession and persisted into the nineteenth century. The 'mechanistic' views of the eighteenth century were declared bankrupt by the adherents of the new 'organic' or 'vitalistic' conception of men and institutions, who, after denouncing their predecessors for crude over-simplification, held in common with them the view that history did possess a pattern.

What the eighteenth century had not noticed, according to the new 'organic' theorists, was that the laws which dominated human affairs were unique; were wholly unlike those which governed inanimate matter; could only be grasped by those who understood the principles not of mere accumulation, or the movement of bodies in space, but of 'growth' or 'evolution'; principles which precluded the analysis of 'wholes', such as human organisms or social units – societies or States or Churches, or languages, legal systems, religions, systems of thought – into their constituent, 'atomic' ingredients, since this left out the impalpable, scarcely describable links and connections, patterns and structures, by which such 'wholes' held together, and which alone explained their unique character, their behaviour and destiny. With this indispensable modification the original programme could be made to work: the experts in 'organic' processes should be able to manipulate – certainly to predict and describe – the behaviour of human beings, no less than the natural scientists the inanimate world with which they dealt. The new 'biological' science of mankind, whether in its metaphysical-Hegelian or evolutionary-Darwinian form, was in principle codifiable, communicable, learnable. Comte, and after him Spencer, made bold attempts to reduce it all to a clear and dogmatic system. The huge cosmologies of Spengler and Toynbee represent the gloomy culmination of this tradition. Karl Marx, who took seriously the proposition that if history was a science, it was concerned with 'inexorable' repetitions of some kind, offered a rival and more fruitful theory.

Yet something always went wrong. Events never took the form in which the experts had so fervently believed, which they had so constantly anticipated. The French Revolution certainly did not produce the results which its makers seemed so certain that they could effect. They were told – such of them as had survived – that the failure of their great experiment was due to the fact that they had, in calculating the future, ignored certain cardinal factors – social and economic ones, for example – and had concentrated too exclusively on political ones. This warning was not forgotten. By 1848 awareness of economic and social facts was very widespread; no one could accuse the new revolutionaries of underestimating them; nevertheless the events of that great year did not fulfil the hopes and plans of those who had worked and prayed for them. They were, in their turn, told by the newest analysts of history that they too had ignored a cardinal factor – perhaps the central factor of all human history – the conflict of social 'classes'. But then the Russian Revolution of 1917, carried out with strict regard to doctrine, produced consequences widely different from those which had been predicted in the simple Utopias of Lenin or the German Communists; the sequence of 1793 and 1848 had repeated itself. Is it possible that there is something amiss in theories which practice so obstinately declines to fulfil? One begins to suspect that we are dealing with something which mere amendment of the theories cannot put right – something which indicates that perhaps the very application of theories of historical development to human societies is doomed to failure as such – that the pejorative sense attached by popular usage to terms like 'doctrinaire' or 'theorist' in politics is not mere obscurantism, but rests on a just feeling that mistakes are being made, that something does not fit.

I do not wish to deny the importance of ideas. On the contrary, unless one is blinded by some over-simple explanation of human affairs, psychological or anthropological or biological, or economic (or by some metaphysics which guarantees an a priori pattern into which all situations must necessarily be arranged), it seems plain that situations do sometimes arise in which groups of men possessed by intense beliefs, given favourable conditions (too various to specify), can cause vast changes to occur. These changes then tend to be retrospectively regarded as inevitable; it is less often remarked that they seldom, if ever, correspond to the intentions of their makers, or embody any considerable portion of their original beliefs.

This seems to demand explanation. Hitherto attempts were made either to explain these failures by the fact that the situation was misconceived by the revolutionaries, or that some factor had not been taken into consideration – all of which implied that, provided the situation was correctly interpreted and all the relevant factors allowed for, a key to the problem could probably be obtained and the human situation transformed by men sufficiently wise and sufficiently strong. And yet it seems amply clear that <u>the most successful among statesmen and reformers have obtained their results by very different means</u>, and that theories of how society could be altered seldom correspond to practice.

Robespierre, Joseph II of Austria, Lenin did not on the whole succeed in translating their ideas into reality. Bismarck, Lincoln, Lloyd George, Roosevelt, on the whole, did so. Austria in 1790, France in 1794, Russia in 1920 did not correspond to the great reformers' dreams. Germany, England, America, at the relevant periods, did not fall nearly so short of what their more practical statesmen attempted. It might be said that these latter were less ambitious, that what they wanted was not so widely different from what existed; but this would not be true. The differences made by Bismarck or Roosevelt were of vast extent, and affected the fortunes of mankind to a radical degree.

There is a sense, seldom denied even by the most biased historians, in which the difference between practical and Utopian statesmen is that <u>the first are said to 'understand'</u>, while the second are said not to 'understand', the nature of <u>the human material with which they deal. It is in the nature of this 'understanding' that the centre of our problem lies.</u> Joseph II, Robespierre, Lenin spared no trouble in attempting to understand the nature of the situation with which they were dealing. They read, they studied, they argued, they reflected. They may have taken too much notice of one aspect and too little of another, but from the point of view of those who regard history as being, in principle, a science, and believe that most effective results are achieved by some combination of induction and deduction analogous to that practised by natural scientists, these men displayed a proper temper: they did all, or nearly all, that was humanly possible, in the conditions of their time, to obtain the right solution; and having obtained it, to apply it, with will and single-minded purpose. Yet they conspicuously failed to achieve what they desired. They succeeded only in violently and permanently upsetting the order which they found, and producing a new situation expected neither by themselves nor by their enemies. Bismarck, Lincoln, Roosevelt did better than this, and the results which they achieved, however surprising or unpalatable to their opponents, approximated to the wishes of their supporters to a recognisable degree.

These are not, in the first instance, value judgements. I merely wish to indicate that the former – the obsessed – were incapable of obtaining what they desired, whereas the latter succeeded. Bismarck did incalculably more harm than the admirable Joseph II; nevertheless, it is reasonable to feel more confidence in the qualities which make up the wicked but 'realistic' Bismarck than in those which composed the idealistic Emperor. And if to be rational is to apply those methods to a given material which produce the results which the experimenter desires, there is a sense in which the official rationalists behaved unreasonably; while the men who worked by 'intuition' (which is certainly a misnomer in this case) employed their reason more successfully.

I do not wish to try to enumerate the differences which divide these two contrasted types, only to remark upon the most salient dissimilarity. It lies in the fact that successful statesmen behave like artists who understand their medium. They undertake courses of action or avoid others on grounds which they find it difficult if not impossible to explain in clear theoretical terms. And not only they, but the historians and psychologists and political analysts who seek to explain their behaviour, are forced to resort to such terms as 'imagination', 'political genius', 'sense of history', 'unerring judgement', which rightly have no place in a scientific treatise. When Bismarck launched his war against the French, or Lincoln his war against the South, or Roosevelt his war against the economic 'Bourbons', they would have found it difficult, to say the least, to state those general propositions from which it followed deductively, as in a properly articulated science, that this was the moment and those the means suitable to that particular operation; difficult in the sense in which the sculptor finds it difficult to explain why he does one thing rather than another with the material which he is moulding. Yet, of course, there is here no question of some mystical intuition or some non-empirical method of guessing at the nature of reality. Judgement, skill, sense of timing, grasp of the relation of means to results depend upon empirical factors, such as experience, observation, above all on that 'sense of reality' which largely consists in semi-conscious integration of a large number of apparently trivial or unnoticeable elements in the situation that between them form some kind of pattern which of itself 'suggests' – 'invites' – the appropriate action. Such action is, no doubt, a form of improvisation, but flowers only upon the soil of rich experience and exceptional responsiveness to what is relevant in the situation – a gift without which neither artists nor scientists are able to achieve original results. This gift seems to be wholly incompatible with faith in the supremacy of some idealised model, which, in the case of fanatical ideologies, takes the place of genuine capacity for responding to impressions. In theory there is perhaps no reason why some omniscient (or nearly omniscient) being should not first patiently accumulate all the relevant facts, and then, by reputable scientific methods – the normal combination of observation, experiment, analogy, deduction, induction and the rest – frame a hypothesis which will enable him to work out correctly all possible alternatives and their consequences. In theory this may be so. In practice the facts are too many, too complex, too brief, too minute, the theoretical weapons at our disposal too abstract, the models too remote from any but the stock, the unusually simple, situations. Leonardo, we are told, imagined that he achieved his effects by precise measurement, although everyone knows that he achieved them by a combination of very different gifts. Similarly, it may be that there are statesmen who believe themselves to be adhering to some cast-iron theory, some precise plan founded upon political and economic doctrines, but in fact achieve their results, if they are successful, by very different qualities in themselves.

This is not a plea for obscurantism, or reliance on immemorial wisdom or ancestral voices, or the inner light. There are regions of social life in which scientific theory clearly applies, and where it is mere ignorance and indolence that make men prefer rules of thumb and ill-digested 'common-sense' beliefs – as often as not, mere disguises for prejudice and boredom – to systematic knowledge. But equally there are regions where gardeners achieve conspicuously more spectacular results than botanists; and to distinguish these areas from one another is one of the first symptoms of a sense of reality. What makes the social theorists of the eighteenth century, and indeed of later times, seem artificial, Utopian and remote is precisely this confusion, which is obscurely felt but seldom formulated, largely because those who are engaged in formulating such distinctions are themselves uneasily committed to the view that scientific method must in principle apply to everything, and that to deny its relevance in any given region is a betrayal of the light.

Yet this is a mistake. When a politician (or even a historian who seeks to *explain* rather than influence human action) is accused of being doctrinaire, this seems a genuine charge – something which politicians (and historians) have genuinely no business to be, which makes them less competent to discharge their task. No scientist can be accused of being 'doctrinaire'; but no one doubts that to be a scientist at all is to have doctrines – which shows a certain instinctive grasp on the part of the users of our common language of the fact that different avocations employ different categories, and that the attempt to apply models which work in one region to another (where a very different method is required) is ultimately a form of irrationalism – of what some have called rationalist obscurantism – the insistence, without evidence, without looking to see, that there is a universal key, that what applies here must necessarily apply there, that what represents progress, knowledge, light in one region must necessarily do so in all others. Because a harmonious system of causal laws – or some corresponding framework – works well in the case of the inanimate world or in biology or zoology or genetics, it does not begin to follow that it alone will work in the field of social history.

Most social theorists in the nineteenth and twentieth centuries start from the naturalistic assumption that men are causally determined, individually weak, and potentially omniscient; that growing knowledge will only progressively reveal their melancholy and complete dependence upon a network of identifiable causal factors; that all else is megalomania and delusion. This bleak doctrine is not based upon observation or experience of human behaviour or social experiment, or any empirical method other than vague analogy with the rest of nature. The most successful statesmen in human history have usually, whether they knew it or not, assumed the opposite: that individuals were sometimes strong (for they so regard themselves and their principal opponents), largely ignorant (ignorant, that is, of the majority of the factors with which they were forced to deal, which had largely to be taken for granted and operated on in semi-darkness), and, within limits, free. So long as the opposite assumptions are made by those who believe in radical reforms of human society, in the name – falsely invoked – of science and reason and unbiased observation of nature, human beings will continue to be offered up to theories and abstractions, a form of idolatry – and of human sacrifice – colder and more destructive than the more intelligible follies of previous generations, and one for which future generations will, with incredulity and anger, rightly condemn our age.

THE ORIGINS OF ISRAEL

I SHOULD like to begin with the strange fact that the State of Israel exists. It was once said by the celebrated Russian revolutionary, Alexander Herzen, writing in the mid-nineteenth century, that the Slavs had no history, only geography. The position of the Jews is the reverse of this. They have enjoyed rather too much history and too little geography. And the foundation of the State of Israel must be regarded as a piece of historical redress for this anomalous situation. The Jews have certainly had more than their share of history, or, as some might say, martyrology. Certainly no community has ever been so conscious of itself, its past fate, its future, and the apparently insoluble character of the problems which beset it. Where were the Jews going? What would happen to them, or should be done about them? Almost every Jew, early or late in his life, has encountered something called the Jewish problem. Englishmen, Frenchmen, Belgians, Chinese, Portuguese are not beset at the beginning of their conscious lives by something called the Belgian, Chinese or Portuguese problem. This consciousness of themselves as being peculiarly problematical rendered the creation of the State of Israel a miracle; for if it had been made dependent on the solution of the Jewish problem by the specialists on the subject, if the Jews had been what either some of their friends or some among their enemies have declared them to be, there might well have been no State of Israel at all.

Perpetual discussions went on, particularly during the nineteenth century – the most historically conscious of all ages – about whether the Jews were a race, or solely a religion; a people, a community, or merely an economic category. Books, pamphlets, debates increased in volume if not in quality. But there was one persistent fact about this problem, which was in some respects more clearly perceived by Gentiles than by the Jews themselves: namely, that if they were only a religion, this would not have needed quite so much argument and insistence; while if they were nothing but a race, this would not have been denied quite as vehemently as it has been by persons who nevertheless professed to denote a unique group of human beings by the term 'Jew'.

It gradually became clear, both to Jews and to those who took an interest in their affairs, that in fact they constituted an anomaly, which could not be defined in terms of the ordinary definition of nations, as applied at any rate to European nations; and that any attempt to classify them in such terms would lead to unnatural, artificial and Procrustean consequences.

One does not need to be old[1] to remember a time when Jews in the West used to grow indignant when other Jews, mainly from Eastern Europe, declared themselves to be members of a nation, and demanded a land in which to lead a national life. And some Western Jews did feel sufficiently assimilated to the natives of the country in which they lived to receive this kind of proposition with much amazement and, indeed, honest indignation. It is said that the late Edwin Montagu described the original draft of the Balfour Declaration as bordering on an act of anti-Semitism. No doubt he was sincere, but the fact that he was both sincere and honest was, in this case, only an illuminating sign of his own and his friends' state of mind. Sincerity and honesty are not always guarantees of knowledge of objective truth. Despite passionate denials of this proposition from many sides, it became increasingly clear to almost everyone who approached the problem from outside that the Jews were a unique combination of religion, race and people; that they could not be classified in normal terms, but demanded an extraordinary description, and their problem an extraordinary solution. The person who saw the problem in the simplest possible terms and provided the most radical solution was Theodor Herzl.

The distinguishing characteristic of Herzl was that, despite his origin and milieu, he came to the problem, as it were, from the outside; and possessed a somewhat romantic conception of the Jews, scarcely recognisable to those who themselves grew up in the thick of a closely-knit traditional Jewish community. There is something about great radical solutions of political questions which seems to make it necessary for them to be born in the minds of those who in some sense stand on the rim, and look in from

[1] It should be borne in mind throughout this essay that it was first published in 1953. Ed.

outside, and have an over-simple ideal, an over-simple purpose, a lucid, usually violent vision, based on an indispensable ignorance of detail. Those who know too much – know too many detailed facts too closely – cannot, as a rule, produce radical solutions. The Jews who grew up in truly traditional Jewish communities, such as those of Eastern and Central Europe, were usually much too conscious of the difficulties and complications, and lived cooped up in too small a world, ever to conceive anything so bold, so simple, so radical, and, in a sense, so fantastic, as Herzl's original idea.

I shall not traverse the familiar ground of how, as a result of the Dreyfus case, Herzl was aware of the total anomaly of the Jewish situation. It presently became obsessively clear to him that the moral and social situation of the Jews was intolerable: that it was painfully and tragically abnormal; that the palliatives had all failed; that the only alternative to apathy or humiliation was a drastic cure. Herzl's original solution was to cause all the Jews to be baptised. That was at any rate simple, general and final; it would surely put an end for ever to all the embarrassment of the ambiguous status of the Jews, their three-quarter citizenships, the peculiarity of their relationships in the various enclaves which they formed within the various communities to which they half believed, and half did not believe, themselves to belong.

It soon became quite clear to him that this was a genuinely Utopian solution, and he abandoned it. The notion of creating a territorial State for his people was in its own way an idea just as audacious and ruthless and direct. It was regarded as absurd by most of those who heard of it, if only because it sprang from a terrible, Napoleonic simplicity of vision. There is perhaps a quality which statesmen of this type have in common, something possessed by Alexander, by Napoleon, perhaps by de Valera, possibly by Disraeli, and I fear by Hitler and Stalin too, which comes of standing apart, at a certain distance, from the people with whose destinies they are engaged, and tending to see things in simple patterns, in contrast to the vision of those who see from within, and, as often as not, simply perceive a patternless heap of minute unending complications, and see every possible path as blocked by a vast number of obstacles which cannot be overcome in their time. Outsiders romanticise and over-simplify more easily: familiarity breeds, if not contempt, then at any rate scepticism and corrosive defeatism.

From this attribute Herzl, who, though he came from Budapest, was not an Eastern European Jew, was free, perhaps too free. His ideas were nationalist, secular, romantic, liberal, and bore more affinity to the enlightenment of Vienna and Paris than to anything specifically Jewish. And this, *mutatis mutandis*, was true of his followers. Each reflected the leading tendencies of his environment, each conceived the Zionist ideal in terms which, to some degree, derived from the national attitudes of his non-Jewish neighbours. The British Jews came with British ideas, the French Jews with French ideas, the German Jews with German, the Russian Jews with Russian, and the American Jews with American ideas. What happened as a result of this confusion of the tongues? The ideas came into collision with one another. In spite of all that we hear about inexorable laws of history (a metaphysical refrain which nowadays comes with almost equally monotonous frequency from the Soviet Union and Chatham House), one thing seems clear: large revolutions, attempts to upheave existing society and alter the course of events, do, at times, produce a break and change things deeply, but seldom in the direction which their initiators anticipated or desired. Why this is so, I do not propose to discuss – this must not become a lecture on the philosophy of history. It is enough to note that the State of Israel emerged with attributes quite different from those which anyone had previously intended. The intentions and purposes and motives had been many: and differed at times from individual to individual. Nevertheless, certain common national and cultural 'patterns' are discernible among them; and the influence of each is still identifiable in Israel today.

Thus the small group of English Jews who accepted Herzl's ideas were to some degree affected by the liberal imperialism of their surroundings. What some among them wanted was a spiritual centre, a source of spiritual light, in a rather nebulous, idealistic sense. Others were more political. What they wanted was a Jewish community which would constitute a Western outpost in the East, a body of missionaries of Western culture, with peculiar duties and responsibilities towards the undeveloped communities of the East, both Jews and Arabs. This was, however unconsciously, a kind of Jewish version of something very British – of the most idealistic liberal conception of the White Man's Burden. The English Jews of whom I speak conceived of the Jewish establishment in Palestine as essentially a civilising mission carried on by dedicated personalities who would bring the maturest fruit of the most peace-loving and most humane culture of the West to these inchoate, rather wild, rather barbarous Eastern peoples.

The French Jews were on the whole less interested in Palestine; but there were exceptions; and at the most notable among them, the great Baron Edmond de Rothschild. His villages – the colonies which he founded – represent a French ideal with pretty French vines and olive trees, elegant, charming and self-contained, an expression of a peaceful, rural, slightly nostalgic nineteenth-century view of the life of tenant farmers and their labourers; of Jewish farmers on the hill and Arab labourers below, and of the great landlord who owned the land, remote, mysterious and benevolent, far away beyond the sea.

The German Jews wanted an orderly, modern, spick and span world, with a sufficiency of applied economic and technological knowledge, and a certain degree of democracy, but on the whole a well-disciplined, tidy, competent, late-nineteenth-century – I will not say Prussian, but at any rate properly regulated and firmly founded – political and economic organisation.

The American Jews wanted something perhaps a little more streamlined and yet sentimentally affecting. They wanted something embodying a great deal of passionate and romantic popular enthusiasm, and, with it, the newest, most up-to-date, most labour-saving, mechanically fertile, twentieth-century gadgets and improvements imaginable anywhere. They wanted Palestine to lead in the van of all spiritual, artistic, material progress, tangibly, palpably, for all to see and admire. And they wanted it at the same time to be the idealised home country, at once biblical and sweetly familiar, by which they could themselves be identified in America among the great groups of immigrants of which that country is composed.

But by far the most important community to be considered is the community most closely concerned with the early foundations of Israel: that is to say, the Jews of Russia and Poland. Both numerically and in influence they outweighed the Western Jews. It seems almost self-evident that if there had existed only the Jews of the Western world, or, perhaps, the Jews of the West and the Jews of the Eastern, Muslim, countries, there would have been no Israel. Whatever the genuine problems besetting the Jews of the West, however true and sharp and refreshing Herzl's extremely ruthless analysis of their diseases might have been, there were in the beginning of our century no sufficiently compelling causes which could uproot the relatively comfortable and well-set-up Jews of the West, materially provided for, and morally and politically unpersecuted, and send them on a general trek in that particular direction. But for the character and needs of the Eastern European Jews there would have been no Israel. They were, in that sense, absolutely *sine quibus non*; to grasp their role is indispensable to the understanding of what happened later.

For this reason I should like to say a few words about their establishment. The Eastern European Jews, as a result of historical circumstances, possessed a kind of independent establishment of their own. They had, unlike their Western brothers, grown to be a kind of State within a State, with their own political, social, religious and human ideals. I should not like to generalise about the oriental countries, for about them I fear that I know nothing. The Jews of Russia and Poland, as a result of political and social persecution, had found themselves cooped up in a kind of single extended ghetto, called the Pale of Settlement, and although, or perhaps because, they were not well treated by the Russian government and bureaucracy, particularly towards the end of the nineteenth century and at the beginning of the twentieth, they remained within their medieval shell and developed a kind of internal structure of their own. They developed a very powerful inner life and, in a certain sense, remained less touched by modern developments than almost any community of Jews in Europe. If one finds difficulty in conceiving what life was like in the Middle Ages in Europe, I think that the life of a truly religious Jewish small town in Western Russia, even as late as 1890 or 1900, probably bears a closer relationship to it than any other modern community anywhere. Its inhabitants were affected by, but on the whole comparatively preserved from the intrusion of, outside forces. They lived their own rich, and despite economic misery and social ostracism, often gay, imaginative and morally satisfying lives. They were surrounded by Russian peasants, against whom they felt no hatred, but whom they regarded as a species of lower beings with whom their contacts were restricted. They lived inside the walls of their own community, leading a closely knit traditional, tight-woven form of existence, and they developed their own inner institutions. There was a great deal of persecution and pressure by the Russian government outside; but if you were inside this establishment, you felt morally and spiritually secure; it was a home, and built on solid foundations.

These were the people who to some extent transferred their own institutional basis to the new country. That is what gave Jewish Palestine its profound continuity with the immediate Jewish past. It might well be asked how a State can be constructed artificially. Is it really feasible to put up a prefabricated society? Even if one does not fully accept the traditionalist views of Burke and his brand of conservatives, one is liable to be told that States cannot be made, they must grow; that there is such a process as the insensible growth of a civilisation by small, scarcely measurable steps; there are imponderables, there is the crucial influence of a multiplicity of untraceable small causes, leading to vast, but individually invisible, unanalysable effects. One cannot, one is informed, create a State in the way in which one makes a machine, or the way one creates any artificial object. There must be roots, growth, soil. There must be an imperceptible traditional accumulation, a sort of precipitate of tradition throughout the ages. And yet the impossible has apparently occurred; we are witnessing the rise of a State which in a few years' existence has been created by, to all appearances, prefabricated means: bits of Italy, bits of England, of Germany, bits and pieces from everywhere, quickly screwed together. And yet, like Aaron's rod, this apparently dead entity, this artificial wooden object, hammered together in a haphazard manner under critical conditions and in terrible haste, has burst into green leaf.

This is a very astonishing fact. It is less astonishing only if one realises that the Jewish community lived by a set of portable values, a tradition on wheels, which, like the Ark of the Covenant, travelled from Jerusalem back into the wilderness of exile across central Europe to Russia and Russian Poland. There it halted, a kind of temporary establishment; a tradition with no roots in specifically Russian or Polish soil, for its roots were not territorial or geographical. It was a very genuine institutional unity, a real pattern of life, a way of living unrelated to almost any other. The Jews of England, Holland, Germany, America could not claim and would not wish, perhaps, to possess anything like it; their histories in modern times have been different: before Hitler, happier and, it may be, less interesting.

What kind of institutions were these? They were compounded of at least two elements. On the one hand there was the Jewish religion and the traditional religious Jewish way of living, which, in conditions of common depression, common misery and common suffering, developed a deep sense of equality, so that all, whether rich or poor, men who were relatively influential and men who were not, felt themselves bound together by the particular ties of solidarity and fraternity which common slavery commonly induces. For this reason it was a more tightly woven community, with more intimate relationships within it, than the freer and looser communities outside. On the other hand, the Jews of every country tend to assimilate to some degree to the movements round them. In Russia and Poland they assimilated the humanist-liberal, radical and social-democratic traditions of intellectual revolt which the best elements in those countries developed in response to the harsh and unbelievably stupid form of despotism maintained by the tsarist regime.

It is not easy for those who have not met it to conceive this queer combination of ancient pious, medieval religion with its immense preservative centripetal power on the one hand, and nineteenth-century liberal-democratic ideals on the other. The emancipated ex-inhabitants of the Pale of Settlement preserved traditional tastes but acquired new beliefs, the creed of the liberal intelligentsia. They believed in human virtue, in knowledge, in science, in reason; they believed in everything in which the Western revolutionaries of 1848 had believed. And if you go to Israel today, a far better key to understanding the minds of the rulers of that country and the methods they employ would be found in the study of the ideals of the nineteenth century than of those of the twentieth. In a certain sense, Israel is an anachronism: a very valuable, interesting and inspiring anachronism; but still, in the twentieth century, odd and unique. The ideals which the Jews imported, and the culture they were able to build in the relative vacuum of Palestine – with a minimum of counter-influence on account of the evident feebleness of the Muslim culture in this corner of the Arab world – were founded upon typically nineteenth-century principles: belief in freedom from government dictation; in civil liberties, in equality, in human rights, in a form of democracy which in the twentieth century has, alas, proved not very reliable in the face of the furious new forces which have been unleashed against it.

Israel is an enclave, a curious corner of the liberal past in which these things were – and are – believed with passionate and single-minded sincerity; and this is what gives it a curiously unfamiliar air.

Anyone who wishes to understand the political structure of Israel had best study the nineteenth-century history of liberal ideas in Europe, and then the story of these ideas as reflected in the minds of Russian liberals and socialists. The Russian Jews who set their stamp so deeply on the social and political structure of Jewish Palestine under the Mandate – and Israel is faithful enough to that inheritance – were brothers and heirs to the idealistic Russian intellectuals, and to the poor artisans, struggling land-labourers, factory workers whose cause they fought. Any student of political institutions who wishes to understand the State of Israel must remember that its political parties derive from Russian Westernism, Russian liberal enlightenment, the ideas and aspirations which united the entire opposition to tsarist oppression, and were, after their short-lived triumphs, so easily and cynically thrown overboard by the Bolsheviks. Nineteenth-century Russian liberals, without the scars of the disenchantments and failures, the crippling frustrations which democrats and liberals had suffered in Europe, remained hopeful; and their Jewish disciples still possess a great deal of hope, optimism, enthusiasm and a certain inner strength. If you examine, for example, the Mapai and Mapam Parties – the Labour Party and the Left Radical Party, which has mysterious sympathies with the Soviet Union – you will find that they both resemble the idealistic members of Russian Menshevik or Socialist-Revolutionary Parties, the latter with its agrarian mystique, the former with its peculiar belief in a possible combination of socialisation of the basic industries with the preservation of an almost maximum degree of cultural liberty on the part of individuals.

There is a direct link between Russian Socialist-Revolutionaries and the early Jewish colonists in Palestine, with their Rousseau-like belief in the healing power of contact with the soil, and their affinities to the Russian students who wished to 'go among the people' in the 1870s and 1880s, and were brought up on the purest principles of agrarian liberalism. Both believed in life on the land, contact with the peasants, a healthy existence away from the contaminating sophistication of the great cities, escape from factors morally destructive for people deformed and maimed by the particular development of modern society which both – in one case intellectuals, in the other Jews – experienced; namely, an abnormal situation of isolation from, and liability to persecution by, the barbarous majority. Not everything came from Russia, of course. The Irgun, a quasi-Fascist Party, is not an imitation of anything Russian, but far more like its Polish origins, having something in common with Pilsudski's colonels of the 1920s with their belief in honour. It is thence that it derives its terrorism, its heroism, its brutality, and a certain kind of romantic, Byronic inhumanity. And if you look to the opposite end of the scale, at the left-wing terrorists of the Stern Gang, they are the direct heirs of those small groups of the terrorist section of the Russian left-wing Socialist-Revolutionary Party, which believed in individual assassination as a politically necessary method. Misguided – deeply so – they may have been; but the roots from which they sprang are in these same humanitarian, idealistic, these now no longer existent, obsolete circles of the liberal intelligentsia of Russo-Polish society of the nineteenth century. To fail to see this is to misinterpret the facts.

The ideals which inspired the early Russian and Polish Zionists who emigrated to Palestine – ideals which are still dominant – came from Russian liberals. They filled the people who arrived earliest, the people who went without compulsion. There is a very great difference between the moral force exercised by those who went with no obvious economic need and no obvious political pressure, and those who went because they were expelled from the countries of their origin by violence. Obviously the moral influence of people who go of their own volition, and as an act of deliberate moral choice, is likely to be greater than that of people who, dazed and thrown about by the waves of misfortune which they neither have brought about nor understand, find themselves, in a large number of cases, cast up on this shore of refuge, to which they gradually grow assimilated, but which begins by being perhaps as bewildering to them as any other remote and unfamiliar country might have been. The people who went voluntarily, the early generations, certainly imported a flavour of liberal enthusiasm and a kind of mild half-socialist faith (I do not think one can go much further than that) – not very Marxist for all its Marxist phraseology, modified by boundless scepticism, individualism, empiricism – a particular brand of outlook which the Jews, particularly in Russia and Poland, derived partly from their own miseries and sufferings, partly from the soft, porous, chaotic, not very well-organised political system in which they were themselves brought up.

In giving this very definite primacy to the Russian settlers and their ideas I may seem guilty of exaggeration. What, it may be asked, of the German element? Where would Israel have been in its most critical hour, at war with the Arab States, and given up by its Western friends, without German skills and capital and talent for organisation alike in peace and war? Where indeed? Lost, perhaps; defeated and destroyed. And yet, for all the crucial contribution which the German settlers have made – to the arts and sciences, to the army and the civilian administration, to the judiciary and to manufacture and commerce, to every walk of life and every profession and technique – in spite of all this, the heart of the national life is almost untouched by the values dearest to the German Jews. It is they who are expected to adjust themselves to an outlook often alien to theirs.

Very little in Israel today can be derived from the views or practices of civilised immigrants from Berlin or Vienna or Frankfurt: much by going farther east. Israel is today a kind of Welfare State, the kind of State which, by the end of the war, many people wished to see everywhere – a country which is neither Communist, nor moving in a Communist direction, nor yet one in which rampant individualism breeds a great deal of violent social injustice. How has Israel come to embody this ideal? Partly, no doubt, as a result of the pressure of the facts themselves. The country was poor, and its original immigrants came from among the poor; it was founded in an irregular fashion; socialism preceded capitalism; trade unions acquired power before industrialists could possibly have done so – Jews, it might be remarked, do everything in the reverse order. But – and this needs some emphasis – it is partly due to the beliefs which these early pioneers brought with them. These are scarcely intelligible unless one knows the peculiarly idealistic political climate, which included an almost mystical worship of British liberalism and British parliamentary institutions, in which the founding fathers (some of whom must surely still be among those whom a celebrated British officer is reported as having this year[1] described as criminals from the ghettos of Europe) obtained their education in the countries of their origin.

One of the remarkable facts which have helped to form the new society is the recreation of the Hebrew language. Much has been alleged against it. It was maintained that the *réchauffage* of a classical tongue, used largely for ceremonial purposes, would lead

---

[1] 1953.

to great artificiality; that the language was outlandish, and would isolate those who used it from the community of civilised peoples; that it was violence done to the 'true' language of the Jews, the popular Yiddish language, which was rooted in the life of the people. These arguments have been blown to pieces by events. Hebrew has achieved a remarkable triumph, partly because it was the only common medium which was equally sacred to all the immigrants, partly because it was the ancient vehicle of a noble literature, the associations of which have affected the roots of all European thought and imagination. Because of this it has acted as an educational instrument of unique power. Words, thoughts and behaviour are not easily divorceable elements. All the warmth, the humour and the raciness, the splendid expressiveness of Yiddish, all the gaiety and tears of the many centuries of exile embodied in it, cannot compensate for the fact that it is an argot; that, like all things created under degraded conditions of life, it is formless, insufficiently disciplined and strict, over-elastic, whereas Hebrew (like much else in Israel, but perhaps more than any of the other factors) became an instrument for the increase of human dignity, a means of recreating a minimum degree of discipline of both emotion and reason. It is an adaptation of a genuine tradition, of long desired, long craved-for forms imposed upon the chaos of bohemian homelessness and blurred outlines, the cosy makeshifts of vagrant exiles – the obliteration, by means of something firm and yet deeply familiar and traditional, of the memories of past wounds and past servitudes. Of all the factors at work in creating a democratic and liberal nation in Israel today, not even excluding the army, it is the most penetrating, the most influential and the most successful; and not, as is often maintained, a mere means of increasing chauvinism and isolationism.

Another of the factors which welded the diverse elements together and overcame those differences which might otherwise have been too pronounced was the fact of war, the war with the Arab States. It is a sad and melancholy fact, and highly discreditable to human nature, that wars produce a cohesion, solidarity, common enthusiasm which few other phenomena create. I remember being told by a celebrated Israeli statesman that he had been brought up as a social democrat in strict hatred of war, that he regretted the Arab War, had done nothing to bring it about and much to prevent it, and thought it a sad and calamitous thing; but that he could not deny that as a result of this war a tradition had grown up, a basis for the State had come into being. The blood of the martyrs had undoubtedly quickened those seeds of the national spirit which otherwise might have taken much longer to develop. There is no doubt that, as during the Blitz of 1940–1 in England, a bringing together and a violent fusion of very different ideals occurred, which, although the end of the war to some extent (as in Britain) dissolved it, nevertheless still continues to be the essential moral basis of the common endeavours of the people of Israel.

Unless one understands that in some sense these citizens of a new State feel that they live in a kind of bivouac; if not in an actual armed camp, at any rate at the crossroads of hostile armies; unless one realises that they feel themselves in constant danger, if not of extermination, at any rate of attack, and that this, besides intensifying the vices of chauvinism and puritanism, brings out certain virtues in human beings, certain forms of altruism, a genuine opportunity for generosity and even toleration which they otherwise seldom show, the whole of their progress becomes unintelligible. Certainly, in terms of the laws of economics and sociology and many other respected social sciences, they should have collapsed a long time ago.

The result of the impact of so many abnormal forces was the emergence of a new species of human beings. If you ask what the founders of the Zionist movement wanted – they wanted to create Jews each in his own image. The English Jews doubtless wanted to see the best kind of English Jew flourish in Israel. The Russian Jews wanted the best kind of idealistic liberal Russian Jews to predominate; the Australian Jews hoped for the best-liked Australians, the Iraqi Jews might desire the most admired Iraqi character. None of this was to be, because, although man proposes, the forces of history dispose very differently. There has come into being the embryo of an Israeli nationality, the like of which has not existed for two thousand years. What, you may well ask, are these new human beings like? They are not easy to describe. Their most striking characteristic seems to me to be their dissimilarity from the concept of the Jews which is lodged in the minds of almost all non-Jews. This may be a matter of pride or regret, pleasure or pain, depending on what one's tastes may be.

There are in Israel very few eminent bankers, very few eminent lawyers, not many scientists of genius; there are very few persons principally occupied with the accumulation of wealth. Again, there are few professional critics (I say nothing of the amateurs); there are few sophisticated, chess-playing, café intellectuals – late-night figures, dispensers of a peculiar compound of Freud, Marx, Sartre, or whatever else is at once shocking and fashionable; seekers after strong sensations, partly genuine, partly fraudulent, sometimes interesting, at other times deliberately sordid and obscene, amusing, destructive, superficial, and liable to exhibitionism and vulgarity; with a tendency to flourish within declining or insecure cultures – in the Weimar Republic of Germany, or in certain sections of the United States today. Of such there are very few to be seen in Israel, and such forms of activity are not held at a premium there. Tourists who visit Tel Aviv with the expectation of Jewish activities of this particular kind, and look for these sharp flavours – the fruits of decadence and self-critical desperation – are much disappointed by the relative placidity, relative coarseness; a kind of stubborn normality and a complacent soundness, wholesomeness, dullness which the Jews have surely richly deserved. For certainly there has been no absence in their lives hitherto of condiment, no absence of salt or acid and exotic spices of all types. They have had these elements, if anything, in rather too high proportions, so high that they tended to poison both themselves and their neighbours. In Israel these elements are at a discount. What you find are natives of a country, not unlike the natives of some other Mediterranean State, and not the artificial products of a liberal European intelligentsia in decay.

That may be a cause for regret, or it may not. Certainly I have known some people who went to Israel and were bitterly disappointed by the fact that the arts do not sufficiently flourish there. There are no great Israeli novelists; there are some good short-story writers, but they are older men who perfected their genius before they went to Palestine. There are on the whole no great thinkers, poets, painters, sculptors, composers; Israeli music is respectable, painting is far from deplorable, writing is moderately good, architecture is improving; and so on. All these activities are reputably carried on. They do not, certainly, lag behind the civilisations of the Middle East, nor, perhaps, even some among the less advanced countries in the West. But the expectation of a sudden efflorescence of genius, this curious hope that the light will come from the East immediately and without delay; that a nucleus of men of superlative gifts would spring forth in this new soil, and at once burst upon the world with a new moral and intellectual message, so that men would wonder how so much astonishing genius could be so marvellously gathered together – this, fortunately, has not happened.

Israel, consequently, has a chance of continuing to grow, under conditions which may be described as almost normal. This is surely what Herzl wanted to see, although whether all his followers were equally won to the idea of something normal and ordinary is not clear. Certainly among the early Zionist pioneers there were those who spoke as if what they wished to create was a cultural enclave, a super-university, a shrine, a temple at once sacred and secular whose task would be spiritual and educational, and not a community occupied with the daily tasks of ordinary life. Yet I cannot think that it is the duty of any man to produce works of genius and irradiate the world with wisdom. If he does, so much the better for him and for the world. The principal obligation of human beings seems to me to consist in living their life according to their lights, and in developing whatever faculties they possess without hurting their neighbours, in realising themselves in as many directions as freely, variously and richly as they can, without worrying overmuch whether they are measuring up to the peaks in their own past history, without casting anxious looks to see whether their achievements reach the highest points reached by the genius of their neighbours, nor yet looking at other nations, or wondering whether they are developing precisely as they expect them to develop.

I spoke earlier of the peculiar self-consciousness – the heightened, sometimes over-acute awareness of themselves and their condition – which is itself a large element in the 'Jewish problem'. To this there was bound to be a reaction. And so in Israel one comes across individuals who say: 'We are not greatly interested in the outside world. We are the natives of this land. No doubt we did come from outside. And the Americans came from Europe, and so did the Australians and Canadians. But it is a mistake to regard the Australians and Canadians as a species of Englishman, and it is a mistake to regard the Americans as a species of Germans, Italians, Dutchmen, Czechs and so on; they have a mentality of their own. This is more obvious if you go to America, Australia and Canada than if you simply study history and look at them from a distance as a kind of extension of a mother country. No doubt we too come from outside and we are composed of very varying elements from different countries; but the "pressure-cooker" is working well. We are gradually assimilating to a common type; and we cannot be tied in our history to perpetual dependence upon, and concern with, the fate of those Jews who have not followed us, and whose fate is determined by their local position in their local communities, in which they have either chosen to stay, or were forced to stay by circumstances.'

This is a very extreme position, and I do not for a moment pretend that it is morally tenable or at all widely held. But in a milder and humaner form it will surely spread. There is nothing unnatural in the fact that there exist people who do not wish to spend their lives in mourning for the six million Jewish dead. They cannot forget them; but neither do they wish to start their lives as the gloomy heirs of a black tragedy; they want to start their lives afresh. Some of them are young, healthy, ordinary men and women who are looking forward to a future of normal activity. They wish to be simple, uncomplicated, and shed the neuroses of their ancestors, without perpetual reminders of their past misfortunes. They cannot develop independently so long as they remain a colony with infinite strands binding it to the entire Diaspora, feeling in its body every tremor of what happens to the end of these strands in other countries. They are today economically dependent on the Jews in the rest of the world; they are, in general, excessively dependent on the rest of the world, because they are not economically viable, their imports exceed their exports, and so forth. Nor is autarky a desirable ideal for any country. But in the end, if they survive at all (as they surely will), this excessive dependence will cease, and a new type of man and citizen will develop. He may produce no very sophisticated art, may produce nothing culturally startling or arresting, but he and his fellows will exist, and be happy, and be a people, and that is surely sufficient.

If a new nation is born which differs from the Jews of the outside world, if a gap occurs – if the Israeli nation gradually becomes almost (never wholly) as different from the Jews of the outside world as other nations are, we should have no ground of complaint. There are those, even among Jews, who say that the entire experiment is a kind of 'exile from exile'. The Jews have been in exile in the Diaspora; and now, in order to escape from its difficulties and burdens, they have voluntarily exiled themselves into a kind of vast ghetto of their own, which still possesses all the properties of those from which they emerged, plus the discomforts of the Middle East. But this, in my view, is quite false. No country gives less of an impression of being a self-enclosed, timid, cowering body of persons, huddling together for mutual protection, which is the idea that a ghetto conjures up.

It is true that Israel's problems are many. Apart from terrifying economic problems which I am incompetent to appraise, it is afflicted, at the fringes of the great liberal, semi-middle-class body of its population, with political unwisdom of both right- and left-wing kinds: not more so than other countries; but, alas, not less. There is the problem of its relations with its neighbours, and perhaps the greater problem of its relations with the outside world. Israelis are of course a predominantly Western people, they read Western books, they think Western thoughts, they go to Western films. Their outlook is a Western outlook. The symbols, the words in which they think have largely been derived from the traditions of England, of France, of Germany, of America, of all the countries of Western civilisation. They are today faced with the problem of assimilating with – or to – their new immigrants from Oriental countries; the army training which the newcomer undergoes is a great leveller. Will the result be Westernisation or 'Levantinisation'? It is too early to tell.

There is no doubt, moreover, that there is a vast gap between them – even their Oriental portion – and their Arab neighbours, and the Arabs are certainly consumed with hostile sentiment towards them; indeed, with the desire to exterminate them. Not as great, perhaps, as Arab leaders find it necessary to proclaim; but violent enough. Neither they, nor their Western friends in or out of government offices in London and Washington and New York, are reconciled to the notion that Israel has come to stay. The relations of Israel with the outside world are difficult. Israel is aware that it has relatively little of material value to offer. It realises that in some sense it is the plaything of the Great Powers: Babylon, Assyria and Egypt in ancient days; America and the Soviet Union and Britain today. They are still at the crossroads between the Great Powers, which may support them one day, and desert them the next. The clash of ideologies between the major powers comes into violent play on the soil of Israel, which is a more impressionable medium than almost any other place in the world. In the circumstances Israelis realise that they are a kind of political and intellectual microcosm, in which almost any tendency of the modern world is more clearly visible, more acutely felt and more traceable than anywhere else. They realise this, but there is nothing that they can do to escape it. Their daily cares are greater than the anxieties induced by long-distance prospects. They feel – I think perhaps rightly – that if they behave themselves in an intelligent and constructive manner, they will survive. Late or soon a settlement with their neighbours will take place. The geographical and ethnic factors are inescapable. On the whole, I should say, they are too wise to brood too gloomily about them: day-to-day anxieties sufficiently absorb their energies.

If one were a serious sociologist, it is to Israel that one would surely go today. There is no place in the world where a greater degree of variety of humanity is observable. Social scientists complain of the absence of 'laboratory conditions' in which experiments can be conducted in their disciplines. But these almost obtain in Israel. Nowhere else can one witness so extraordinary a collision and 'cross-fertilisation' of types – of representatives of some ancient pre-classical culture coming into contact with the most sophisticated modern products of the United States; of the most theoretical, intellectually coherent form of, let us say, Marxist ideology coming into collision with some dim, mystical, almost inexpressible Oriental attitude to life. There is no country where so many ideas, so many ways of living, so many attitudes, so many methods of going about everyday things have suddenly been thrown into a more violent clash. It is one of the most fascinating spectacles in the world. Yet the sociologists have paid relatively little attention to Israel, and prefer to study routine phenomena in, let us say, the US Midwest. This is virtuous, there is nothing to be said against it. Nevertheless it seems curious to me that sociologists, with the opportunity of studying a phenomenon unique in their field, obstinately avert their gaze and go on burrowing into the dullest and most uniform forms of life that they can find. It is as if there were an eclipse only once in the history of the world, from which some kind of crucial data – refuting and confirming essential hypotheses – could be deduced, and as if the world's astronomers were found firmly pointing their telescopes in some other direction.

From the point of view of Israel itself, as a result of this violent clash and collision of various cultures a common denominator is emerging, something identifiable and fascinating, namely a politically liberal, egalitarian human being with a mentality not unlike that of the Italian Risorgimento: on the whole left of centre, of a kind rightly admired by English liberals and radicals in the nineteenth century. This is the kind of outlook which has set its stamp upon the whole economic and social development of Palestine. None of this could have been deduced solely from economic needs or the social necessities of the Israeli community.

This seems to me interesting, because it shows the power of ideas, and not merely of economic and social pressures. It upsets materialist theories of history according to which environment, or economic factors, or the collision of classes is mainly responsible for what happens. It upsets the various doctrines in accordance with which Israel could not have arisen at all; the doctrines which the German Marxists and Russian Bundists used to adduce in order to prove the impossibility of a Jewish State, and all the various doctrines about the inevitable assimilation of the Jews, advanced by both Jews and Gentiles on the basis of some set of cut and dried premisses, or historical theory, or sociological law or system. Nor did the empiricists in the foreign offices of the Great Powers do much better. Very few of the chancelleries of Europe or America seriously believed in the possibility of the rise of even a short-lived independent State of Israel. Very few believed that it would ever have the fighting strength, the unity of spirit which would enable it to triumph over so many obstacles. A great many of the prophets were in the grip of various obsolete theories of how nations rise and fall, or simply of powerful prejudice and emotion; and on the whole they tended to discount too much the sheer power of human idealism and human will-power.

Israel is not a large-scale experiment. It occupies a very small portion of the earth's surface; the number of persons comprising its population is relatively small. But its career confutes a number of deterministic theories of human behaviour, those offered both by materialism and by the fashionable brands of anti-materialism. And that, I will not deny, is a source of great satisfaction to those who have always believed such theories to be false in principle, but have never before, perhaps, found evidence quite so vivid and quite so convincing of their hollowness. Israel remains a living witness to the triumph of human idealism and will-power over the allegedly inexorable laws of historical evolution. And this seems to me to be to the eternal credit of the entire human race.

JEWISH SLAVERY AND EMANCIPATION

I

SOME TWENTY years ago or so there appeared, in a weekly periodical, an essay by L. B. Namier.[1] It was concerned with the problem of the Jews of our time. If I recollect it correctly, Namier proceeded in a simile of characteristic precision and brilliance to compare the effect of enlightenment upon the Jewish masses in the last century with that of the sun upon a glacier. The outer crust disappeared by evaporation; the heart of the glacier remained stiff and frozen; but a great portion of the mass melted into a turbulent flood of water which inundated the valleys below, some flowing on in rivers and streams, while the rest collected into stagnant pools; in either case the landscape altered in a unique, and at times revolutionary, fashion. The image was not merely vivid but accurate, because such evaporation does, of course, occur despite all denials; assimilation can sometimes be total. In England alone the main branches of such families as the Ricardos, the Disraelis, the Levy-Lawsons have entered the general texture of Gentile society and become divorced from their origins in the minds of both themselves and their neighbours. This phenomenon will be condemned by those who believe the Jewish religion alone to be the truth and, consequently, regard all forms of departure from it, particularly on the part of those who once believed it, as being treasonable and, moreover, wicked in so far as it tends to spread false beliefs; and again, by those who believe in the inner solidarity of races or communities as such, and view abandonment of them by their members, on any ground, as a species of disloyalty and desertion. Nevertheless, the phenomenon does occur: and if, under present-day conditions, it looked feasible on a mass scale, and not merely in the case of a minute percentage of the Jewish people, it

[1] This was written in 1951. Namier's essay is 'Zionism', *New Statesman*, 5 November 1927, 103–4, reprinted in his *Skyscrapers and Other Essays* (London, 1931).

would perhaps not be as easy to argue against it as in fact it is.

It is as well to say at the outset that there is no possible answer to, or argument against, those truly religious Jews to whom the preservation of Judaism as a faith is an absolute obligation to which everything, including life itself, must without hesitation be sacrificed, should such a choice ever become inescapable. The position of all true believers, since their position is in principle not susceptible to any empirical argument from history or experience, nor to the claims of any form of happiness on earth, can for these reasons be made impregnable. But it is not so clear that those who believe in the preservation and transmission of 'Jewish values' (which are usually something less than a complete religious faith, but rather an amalgam of attitudes, cultural outlook, racial memories and feelings, personal and social habits) are justified in assuming without question that this form of life is obviously worth saving, even at the unbelievable cost in blood and tears which has made the history of the Jews for two thousand years a dreadful martyrology. Once the absoluteness of the values of unreasoning faith is diluted into loyalty to traditional forms of life, even though it be sanctified by history and the suffering and faith of heroes and martyrs in every generation, alternative possibilities can no longer be dismissed out of hand, if only because so much torment accompanies any choice. However, fortunately for those to whom moral problems of this type tend to be painful, the question in this case turns out to be merely academic. Large-scale assimilation has not in modern times – whatever may have occurred in earlier ages – proved to be a practicable alternative. The German Jews who believed and practised it with the most sincere conviction have suffered the most tragic fate of all. Evaporation, in Namier's sense, occurs, indeed, but on too negligible a scale; consequently the question of whether or not total assimilation is permissible or dignified or justifiable, or in any respect desirable, is, for good or ill, irrelevant to the Jewish problem. As a radical solution – that is as an answer to the problems of more than a few individuals in exceptional circumstances – it has failed. Nor is there any reason, if history and sociology have any lessons to teach, for thinking that it will ever succeed.

But neither is there any 'future' in the life of the still-frozen heart of the glacier. However powerful the bonds of an ancient and rigid religion which permeates the whole of the individual's life and organises it into a unique discipline, the social disintegration of the old world which once made such a life possible for entire communities has gone too far. The Jews have undergone, in a somewhat peculiar and abnormal fashion, and after a certain time-lag, a historical process similar to that of other European nations. The European Jews were the last community to emerge from the Middle Ages; the last to be carried into statehood by a national and cultural Risorgimento, which *mutatis mutandis* (and there are fewer *mutanda* than is usually supposed) resembles those of other late-comers – particularly the political resurrection of the great historical partners of Israel in the creation of Western civilisation, the peoples of Greece and of Italy. The transforming process, once it has begun, cannot be evaded: the ancient establishment wherein the Jews were enabled, even after the Spanish expulsion, to lead a social and religious life which was completely *sui generis* – in Germany, in Italy, in Provence, and later in the Russian, Austro-Hungarian and Turkish Empires – has collapsed. It was, at its height, one of the most complete and powerful civilisations, albeit persecuted, insulated, and without influence outside the ghetto walls, that can be conceived. It lingered into modern history, mainly within the frontiers of the Russian Empire, and owing its strength to the suspicion and active hostility of the government of that Empire, caused the Russian Jews to become a community within a community. Within this framework, despite appalling poverty, the most violent political and economic discrimination, and every form of material and moral discouragement, the Jews developed a rich and independent inner life of their own, from which sprang those generously endowed, imaginative, free, un-broken Jewish personalities who, even today, compare so favour-ably with the better-educated but, at times, less spontaneous and morally and aesthetically less attractive Jews of the West. Born and bred, as these latter were, in a more tolerant, but also more ambivalent, atmosphere, in which the Jews were half accepted by their neighbours, and lacking the protective influence of a social establishment of their own, they turned out to be, at times, embarrassed, inadequate and wanting, a species of spiritual casual-ties, often gifted and interesting, subtle, sensitive and exceptionally penetrating, but for some unexplained reason a source of disquiet and *malaise* to themselves and others. For it is difficult to deny (even though it has been often denied) that the recent history of this category of Jews – those who failed equally to evaporate and to stay frozen – has been, save in those peaceful communities in which they have formed quiet and largely unnoticed pools, one of anxiety and discomfort; sometimes, indeed, tempered by periods of relative tranquillity in which it has seemed as if some stable condition might be achieved at last; but such periods were succeeded inevitably by some cruel upheaval in which illusions were shattered, and the precarious search for security and happiness, even when there was little hope of stability, began again.

In the course of their troubled and frustrated history during the last two centuries the Jews have created works of lasting genius in almost every sphere of life; Jews have served the communities in which they lived faithfully in many diverse capacities, often more devotedly than the other natives of the lands in which they lived; they have taken every conceivable step to adapt and adjust themselves consciously and unconsciously to many societies and institutions, they have with painful anxiety tried to avoid causing irritation to their neighbours; they have often hushed their voices to something below a whisper; they have imitated others with astonishing skill, and adopted the colouring of their environment at times with unheard of rapidity and success. And yet it has all proved unavailing. They have throughout carried within them the uneasy feeling that their stoical ancestors, locked nightly into their narrow and hideous ghettos, were not merely more dignified, but more contented, than they; prouder, better, more hated, perhaps, but less despised by the outer world. And this uneasiness, which rational argument failed to dispel, has troubled the Jews and troubled their friends, and has infected all discussion of the subject, as if something lay concealed which could not be mentioned in the course of it and yet was the centre of the entire problem. This queer status of the problem itself – that its mere mention should tend to cause suspicion and embarrassment – is a fact which those interested in the Jewish destiny, Jews and Gentiles, friends and enemies, have, during the last hundred years or so, tirelessly but not very successfully sought to explain. Perhaps another simile may throw some light, if not upon the solution, at any rate upon the nature, of the ancient *Judenfrage* itself.

II

The position of the Jews, so suddenly liberated towards the end of the eighteenth century and the beginning of the nineteenth, might be compared to that of travellers who by some accident find themselves among a tribe with whose customs they are not familiar. The reaction of the tribe to the strangers is uncertain. It may or may not welcome them. It may kill them or expel them or, alternatively, accept them, or even worship them. The first thing that the strangers must do, if they are to survive at all, is to make themselves familiar with the habits and modes of behaviour of the tribe. The members of the tribe themselves do not need to do this; they live the life they live, they eat, drink, talk, sing, look for means of subsistence, love and hate, without needing to be aware of how these processes are carried on, or what each next step will be. The strangers, on the other hand, being alien to this mode of life, find little they can take for granted; on the contrary, they find it necessary to do everything they can to find out how their hosts 'function'. They must get this right, otherwise they may easily find themselves in trouble. They must not miscalculate, or their survival is in jeopardy. Their principal purpose is to investigate and form a clear picture of how members of the tribe think and act; and then try to fit themselves into the tribal form of life. Consequently, if the travellers are at all gifted they presently become exceptionally knowledgeable about the life of the tribe. They come to know far more about its habits than the members of the tribe themselves know or need to know; for upon accurate knowledge of this kind the strangers' freedom and happiness – their life itself – directly depend, whereas those of the tribe do not.

So much labour and devotion to the life and outlook of other people must in time induce a natural affection for, and devotion to, it – a sense of personal identification with, and dedication to, a subject which has absorbed all the time, gifts, energy, all the mental and emotional resources of the researcher. The strangers become primary authorities on the natives: they codify their language and their customs, they compose the tribe's dictionaries and encyclo-paedias, they interpret the native society to the outside world. With every year their knowledge and love of it, their fascination with all that it is and does, become greater. If their enterprise is successful, they feel that they understand the natives so profoundly, so much better than they understand themselves, that they feel at one with the native civilisation; they feel – not unjustifiably – that they are its best friends, its champions and its prophets. In the end they are prepared not merely to live but to die for it and, if need be, with it, no less bravely, and perhaps with greater passion, than the natives themselves. Nevertheless, the natives often fail to reciprocate these sentiments. They may wonder at, admire, sometimes be spellbound by the strangers, grow fond, even very fond, of them, but their feelings, however benevolent or respectful or fascinated, are, at best, those felt toward strangers – persons the very quality of whose excellence goes with their being in some sense different from, and outside, the tribal structure.

The strangers are at first puzzled by this sense of distance, and then become indignant and protest; how can it be that they are treated as being in some sense alien, they who have given their life and treasure and all their intellectual and moral energies to the welfare at home and justification abroad of the native community – they who have done so much more than the natives themselves seem prepared to do? But then this is precisely the reason for which they are felt to be outsiders – their understanding is too sharp, their devotion too great, they are experts on the tribe, not members of it. They are its servants, perhaps its saviours, but they are not homogeneous with it. They are altogether too anxious to please; indeed, too anxious to be whatever it is that they protest so much – and to all appearances so plausibly – that they surely are. One of the factors which make them different is precisely this excessive interest in the tribe and its fortunes; and, as an inevitable concomitant of it, their unique passion for getting things right and for arriving at the truth. For without this they cannot function; *they* cannot afford to look on the world with uncritical eyes, and merely live and die, suffer normal pains and enjoy normal pleasures, like the natives; for not being automatically adjusted to the life of the native community, they must perpetually, and particularly when some failure to connect with the natives occurs, examine and re-examine their situation, and in particular their relationships with their neighbours; for unless they do this they may commit blunders, and fall foul of the tribe, and perish. This puts a premium no less strong, because only half-conscious, on obtaining the correct view of the facts, lack of which may prove fatal to them. Hence the strangers grow to be peerless analysts of the social conditions of the tribe. During periods of boom they describe the tribal successes accurately, and, indeed, advertise them with pride and enthusiasm and are correspondingly popular. But their sense of truth never abandons them; they analyse slumps with equal fidelity and sharpness, and make themselves correspondingly disliked.

At such moments the natives feel not so much that what they are being told is in itself unpalatable, though it may well be so, but that those who say it occupy some outside vantage-point, and that the diagnosis is a little too objective and too cool, that those who pronounce it are in some sense foreign specialists, identified with the fate of their client not 'organically', but by some fortuitous accident. Consequently the tribe turns upon them, and pursues them with particular ferocity the more they speak, however true or valuable or important their words may be. The strangers, who are by this time so thoroughly identified in their own minds with the natives that these attacks seem to them gratuitous as well as cruelly unjust, cannot as a rule understand what causes them. For, shrewd and self-critical as they may be in other respects, they must harbour at least one illusion – that they are truly and fully members of the tribe; for upon this their entire position and capacity for working for the tribe must necessarily rest. This is so because their whole existence and all their values depend upon the assumption that they can by conscious effort live the life of the natives, and acquire complete security through pursuing, if need be by means of artificial techniques, those activities which the natives perform by nature and spontaneously. This must not be questioned, since, unless it is true, the presence of the strangers among the natives can never be wholly free from danger, and their enormous sustained effort, culminating in the acquisition of a special kind of intellectual and moral vision with which they have seen into the heart of the native system, might turn out to derive from a gigantic delusion: a delusion which has taken them in, perhaps, but has not taken in the natives whose instincts continue to tell them that the strangers, who by this time look like natives, speak like them, even react like them, nevertheless lack something, want of which prevents them from being natives. What that something is neither the natives nor the strangers can precisely specify, the strangers being particularly skilled at refuting crude or malicious native theories about what the impalpable something is. Nevertheless it is there – the difference – and the strangers' anxiety to deny it merely attracts further attention to their un-native conduct: for the natives would never dedicate themselves to refuting something alleged to be so patently false with so much fervour and such a wealth of apparently unanswerable yet, in the end, unconvincing argument. The more desperately the strangers argue, the more vividly their differences from the natives stand out; indeed, the anxiety to deny the difference is itself a barrier to its disappearance. Other strangers – Normans among the Franks, Huguenots among the English, Gauls in Asia Minor – have been content to recognise themselves for what others took them to be – strangers, believers in strange religions, followers of unfamiliar customs. And this may have involved them in unpopularity or even acute persecution. But there was nothing obscure or problematic about their identity or status; and they merged with the surrounding population only when they lost their special physical, or social, or spiritual characteristics, by intermarriage or other forms of social fusion. But the strangers we speak of are unique in retaining their peculiar attributes, especially their religious views, while stoutly denying that these peculiarities are of crucial importance, or relevant to their relationship to the society in which they dwell. This attitude rests on an illusion which is nevertheless, for the most part sincerely and honourably, accepted as a reality by both sides, but which, being half felt as delusive, communicates a sense of desperate embarrassment to those who seek to examine it: as if a mystery were being approached to the belief in the non-existence of which both sides are pledged, yet the reality of which both at least suspect.

III

This is a parable of the fate of the Jews in Europe and America. Perhaps the most vivid example of it is the fate of the German Jews. In a sense no community ever succeeded in identifying itself more closely with the nation in which it lived. When a German Jew, shortly after Hitler's rise to power, declined to go to France, saying, 'I cannot go to the country of our enemies', the pathos of the situation which this underlined could not, perhaps, be paralleled in any other country. Some German Jews seemed to understand far less clearly than almost anyone else what it was that had struck them, and how it had come to do so. After all, they pleaded, what poet was more German than Heine? What composer more German than Mendelssohn? But then this is precisely the point. Goethe was a poet and wrote about nature or love or the human predicament, and because he was a German the quality of his genius was German, and he was a great German poet. Beethoven was a composer, and being a German, was a great German composer, and in specific respects differed, by possessing certain German attributes, from French and Italian composers. But

Heine wrote for the most part not about love and life directly, but principally about Germany, about what it was to be a German and also not to be a German. Much of what he wrote was derived not from a first, but from a second, order of experience – he saw himself as a German, as a Jew, as a poet, as an inhabitant of too many worlds, and wrote with a particular kind of self-consciousness alien to a normal member of a recognised community. There never was so consciously German a composer as Mendelssohn: he set himself to revive the national heritage contained in the Protestant liturgy; he rediscovered and reinstated the great J. S. Bach; he wrote the Reformation Symphony to the greater glory of his adopted Church; towards the end of his life he had become a great neo-Lutheran musician as neither Schumann, nor even Brahms, was or could have been. Of Mendelssohn it could truly be said that he had done a great deal for German music, and German culture; but no one has ever felt inclined to say this of Mozart or of Schubert. They were merely composers of genius and also Germans (or Austrians) – they did nothing 'for' German (or Austrian) music: they only wrote it. Traditional German music was an ideal to Mendelssohn as the British Empire was to Disraeli; he believed in it more passionately than the average German artist.

Such passion surely often derives from a feeling of insufficient kinship and a desire to obliterate the gap; the more obstinate the gap, the more violent the desire to close it, or to act as if it did not exist. And this strikes an unnatural note, audible to all but the stranger himself – whether he be a Jew or some other kind of half-assimilated foreigner, whose very devotion to his second home, whose very passion for a second nature, causes the false note to sound. But second nature is different from nature, and the desperate self-identification of the Jew does not ring wholly true. Walter Rathenau once wrote, 'My people are the Germans, no one else. For me the Jews are a German tribe, like the Saxons, the Bavarians or the Wends.'[1] No sensitive person – particularly if he is a German – can read this without embarrassment. And when he was killed by the kind of young German nationalist whom, in some moods, he seemed to admire most, his assassination was

---

[1] Letter to Wilhelm Schwaner of 18 August 1916: p. 155 in Walther Rathenau, *Ein preussischer Europäer: Briefe*, ed. Margarete von Eynern (Berlin, 1955); cf. Rathenau's *An Deutschlands Jugend* (Berlin, 1918), p. 9, where he says he is 'a German of the Jewish tribe': vol. 6, p. 99, in Walter Rathenau, *Gesammelte Schriften* (Berlin, 1925–9). Ed.

doubtless a great crime and a tragedy for his country, but it had a dreadful pathos about it too – since it was something which Rathenau himself was all his life too blind, or too self-blinded, to allow even to be possible. If he had conceived its possibility, his life and attitude would have been very different; possibly he might have escaped assassination: or, at the very worst, he would have fallen as a martyr to a clearly pursued cause, and not as a sad victim to his own delusions.

IV

It has often been remarked that the Jews are better interpreters than creators; and this contains some truth but needs radical qualification. To say, as some do, that interpretation is itself a kind of creation – that journalists or violinists or translators of genius are fully creative – is, of course, true, but as a comment on the original thesis it is a sophistry. The difference between properly creative and properly interpretative activities is something which is familiar to everyone – although insistence upon drawing a precise frontier between the two provinces would doubtless lead to foolishly pedantic and unplausible conclusions. There is surely a clear sense in which Tolstoy or Bach were primarily creative artists – and in which such men of unique gifts as Paganini or Sainte-Beuve were not. Such descriptive terms as 'creative' or 'interpretative' are not judgements of value, they are merely categories of classification, although, at times, vague or unsatisfactory ones. If we allow such classification at all, it becomes fairly clear that in the province of the humanities the Jews, for whatever reasons, have made their deepest mark as interpreters and not as creators. This is conspicuously not so in the region of mathematics and the natural sciences. Here the Jews have contributed men of genius as great and as numerous as any people (the list has in recent times been reiterated with a pathetic frequency and need not be recited again).

The reason for this is not far to seek. If we may be allowed to revert to our simile: the Jews, like the strangers seeking to lose themselves in the strange tribe, find themselves compelled to devote all their energies and talents to the task of understanding and adaptation upon which their lives depend at every step. Hence the fantastic over-development of their faculties for detecting trends, and discriminating the shades and hues of changing individual and social situations, often before they have been noticed anywhere else. Hence, too, their celebrated critical acumen, their astonishingly sharp eye for the analysis of the past, the present and sometimes the future also – in short, their well-known genius for observation and classification, and explanation – above all for reportage in its sharpest and finest forms. What one has discovered for oneself one often loves beyond its deserts – one tends to exaggerate its merits or importance. So we find Jews prone to a peculiar kind of worship of the heroes or institutions of the nations among which they live. We find Stahl and Friedjung among the prophets of German nationalism, Disraeli as the inventor of the mystique of British imperialism, and Ludwig, Guedalla, Maurois as the best-known popular biographers – and hero-worshippers – of our time: court painters with a capacity for romanticising their subjects, for seeing them with bemused eyes, perceiving in them much that natures less hungry for a happier, more brightly coloured world would, perhaps, pronounce non-existent. There is no need to appeal to abstruse or dubious psychological techniques to realise how much yearning for what the world has denied the author there is in Ludwig's portrait of Goethe, or Guedalla's (for all his wit and apparent sophistication) naïvely romantic visions of Wellington or Palmerston, or Maurois's almost painfully self-revealing study of Disraeli (and one might add the exquisitely elegant and flattering portrait of Catholic ideals in the work of Bergson's later years). In a sense this is the modern equivalent of the knowledge, devotion and imagination which Jewish physicians or financiers offered to their patrons in the Middle Ages, for which, when all went well, they were rewarded with kind treatment and vouchsafed glimpses of a more glorious world.

For this reason there is at times something self-conscious and palpably imitative about direct ventures on the part of Jews into art or imaginative literature. There is no need to subscribe to racist or other repulsive brands of dangerous nonsense in order to hold that art and literature are inevitably rooted in the traditional experience of the social unit to which the artist belongs; for it is true (even though this truth has been too violently exaggerated by nationalists and other extremists in recent years to be as obvious as it should be) that the language, or the musical forms, or the colours and shapes in terms of which he expresses himself are the product not merely of his own individuality, but of a wider social tradition, of which he himself is largely unconscious and which alone puts him in harmony, and gives him the possibility of instinctive communication, with those to whom he speaks. But here the Jews start, as it were, below scratch. They must spend much preliminary effort and ability on merely adapting themselves to a medium in which their neighbours move naturally and without effort. It is, therefore, not surprising if, after so much expenditure of their emotional and intellectual substance on the process of self-adjustment – on trying, as it were, to become 'naturalised' – there is often not enough left for a genuinely strong, free, original creative effort. The process of learning how to make use of a medium less or more alien is necessarily self-critical, full of conscious awareness of one's relationship to this or that standard, this or that artist or school of thought. The music of Meyerbeer or Mahler (as of the non-Jewish, but equally 'assimilated' half-German, half-Italian Busoni) is, at its best, abnormally full of memories of other music, and is adulterated by much that is non-musical, extraneous and highly self-conscious; and the same holds of the novels of such very diverse writers as Auerbach and Disraeli, Wassermann and Schnitzler – to mention only the genuinely good. In the case of the inferior novelists and poets and composers this is even more obviously true.

It is not natural gifts, or integrity, or opportunity that is lacking, but an environment in which capacities and energies need not be half used up in the process of establishing foundations upon which an artistic edifice can be built – foundations which the non-Jews find ready-made, since they are the basis upon which their normal lives are lived. And it is interesting that, while this holds good of the arts and humane activities generally, where words and symbols which are the fruit of the unconscious growth of traditions are the vehicles of expression, it does not apply nearly so much to the sciences. There the vehicles – the symbols – are, in any case, something artificial, made to order by experts and intended to be neutral and international. In the humane arts the rich associative quality of a symbol is indispensable; almost everything depends upon the interplay of such non-artificially made nuances. In the sciences and mathematics this is merely an obstacle to clarity and precision, and is ruthlessly and rightly eliminated. In a world of abstract symbols, divorced from national cultures and times and places, the Jewish genius finds full freedom, and, consequently, is capable of magnificent creative achievement. Here Jews start not below scratch, but at the same level as others, and their intellectual and imaginative qualities, trained by the centuries of solitary confinement during which they were turned in upon themselves, have produced prodigious results. Here Jews are no longer interpreters, explainers, translators, but independent creators in their own right. This is but an earnest of what the Jews could create in cultural conditions similar to those of other nations – and is much the strongest of all arguments for that 'normalisation' which has always been the whole, or nearly the whole, case for Zionism.

V

Persons, like things as a rule, are what those who deal with them take them to be, and not necessarily what they think themselves to be. A table is what most people would treat as being a table; we do not know what the table would say if it could speak; if it told us that in its own view it was not a table, we should not, in spite of this, cease to think it to be a table. This holds no less of persons. After telling themselves for half a century that they were perfectly normal Germans in Germany, Frenchmen in France, Peruvians in Peru, the Jews of the Western world, in the end, could not altogether ignore the view that they were not altogether as others were, a view only too obviously held with remorseless persistency by some of their neighbours during, at any rate, some of the time. The view was sometimes described as anti-Semitism, sometimes as ignorance, sometimes as an illusion spread by wilful obscurantists or chauvinists among the Jews themselves. But the problem which could be treated by the optimists of the nineteenth century as unreal, or in process of liquidation, became recognised as something genuine in the most assimilationist Jewish circles of our time, and led to various equally peculiar psychological consequences. If we may be allowed to employ yet another analogy, the situation grew to be somewhat as follows. Jews in such circles acted like a species of deformed human beings, let us say hunchbacks, and could be distinguished into three types according to the attitudes they adopted towards their humps. The first class consisted of those who maintained that they had no hump. If challenged, they were prepared to produce a document signed and countersigned by all the nations, in particular by their most enlightened leaders, solemnly declaring that the bearers were normal, full-grown persons, with no marks to distinguish them from other healthy human beings, and that to think otherwise was an offence against international morality. If, nevertheless, someone persisted in staring at their backs, the hunchbacks maintained that this was due either to an optical illusion, or to a violent form of prejudice dating from a period when they were thought, however mistakenly, to have humps, or perhaps to a remote time when there were in fact hunchbacks in the world, although these were now extinct. At times they were sure that they observed furtive glances thrown at that portion of their backs where they maintained no hump was discernible, even when, in fact, no one was looking at them. When they did not actually produce international certificates of hump-lessness, they quoted enlightened nineteenth-century liberal intellectuals, or learned anthropologists, or socialist theorists and the like, who explained that the very notion of hunchbacks was due to a confusion – since no such beings existed, or if they did had disappeared a long time ago – or was, even if the creatures existed, not relevant to any possible enquiry.[1]

The second attitude was the opposite to this. The hunchback did not conceal the fact that he wore a hump, and declared openly that he was happy to do so, that to own a hump was a privilege and an honour, that it set him apart as a member of a superior group, and that those who persecuted and threw stones at him did so out of concealed envy – a conscious or subconscious jealousy of so rare a possession, and one which could not be acquired at will. These persons said in effect, 'I am not ashamed of being a hunchback; very far from it; certainly I am a hunchback, and proud of it.'

The third type consisted of those timid and respectful cripples who found that, by never mentioning humps at all, and by inducing others to regard the very use of the term as virtually implying an unworthy discrimination, or, at the very best, lack of taste, they could reduce discussion of the topic to manageable and ever-diminishing dimensions, and move among the straight-backed with almost no sense of embarrassment, at any rate to themselves. They tended to wear voluminous cloaks which concealed their

---

[1] This was the attitude of those who, like the well-meaning (Gentile) social democrat Karl Kautsky, wrote books to prove that, in terms of current criteria of what constituted a race or nation, the Jews could not be described as constituting one; or like the rabbis who declared Judaism to be only a religion; or only a system of ethics, or an outlook, or a memory. If any of these propositions had been true, they would have been too obvious to need proof. It is not necessary to prove that the Methodists are not a race or a nation, that utilitarianism is only an ethical system, that united Christendom is only a memory, or that the Jews are oddly unlike any and all of these.

precise contours. Among themselves they did occasionally mention the forbidden topic, and even recommended one another various kinds of ointment, which, it was rumoured, if rubbed in nightly, for many hundreds of years, would very gradually lessen the size of the hump or – who knows? – might even remove it altogether. Cases of complete disappearance were not altogether unknown, particularly in remote places or the very distant past. There was hope for everyone, provided as little as possible was said, and the ointment used regularly and assiduously.

These were for a long time the three principal categories of 'assimilated' Jews, enjoying varying degrees of discomfort about the abnormality of their status. Each category regarded the members of the other two with some disfavour as pursuing an absurdly mistaken policy and therefore liable to compromise the wise together with the foolish. But presently there came those who said that a hump was a hump, an appendage which was neither desirable nor capable of being disguised, nor yet of being slowly diminished by application of mild palliatives, and, in the meanwhile, a cause of grave distress to those afflicted with it. They recommended – and this was considered audacious to the point of lunacy – that it be cut off by means of a surgical operation. This, like all operations, admittedly involved a grave risk to the life of the patient; it might lead to disorders in other parts of the body; it might have unexpected psychical results; but if successful it would remove the hump. Perhaps a hump was not the worst of evils; and the operation was certainly both costly and dangerous. But if what was desired above all things was the removal of humps on a mass scale – if, in short, anything was preferable to a hump – then there was nothing for it: only an operation of this kind would secure adequate results. This, in fact, is what the Zionist solution – in its full political form – advocated. Its triumph consists in the fact – and I believe it to be a fact – that the Jews of Israel, certainly those born there in recent times, are, whatever their other qualities and defects, straight-backed. Whatever the present and future effects of this operation upon Jews or Gentiles, the three earlier attitudes have become historically discredited by the emergence of the State of Israel. This astonishing event has transformed the situation of the Jews beyond recognition, and made all previous theories and activities which flowed from it obsolete: not without leading in its own turn to new problems, new solutions and sharp new controversies.

VI

Arthur Koestler has formulated one of these new issues with great effectiveness.[1] In the old days the Jews prayed thrice daily to be restored to Zion. Material obstacles made it impossible for them to achieve this. Circumstances have now changed, and a great many of those who wish to do so can at least initiate steps which will take them to Israel in the end, or, at any rate, will convert them in due course into being citizens of that country resident abroad. Is it, therefore, not mere hypocrisy to continue to utter such prayers while taking no action appropriate to the end prayed for? Those who wish, politically speaking, to be Jews and nothing but Jews can, and therefore should, do so by identifying themselves thoroughly with the State of Israel. Those who do not wish to emigrate, or apply for Israeli citizenship, should face the fact that they do not actually wish to be Jews in the full sense, and should choose some other nationality. Having decided, let us say, that they would rather be Englishmen or Americans than Israelis, they must cease to irritate their neighbours by a self-imposed exclusiveness, cease to oppose mixed marriages of their sons and daughters, cease to congregate in spiritual and even topographical ghettos round specially Jewish institutions, or cling to the use of Yiddish or other Jewish languages, and generally take vigorous steps to immerse themselves completely (and not, as before, with reservations) in the general life around them. This policy of 'the liquidation of the Diaspora' is in effect an invitation to the voluntary suicide of the *galut* as a specifically Jewish establishment.

From the other shore, the champions of the absolute primacy of Israel in Jewish life have arrived at conclusions not dissimilar to Koestler's. The future of the Jews lies in the State of Israel, and there alone: the value of the Diaspora, therefore, consists solely in the amount of support which they can offer to the new State, still faced with many perils. So long as the Jewish communities outside Israel can serve to support it, they have a *raison d'être*; as soon as they cease doing so, whether because they are unwilling or unable to help, or because their help is no longer needed, this *raison d'être* disappears and they are of no further significance to the destiny of

---

[1] In his *Promise and Fulfilment: Palestine 1917–1949* (London, 1949); cf. 'Judah at the Crossroads' (1954) in his *The Trail of the Dinosaur and other essays* (London, 1955), where he comments on IB's essay. Ed.

the Jews as such – and might as well vanish peacefully by mass emigration to Israel, liquidating the Jewish problems of which they are the focus and which will automatically disappear with them. The difference between the two views seems to consist in this. Koestler wishes the Diaspora to set about liquidating itself at once: the ultra-nationalists wish to preserve it in being so long as it plays the role of a much-needed milch-cow; its 'liquidation' must be postponed until this function is no longer crucial, but, sooner or later, must occur.

Before pointing out the defects of this very clear-cut thesis, it is perhaps as well to concede the large amount of truth which it embodies. The creation of the State of Israel has genuinely transformed the individual problem of the Jews of the Dispersion. The old problem was national in type. The Jews were regarded as something of an embarrassment everywhere, and even where they were not actually persecuted, the temptation either to assimilate or to segregate themselves was very great; but segregation did not protect them from persecution; and to order individuals voluntarily to 'assimilate', whether this advice was worthy or unworthy, was to make it virtually impossible for them to do so. I have never thought about a pink elephant in my life, but if I am told that above all things I must never think of one, I find that I can think of little else. Told to lose or forget their distinguishing characteristics, some Jews will try to do so desperately, but the more desperate their efforts the more unsuccessful they are and the more conspicuous this makes them. Associations of Jews for the purpose of promoting assimilation resemble nothing so much as public meetings of persons assembled to protest against the dangerous practice of holding public meetings. Hence the self-defeating nature of such policies, and the grotesque and pitiful human casualties by which they have been attended. The problem of the Jews was not individual but communal: individual Jews might disappear or establish themselves comfortably somewhere; communities could not do this of their own will. Literal mass suicide was not feasible as mass murder was, for example, where force was employed, as it was by the Inquisition in Spain, which probably did effect the permanent baptism of many Jews who preferred it to exile. But even there generations had to pass before Jewish memories died; some Marranos returned to the faith of their fathers; and no Jewish community gave in wholly: everywhere there was a toll of martyrs and exiles. Driven from one country, the expelled wandered to another, with no real hope of finding a permanent home. This very sense of insecurity – both inability to assimilate at will, and the shame and humiliation born of trying to do so, or of seeing others engaged on this harrowing procedure, caused acute psychological discomfort within individual Jews, caused them in fact to fidget uncomfortably wherever they were, to attract unwelcome attention to themselves, to excite contempt, dislike and persecution. This was produced equally by those over-anxious to assimilate and by those engaged in fighting this phenomenon.

This situation is now at an end. Most of those who feel the discomfort of their situation to be too great, and those, no less, who, whatever their feelings about life among their neighbours, wish for religious, or national, or any other reasons to live the full life of the members of a majority and not of a minority of a modern nation, have today a reasonable hope of reaching Israel and living its life. But there are others who, rightly or wrongly, openly or secretly, are not prepared to do this. For one reason or another they wish to, or at any rate do, continue to live as Jewish citizens of politically non-Jewish States. One may take up whatever attitude one wishes towards these people, who may well form the majority of the present (and future) Diaspora; one may defend or attack them, or have no particular attitude towards them; but the point is – and it is new and cardinal – that their problem of whether to go or stay, to assimilate or to remain in a betwixt-and-between condition, is now a purely individual problem which each Jew is free to solve as he chooses, and for which he bears responsibility not as a member of a nation but as an individual human being. If a man chooses, whether actively or passively, the discomfort, the insecure status, the social humiliations of living as a Jew, whether concealed or open, in a country which does not like Jews, that is to a large and increasing degree his own or his family's affair. We may despise him for insufficient pride, or denounce him for deceiving himself and predict disasters for him in the future, or congratulate him on a far-sighted utilitarianism or on bravely sacrificing himself to the future of his children, or on a commendable independence or disdainfulness of prejudice; that is our right. But it is no less his right to live the life he chooses, unless thereby he brings too much pain or injustice into the world.

Before the present situation the tragedy of the Jews was that no real choice was open to them. Men's beliefs are not in their own control; assimilation – except by mass conversion to religions in which they could not, or did not, believe, and in the intellectual climate of the last three centuries could not even pretend to believe – was impracticable for the majority. And there was no other solution which guaranteed their security except the growth of liberal institutions in the world; and this last was a hope which has been too cruelly betrayed in the last half-century to seem today more than a noble but somewhat remote ideal. As for the hopes set up among many despairing souls by Communism, they have led to the bitterest of all disenchantments; so far from providing a method of mass assimilation, Communism has left many of its Jewish victims largely incapable of readjustment to any normal, peaceful, civilised, productive kind of life. But today this problem is not nearly as difficult to solve as it once used to be. Each and every individual Jew is in a far better position than he has been since the destruction of the Jewish State by the Romans to choose his own mode of life for himself, with all its attendant qualities. Koestler seems to think that the Jews who refuse either to emigrate or to assimilate will for ever remain a troubled element in the countries of their settlement, causing distress to themselves and others, inviting ill-treatment by the very falsity of their position. Perhaps so. There are still to be met among us the pathetic descendants of the old Bundists and Yiddishists, the modern advocates of 'galut nationalism', which is based on the notion of modern nations as a motley amalgam of highly diverse and quasi-autonomous communities, in which Yiddish-speaking Jewish groups, living lives full of picturesque native colour, with folk-song and ancient crafts, and quaint traditional customs, would form a rich, if exotic, ingredient. These sorry absurdities, which recall the neo-medieval day-dreams of such eccentrics as Belloc and Chesterton, would scarcely be worthy of mention if they did not, by offering a totally unreal vision of what modern societies were or could be, succeed in deluding innocent persons, even at this late hour, to their personal doom. Against such blind leaders of the blind Koestler's most violent phrases hold good. They, if anyone, fully deserve the Russian socialist Plekhanov's bitter gibe at the Bundists as being in reality only Zionists who are afraid of sea-sickness. Since all the horrors of recent history have failed to bring the truth home to them, they must be reckoned incurable.

But even if Koestler's harsh words apply to such small, if maddening, minorities, there are too many individuals in the world who do not choose to see life in the form of radical choices between one course and another, and whom we do not condemn for this reason. 'Out of the crooked timber of humanity', said a great philosopher, 'no straight thing was ever made.'[1] No doubt an artist may sometimes be faced with such a crisis – with a choice between abandonment of his home and his family for a form of life more propitious to his art, and the abandonment of his art in order to set up as, let us say, a businessman. But even artists often do neither of these things, and may then be less successful as artists and as husbands and fathers than they might have been; but at least they are all these at once. To tell an artist that he must choose – to force on him quite gratuitously a rigid 'either–or', just because we like 'radical' solutions – is an intolerable form of bullying in a society which recognises the rights of human beings to a certain elasticity, to the right to realise themselves as they wish within the widest possible limits compatible with the existence of a minimum of justice and liberty and well-being. Fearful thinkers, with minds seeking salvation in religious or political dogma, souls filled with terror, like T. S. Eliot and Arthur Koestler, may wish to eliminate such ambiguous elements in favour of a more clear-cut structure, and they are, in this respect, true children of the new age which, with its totalitarian systems, has tried to institute just such an order among human beings, and sort them out neatly, each to his own category, and has suppressed civil liberties in varying degrees in order to achieve this purpose, which is sometimes defended on ultra-rationalist, scientific grounds. Doubtless Eliot and Koestler would protest at being associated with each other or with the *Zeitgeist* in this way. Eliot particularly abhors societies organised on a rationalistic or scientific basis; Koestler is foremost among the enemies of totalitarianism. And yet, to protest about a section of the population merely because it is felt to be an uncosy element in society, to order it to alter its outlook or get out – while the psychological explanation of this tone may be obvious enough (particularly when the accuser is himself prey to doubts and suffering) – is nevertheless a kind of petty tyranny, and derives ultimately from the conviction that human beings have no right to behave foolishly or inconsistently or vulgarly, and that society has the right to try and rid itself by humane means, but rid itself

---

[1] Immanuel Kant, 'Idea for a Universal History with a Cosmopolitan Purpose' (1784), *Kant's gesammelte Schriften* (Berlin, 1900–), vol. 8, p. 23, line 22.

nevertheless, of such persons, although they are neither criminals nor lunatics nor in any sense a danger to the lives or liberties of their fellows. This attitude, which is sometimes found to colour the views of otherwise civilised and sensitive thinkers, is a bad attitude because it is clearly not compatible with the survival of the sort of reasonable, humane, 'open' social texture in which human beings can enjoy those freedoms and those personal relationships upon which all tolerable life depends. Similarly, those Jewish ultra-nationalists (whether within or outside Israel) who look on the Jews as so many *Auslandsjuden* (the concept of *Auslandsdeutsche*, if not the title, is, after all, many decades older than Hitler, and Jews are nothing if not imitative) who have duties towards Israel but no rights – since Jews must live in, or at least for, Israel, or not at all – are guilty of similar exaggeration. The creation of the State of Israel has rendered the greatest service that any human institution can perform for individuals – has restored to Jews not merely their personal dignity and status as human beings, but what is vastly more important, their right to choose as individuals how they shall live – the basic freedom of choice, the right to live or perish, go to the good or the bad in one's own way, without which life is a form of slavery, as it has been, indeed, for the Jewish community for almost two thousand years.

But we must be careful not to confuse this recently won liberty with a new slavery. The old slavery consisted in telling the Jews that their right to the full liberties of men and citizens was at best doubtful so long as they insisted on remaining fully Jewish; and the propaganda of the assimilationists duly produced an indignant reaction among people who wished neither to hide their character-istics, nor to allow themselves to be transformed by some violent process of plastic surgery, or even a slower method, into something totally different from what they were and wished to be. And the Jewish religious revival which stemmed from Frankfurt, as well as the Zionist movement, were each in its own fashion worthy answers to this earlier attempt to re-enslave the newly liberated. Today assimilation is a sad wraith of its former self. But there is a danger that in the flush of the great new victory (and how great a victory it is, and what a thing it is suddenly to be set free and allowed to choose whether to live as other nations do or otherwise, we are perhaps scarcely yet in a position to grasp fully) an attempt may be made to impose new chains upon backs all too used to fetters, although fetters of a different kind; and the notion may be hammered into the heads of the ignorant and the confused that as Jews they have virtually no right to live beyond the borders of Israel, and that, unless they do this because they are specifically required to do it by the State of Israel, they are committing some kind of 'race treason'; and this because, so they will be told, their lives are not their own, but belong to their race and nation and State. In this way the vast wave of generous sentiment which at present flows so freely towards Israel on the part both of those who wish to live there and of those who rightly see in it the guarantee of their own emancipation as human beings, whether they go to live there or not, may be converted into a narrow and fatal and wholly indefensible chauvinism; and, unless checked, lead in its turn to the inevitable, and probably exaggerated, revulsion against such monstrous claims. No responsible leader of opinion in Israel – that last child of the European Risorgimento, the last State built on the humane and liberal foundations heralded by the great French Revolution and the European revolutions of 1848, conceived by the progressive social thought of Western Europe, traduced by Bolshevism and denounced by Goebbels – no responsible leader of opinion in Israel, or outside it, would consciously lend himself to such a policy. Whether the Jewish communities of the Dispersion still have that great and worthy part to play, of which those who are deeply concerned with their spiritual survival seem so confident, may well be doubted. But that is no longer a matter of crucial importance. The communal Jewish future belongs to Israel. The Jewish religion will survive in the hearts of those who believe in it, wherever they may be. And individual Jews will surely claim their rights and perform their full duties as human beings and citizens in the communities in which, at last, they can freely choose to live – freely, because they are physically as well as morally free to leave them, and their choice whether to go or stay, being no longer forced upon them, is a genuine choice.

An American wit once declared that the Jews were a peculiar people only because they are just like everybody else, only more so. There is a bitter truth in this remark. Doubtless no one likes to be aped, to see their characteristics exaggerated to the point, sometimes, of caricature. But to use force to prevent people from doing so, however irritating their behaviour, is nevertheless an infringement of minimal human liberties. To be over-sceptical or over-critical or insensitive or over-sensitive; to lack dignity, or practise vulgar ostentation; to be obsequious or neurotically aggressive, or lack a sense of moral or aesthetic measure or certain forms of spiritual tact, is doubtless unattractive and thoroughly regrettable, but it is not a crime, and neither Plato nor Maurras nor Eliot, nor any of their followers, have a right to place men, for this alone, beyond the borders of the city. If the Jews are to continue to suffer for failing to please their neighbours by behaving like apes and parrots, they will at least do so individually. They are human beings, and have the right to misbehaviour within the limits permitted to human beings in free societies, and neither Koestler, nor the ultra-nationalists whose claims he tacitly recognises, nor the 'galut nationalists', nor the assimilationists, may give them less than that. But neither, unless they go to Israel, have they a right to ask for more: for example, for even an attenuated version of a State within a State, or the enjoyment of any status and privileges in non-Jewish communities. That is how the problem has in our time become transformed. In the Diaspora as much as in Israel some Jews will make themselves agreeable and some disagreeable, some will parade their Jewish qualities and some will conceal them, some will be popular or respected, or disliked and despised, some may be Communists and some advocate Fascism for their own countries or for the entire human race. But none of this is any longer the matter of tragic and desperate concern to the Jews as a whole which once it was. For the fate of individuals (and even of individual communities) – whether to stay or move – is now, morally at least, in their own hands, and each can settle it freely, as he wishes, as best he can, with as much wisdom and good fortune as may fall to his lot. In this sense the creation of the State of Israel has liberated all Jews, whatever their relation to it. And this it will have done even if, in a dark hour, it should be overrun and lose its independence. This is a calamity not to be contemplated; yet even if it occurred, the State would have performed its task of emancipation. This is the answer to those who opposed the creation of a Jewish State because it would prove too weak and indefensible to survive, or too small to contain the entire Dispersion. But then most of those who used to put questions of this type did not, as a rule, genuinely themselves believe in the validity of the questions, and used them as an excuse for averting their thoughts from difficult choices.

A national problem – indeed a world problem – has been solved in our day. Surely, despite those who invent a hideous dilemma and demand all or nothing (all Jews to go to Israel, or in some other way to keep out of our sight), this is miraculous enough for one generation of men. Surely we are entitled to say *dayenu*;[1] and may well wonder whether later generations of Jews will begin to comprehend the problems and frustrations of their ancestors, and explain to themselves the reasons for those narrow and violent claims which, even in the hour of triumph, were put forward by those children of the *dor ha-midbar*[2] who have dwelt too long in darkness to know how to live, and let others live freely, in the light of day.

---

[1] 'This suffices us.'

[2] 'The desert generation' – that is, those who, having wandered for forty years, were in no condition to enter properly into the inheritance of the Promised Land.

CHAIM WEIZMANN'S LEADERSHIP

No one who spent any length of time in Weizmann's company could doubt that he was in the presence of a prodigiously endowed personality, a human being with an intellect more massive and powerful, a will stronger and more concentrated, emotions richer and more responsive, above all a view of human affairs larger and more profound, than are commonly to be found in even the most capable and successful men; in short, in the presence of a statesman of genius.

There are at least two types of political greatness, incompatible with, and indeed sometimes opposed to, each other. The first kind is that amalgam of simplicity of vision with intense, sometimes fanatical, idealism which is to be found in men compounded of fewer attributes than the normal human complement, but those larger than life. At its best such men rise to the noble grandeur of the great and simple heroes of classical antiquity. They tend to see life in a series of simple contrasts between light and darkness, good and evil, their own sacred cause and blind or wicked opposition to it; they attract their followers by the intensity and purity of their mind, by their fearless and unbending character, by the simplicity and nobility of the central principle to which they dedicate all that they have, by the very fact that they impose some pattern so clear, so uncomplicated, upon the manifold diversity of life, that other men, smaller, more troubled and more fearful, weaker, at times subtler and more intelligent than the leaders, feel liberated and vastly strengthened by the very directness and sincerity with which the unadorned central doctrine is presented to them. Sometimes the doctrine is Utopian: but the leader's total self-identification with it cures all anxieties and hesitations by the sheer force of conviction with which it is held and imposed on others.

Garibaldi, the liberator of Italy, is a notable and very noble representative of this type. He was not clever, nor particularly wise; he understood little about politics, still less about social and economic needs; as a soldier he was an amateur, he had little education, little understanding of human beings. But he focused the national aspirations of a great number of Italians, and focused them more directly, more simply, more crudely, perhaps, than the more sophisticated Mazzini; because he was simple, utterly brave, utterly guileless, and large-hearted and generous, and did not begin to understand the difficulties in his path, and applied very few, very primitive moral categories to all the problems which stood in the path of Italian unification, he made some of these problems disappear. Garibaldi untied no knots, but cut wherever he could with that simple sword which every Italian knew to be dedicated to the cause of Italian freedom, and to nothing else.

Such persons often stand, in a sense, outside the movements which idolise them; they are felt to be embodiments of greater virtues – and more mysterious ones – than their followers can emulate: they lead their armies to glory or to destruction, not by taking account of the obstacles in their path but by ignoring them; their faith is their stronger single attribute, the light which it casts is so intense as to obscure the unevenness and lurking dangers of the path which is being trodden, and to create the illusion of something direct, luminous and irresistible – the unique road to salvation. Such leaders tend to be somewhat inhuman – because instead of understanding the details of the lives and characters of their own and other peoples, they over-simplify, they create a radiant myth with which they identify themselves, and which their followers bear in their hearts.

This legendary quality, and this capacity for defying obstacles and dominating history by will-power and the ignoring of complexities, is a quality conspicuous in our day in, for example, General de Gaulle; there is something of it in Kosciuszko, in Kossuth, in Jabotinsky, in Tito and in Trotsky; such men become legendary heroes not merely in the eyes of their followers but in their own; and commit deeds of valour in the name of some externalised concept of themselves in which they believe and which they serve.

The second type of political genius belongs to those who possess the gifts of ordinary men, but these in an almost supernatural degree. So far from ignoring the infinite complexity of the life which surrounds them, they have an unanalysable capacity for integrating the tiny fragments of which it is composed into some coherent, intelligible pattern. So far from imposing their own form upon events without regard for the properties of the material, moulding it by sheer force of will-power and the passionate ideal, these latter are acutely aware of the smallest oscillations, the infinite variety of the social and political elements in which they live. Their antennae are extremely sensitive and record half-consciously a vast variety of experience; but instead of being overwhelmed by so much, their genius consists precisely in the fact that they are able to integrate it – not by any conscious process, but in some semi-instinctive fashion – into a single coherent picture; and then to act in accordance with this picture in a sure-footed, morally confident, firm and supremely effective fashion, responsive to the sharpest needs of their time in an infinity of sympathetic ways.

To this type belonged such men as Mirabeau, Cavour, Abraham Lincoln, Thomas Masaryk, Franklin Roosevelt – men whose outstanding characteristics were an unparalleled understanding of the medium which they were moulding, uncanny skill in dealing with men and situations, an unfailing sense of timing, and all those other qualities which made them so notably human, so delightful to persons of such different types, so ambitious, so seductive and so successful.

If the chief attribute of men of the first type is boldly to ignore obstacles – to ride with supreme unconcern into the heart of danger, to storm the enemy's bastions with simple and fervent faith, to believe in the triumph of their cause with sublime but somewhat inhuman fanaticism – the outstanding characteristics of the latter type are a profound and delicate understanding of the factors involved, a capacity to give the impression (which indeed must have some truth in it if it is to be effective at all) that they do not merely stand for but understand the aspirations of many humble persons, and understand them not merely in the sense of believing in the same ideals, but of knowing precisely where the shoe pinches, understanding the many varieties of frustration and misery from which, by means less or more scrupulous, they are trying to rescue the vast majority of those who put their faith in them. These men are regarded not with awe or religious faith – they are not figures surrounded by a kind of unearthly radiance – but with affection, confidence, admiration, sometimes not unmixed with a certain appreciative irony – a delight in their accessibility, their democratic quality, their human failings.

Both these types of political leaders have altered the history of mankind. Of the founding fathers of Israel, Theodor Herzl belonged to the first type, Chaim Weizmann to the second. The achievements of Herzl do not need to be rehearsed. It is difficult to conceive that without him what was built could have been so much as begun. But his very strength, and the very magic of his appeal, seem to derive partly from his psychological remoteness from his own people. If one is born on the edges of the consciousness of a community, as Herzl undoubtedly was (even though his native town contained many Jews), one tends to construct an ideal which does not precisely fit the real facts and which enables him who holds it to dramatise his task – without being trammelled by too intimate a knowledge of the real situation – and dramatise it in such a way as to dazzle even those who do know the real situation all too well into following the man of destiny.

Thus Disraeli – because of his love of the exotic, his very tendency to exaggerate what was least English in himself – invented the splendid vision of the British Empire, and particularly its magnificent Oriental aspect, as no empirically-minded, sane Englishman with a balanced and moderate view of his own country and the world could possibly have done. Napoleon, de Valera, Stalin came from the outer edges of the peoples to whom they gave legends of national greatness. I cannot help thinking that part of Herzl's immense 'glamour', part of the spell which he cast upon the Jewish masses, came from the fact that he was not of them, that in a sense he did not even understand them, that he conceived an image of them which did not truly correspond to the realities of their situation, and that this purified, idealised image, lifted high above their heads, in which he believed so passionately and to which he dedicated his life, was something that in turn lifted them out of themselves, that inspired them to political action, or at any rate to the transformation of their personal lives, precisely because it emancipated them from the oppressive and crippling consciousness of their real weaknesses and wounds and humiliations.

Napoleon's conception of the French, Churchill's conception of England – these great imaginative creations, in the name of which people are prepared to die, are not the fruit of sober realism as, for example, were Cavour's Italy or Lincoln's America, despite the passionate emotion, the heroism, the drama; and it was Herzl's very exoticism, his remoteness from the common preoccupations of mankind, his deeply romantic conception of the Jews and their past and future, the inspired, somewhat supernatural, quality of his images, that were doubtless needed to create a myth, a tradition, an immortal vision. He was tied to his people, not by the strands of real unbreakable connection, but by something born in his own intense power of political fantasy. And the fantasy became a reality because there was something in it that sprang from a genuine overmastering need, and because it did touch a central chord in Jewish experience. But Herzl remained outside – sublime, remote, an object of worship.

Chaim Weizmann seemed to me to be the exact opposite. Herzl received homage in part because, although he was a Jew, some of his qualities were those of a gloriously free, noble Gentile. Weizmann possessed characteristic Jewish qualities to the highest possible degree. He was sceptical, ironical, acute, humane, perspicacious, brilliant, and possessed a capacity for understanding both human beings and situations given to no one else in the twentieth century. He indulged in no fantasies, he was not a fanatic or a romantic or a national leader of fable. He understood his people through and through; he knew their virtues and their vices and was attached to both. Everything that was exotic, exaggerated, fanatical, obsessed, unnaturally intense, repelled his sane, humorous, harmonious, realistic, generously constructed nature. He was a man of immense inward strength and tranquillity. He marched towards his goal after having calculated all the difficulties, aware of every obstacle, with due allowance for the imperfections of his own nation and for those of other peoples.

Where the 'inspired' leaders burnt with a violent flame, magnetised everything round them, made people lose a sense of proportion, made them throw themselves headlong into unequal battle for the sake, very often, of forms and abstractions – a State, a constitution, a Church, liberty, independence, equality – Weizmann preserved an exquisite sense of proportion, understood things as they were, was never deluded by forms or words or ideals into forgetting the social and economic and human realities which he desired to create, and which could easily be lost, or at any rate damaged and compromised, by fanatical emphasis upon the outer framework to which Herzl, for instance, paid such passionate attention.

For this reason it is difficult to identify Weizmann with political parties, just as it is difficult so to identify Cavour or Lincoln in a strict sense. Was Weizmann a man of the 'right' or of the 'left'? The question appears almost meaningless. He was a national leader, he believed in the Risorgimento of the Jews. He was a complete and unbroken personality of immense strength, dignity and political wisdom, he did not suffer from the usual Jewish disabilities, the 'ambivalences', the lack of social balance, the uncertainty about what one is and where one belongs, the self-conscious vacillations and doubts and hesitations in the matter of one's proper class or outlook or profession or status. And because he was so firm and because he understood the minute elements of the world in which he was living, and moved with confidence and remarkable skill in an area dark and filled with dangers for others, he inspired uncommon confidence in people least of all disposed to feel it: in those Jews who, for one reason or another, felt it oppressive to remain such, who looked upon their Judaism as a yoke to be borne with dignity or to be laid down at the most convenient opportunity, but nevertheless always as a yoke. He impressed such people, not as other Jews impressed them, by their status in the Gentile world, by being eminent in the arts or the sciences or the public life of some great European or transatlantic country, but (despite the fact that he had these last attributes also) as a representative – *the* representative – of the Jews and of no one else.

This extraordinary capacity for creating the illusion that in some sense there existed a fully formed nationality whose true elected representative he was, that there was not only a nation but very nearly a State, a social edifice, a government, legislative institutions (when everyone knew that this was not the case), the fact that a single human individual could, by being as he was, and behaving as he did, cast this spell upon foreign statesmen and assimilated Jews alike, created the greatest single exemplar of what a Jew could be if he was genuinely free.

It was this example, far more than the precepts and preachings of others, that inspired Jews in many lands and made them believe that the dream could be made a reality. Tremulous, half-assimilated Jews who were, whether they admitted it to themselves or not, ashamed of being Jews – at least in some degree – were in his presence released from this feeling, ceased for a brief hour to be ashamed. Jews who needed to wear the clothes of something acutely un-Jewish – Communism, or the romantic chauvinism of some modern State, or the army uniform of some respectable country, or membership in some distinguished social or professional or intellectual group – these Jews, who were normally released only by violent 'transvestism' of this kind, were miraculously restored to their human dignity, if only for a moment, by this man who offered them nothing but their own true attributes.

The success of vehement, fanatical crusaders comes, very often, through the fact that, armed with a doctrine, or 'ideology', in place of humanity and realism, they hurl themselves against apparently insuperable obstacles because they feel that they have nothing of value to lose: the 'cause', the ideology, is all that they hold sacred, they are remote from the sufferings of the human beings upon whom they inevitably trample, and, being morally proof against human considerations, they sometimes triumphantly break through against enormous odds.

These are not the weapons of the kind of statesman to which Weizmann belonged; he relied rather upon his sense of the correlation of real historical forces – the strengths and weaknesses, the purposes and characters of the human beings and institutions with which he was concerned; and these are at once too concrete, too complex and too imprecise to be capable of being formulated in historical 'laws' or formulae, or ideological nostrums of any kind.

I well remember how, in what seemed the darkest days of post-war Zionism, Weizmann would pace up and down in his room in a London hotel, and at each depressing report of hostility here, failure there, keep repeating, 'It will not help them, it will not help them.' 'They' were the makers of British policy, many of whom he understood and often personally liked, but whom he thought to be behaving in a bitter and foolish way because they had lost their appetite for great constructive designs and were engaged in saving their melting strength instead of boldly seeking (as he passionately desired them to do – and he had plans of his own to propose) to build something new on the ruins of the old. And this, he felt with his sure sense of events, was doomed to failure.

The natural bond of sympathy which existed between Weizmann and Churchill was due to the immense love of life in both (which also endeared Weizmann to Lloyd George), to the fact that they were both on the side of whatever expanded, grew, was likely to stand up, to animate and to quicken vital processes, and against all that tended towards contraction, stillness, everything which sprang from caution, hugged the shore, wished to conserve and not transform.

There was an occasion early in the War when Weizmann, speaking to the great Prime Minister who had told him of the very anti-Zionist opinions expressed to him by various of his advisers, said to him (so he told me later), 'You must remember, Sir, that those who are against us are against you too.' He staked a great deal – almost everything – on this belief, and if some of his hopes were subsequently betrayed, those who denounced him as an Anglomaniac and an 'appeaser', whatever their justification in the immediate post-war years, were ultimately as mistaken as those who blamed Cavour for trusting the French and obtaining less for Italy, or establishing a regime less desirable than what might have been gained by a violent republican rising with no foreign alliances. In Italy Cavour won; in Palestine Weizmann's ideals were set aside.

Perhaps this turn of events was inevitable, perhaps this was the only way in which the Jewish cause could have been saved; yet one cannot help wondering whether, with better understanding between the two sides, and perhaps less disdain for some of his colleagues and followers on the part of Weizmann (who in this was like Parnell), the Jewish State might not have been today in a somewhat sounder political position. But these are might-have-beens, and it is unprofitable to investigate them.

If Weizmann was punished it was for his excessively clear sense of reality and for his love of the English. And these two attitudes are not unconnected, since it was his distaste for myths and drama (the very sources of Herzl's powers) that made Weizmann so deeply devoted to the English. Weizmann believed in the English because he believed in the sane, balanced, empirical quality of their lives; in their distaste for theories and ideologies; in their respect for individuals; in their love of genuine liberty and genuine contentment; in their capacity for not sacrificing live human beings on the altar of abstractions and ideals. They responded by realising that he was not a political agent, or a representative of an *exalté* movement, or a single-minded leader, or even an isolated great man in his own right; all this he was, but he was also an authentic statesman – someone who understood the texture of public life, distinguished the trivial from the important, to whom it was not necessary to explain that which they, the English, had accumulated during centuries of ripe experience.

On the whole it was a happy marriage and it needed all Ernest Bevin's colossal *amour propre*, his wounded vanity, and the blindness or pettiness of his officials, to cause a breach. And when it happened, Weizmann, who could not avoid continuing to like and admire this most tolerant, most sensible, most political of peoples, could scarcely bear it. It is by now a commonplace of history that Bevin brought the State of Israel into being very much as Lord North and George III founded the United States.

Weizmann felt betrayed by his old friends in Whitehall and Westminster, he felt betrayed by the turn which events in general had taken: but nothing could alter his sense of glory in the fact that an achievement without parallel had come to crown his life. He too is now an eponymous hero – a gigantic figure standing at the head of the new history of the Jews – but the strands which unite him with his people are infinitely more intimate than those which stretch from the remoter, colder, heroes.

The Jews of the entire world, when he died, mourned not only the greatest of their sons in this century (and as the years pass his figure will inevitably grow larger), but a human being whose qualities were a more intense and nobler version of their own, a being compounded of qualities which Jews and only Jews have ever possessed in the peculiar combination in which he showed them. His face, his figure, the fabulous charm of his manner, his memorable interventions in the councils of the nations, his wit, his mordant epigrams and the sublime moments of reasoned and noble indignation, his command of all the Jewish languages, his roots in the heart of the Diaspora in a Russian Jewish town; the fact that, despite his eminence in the world, he sacrificed nothing – he compromised not a whit – and retained all his Jewish qualities intact, and was accepted by the world neither in spite of them, nor even because of them, but as a matter of course, quite naturally and normally, as a representative of one people among others, neither superior nor inferior, but an equal – all this makes his image unique in the annals of the Jews.

When Weizmann died, it was as if some personage of vast historical magnitude had passed – Oliver Cromwell or Abraham Lincoln – not an inhabitant of the twentieth century. To his own people he remains a figure full of imaginative humour, human, ironical, wise, amused, warm-hearted, a microcosm of all the extravagant yet not inharmonious variety of Jewish life in the last century; and, with it all, a figure of more than human size, an immortal hero, someone who overshadowed his contemporaries and will continue to do so for all foreseeable time.

THE SEARCH FOR STATUS

WE OFTEN speak of demands for liberty made by oppressed classes or nationalities. But it is not always individual freedom, nor even individual equality, that they primarily want. What they aspire to is not simply unhampered liberty of action for their members, nor, above everything else, equality of social or economic opportunity, still less assignment of a secure and carefully determined place in a frictionless, organic, 'monolithic' State devised by the rational lawgiver. What they want, as often as not, is simply recognition – of their class or nation, or colour or race – as an independent source of human activity, as an entity with a will of its own, intending to act in accordance with it (whether it is good, or legitimate, or not), and not to be ruled, educated, guided, with however light a hand, as being not quite fully human, and therefore not quite fully free. Paternalism is 'the greatest *despotism* imaginable', said Immanuel Kant;[1] paternalism is despotic, not because it is more oppressive than naked, brutal, unenlightened tyranny, but because it is an insult to my conception of myself as a human being, determined to make my own life in accordance with my own (not necessarily rational or benevolent) purposes, and, above all, entitled to be recognised as such by others. For if I am not so recognised, then I may fail to recognise, I may doubt, my own claim to be a fully independent human being. For what I am is, in large part, determined by what I feel and think; and what I feel and think is determined by the feeling and thought prevailing in the society to which I belong. I may feel unfree in the sense of not being recognised as a self-governing individual human being, but I may feel it also as a member of an unrecognised or insufficiently respected group: then I wish for the emancipation of my entire class, or nation, or race, or profession. So much can I

[1] *Kant's gesammelte Schriften* (see p. 181 above, note 1), vol. 8, p. 290, line 35.

desire this that [if I am a slave, a colonial, a member of an 'oppressed' class, I may prefer, in my bitter longing for status, to be bullied and misgoverned by some member of my own race or social class, by whom I am, nevertheless, recognised as a man and a rival – that is, as an equal – to being well and tolerantly treated by someone from some higher and more remote group who does not recognise me for what I wish to feel myself to be.]

This is the heart of the great cry for recognition, on the part of both individuals and groups, and, in our own day, of professions and classes, nations and races. Although I may not get liberty at the hands of the members of my own society, yet they are members of my own group; they understand me, as I understand them; and this understanding creates within me the sense of being somebody in the world. It is this desire for reciprocal recognition that leads the most authoritarian democracies to be, at times, consciously preferred by their members to the most enlightened oligarchies, or sometimes causes a member of some newly liberated Asian or African State to complain less today, when he is rudely treated by members of his own race or nation, than when he was governed by some cautious, just, gentle, well-meaning administrator from outside.

Yet it is not with liberty, in either the 'negative' or in the 'positive' senses of the word, nor with equality, that this desire for status and recognition can easily be identified: it is something no less profoundly needed and passionately fought for by human beings. It is something akin to, but not itself, freedom: it is most closely related to solidarity, fraternity, mutual understanding, need for association on equal terms, all of which are sometimes – but misleadingly – called social freedom. Social and political terms are necessarily vague. The attempt to make the vocabulary of politics too precise may render it useless. But it is no service to the truth to loosen usage beyond necessity. The essence of the notion of liberty is the *holding off* of something or someone – of others, who trespass on my field or assert their authority over me, or of obsessions, fears, neuroses, irrational forces – intruders and despots of one kind or another. The desire for recognition is a desire for something very different: for union, closer understanding, integration of interests, a life of common dependence and common sacrifice. It is only the confusion of desire for liberty with this profound and universal craving for status and understanding that makes it possible for men, while submitting to the authority of oligarchs or dictators, to claim that this in some sense liberates them.

But is the struggle for higher status, the wish to escape from an inferior position, to be called a struggle for liberty? Is it mere pedantry to confine this word to the main senses just mentioned, or are we, as I suspect, in danger of calling *any* adjustment of his social situation favoured by a human being an increase of his liberty, and will this not render this term so vague and distended as to make it virtually useless? And yet we cannot simply dismiss this case as a mere confusion of the notion of freedom with those of status, or solidarity or fraternity, or equality, or some combination of these. For the craving for status is, in certain respects, very close to the desire to be an independent agent.

We may refuse this collective goal the title of liberty; yet it would be a shallow view that assumed that such analogies between individuals and groups are merely misleading, that organic metaphors, or several senses of the word 'liberty', are mere fallacies. What those people want who are prepared to barter their own and others' liberty of individual action for the status of their group, and for their own status within the group, is not simply a surrender of liberty for the sake of security, for the sake of some assured place in a harmonious hierarchy in which all men and all classes know their place, a structure in which they can, with relief, give up the painful privilege of choosing – 'the burden of freedom' – for the peace and comfort and relative mindlessness of an authoritarian or totalitarian structure. No doubt there are such men and such desires, and no doubt such surrenders of individual liberty can occur, and, indeed, have often occurred. But it is a profound misunderstanding of the temper of our times to assume that this is what makes nationalism, or Marxism, attractive to nations which have been ruled by foreign masters, or to classes whose lives were directed by other classes in a semi-feudal regime, or some other hierarchical form of government. What they seek is more akin to what Mill called 'pagan self-assertion',[1] as opposed to Christian self-sacrifice, but in a collective, socialised form.

The bulk of humanity has certainly, at most times, been prepared to sacrifice individual liberty to other goals: security, status, prosperity, power, virtue, rewards in the next world; or to justice,

---

[1] J. S. Mill, *On Liberty*, chapter 3: vol. 18, p. 266, in *Collected Works of John Stuart Mill*, ed. J. M. Robson (Toronto/London, 1981–).

equality, fraternity, and many other values which are wholly, or partially, incompatible with the greatest degree of individual liberty, and certainly do not need such liberty for their own realisation. It is not a demand for *Lebensraum* for each individual that has stimulated the rebellions and wars of liberation for which men have been ready to die in the past, or, indeed, in the present. Men who have fought for freedom have commonly fought for the right to be governed by themselves or their representatives – sternly governed, if need be, like the Spartans, or the Puritans in Geneva or New England, with little individual liberty, but in a manner which allowed them to participate, or at any rate to think that they were participating, in the legislation and administration of their collective lives. And men who have made revolutions have, as often as not, meant by liberty simply the conquest of power and authority by a sect of believers in a doctrine, or by a class, or by some other social group. Their victories certainly frustrated those whom they ousted, and they sometimes repressed, enslaved or exterminated vast numbers of human beings. Yet such revolutionaries have usually felt it necessary to argue that, despite this, they represented the party of liberty, or 'true' liberty, by claiming universality for their ideal, which the 'real selves' of even those who resisted them were also alleged to be seeking, although these unfortunate men or groups were held to have lost the way to the goal, or to have mistaken the goal itself, owing to some moral or spiritual blindness.

All this has little to do with the classical Western notion of liberty as limited only by the danger of doing harm to others. It is the non-recognition of this psychological and political fact (which lurks behind the apparent ambiguity of the term 'liberty') that has, perhaps, blinded some contemporary liberals to the world in which they live. Their plea is clear, their cause is just. But they do not allow for the variety of human wishes, for the different, quite incompatible, kinds of life for which men are ready to fight and, if need be, die. Nor do such good and rational men allow for the terrible ingenuity with which men can prove to their own satisfaction that the road to one ideal also leads somehow to its contrary. Men want too much: they want what is logically impossible. That is why such sacred symbols as 'liberty' and 'democracy' and self-governmental 'rights' cover such a multitude of ideals which conflict with one another. It is as well to realise this. Things are what they are; status is one thing, liberty another;

recognition is not the same as non-interference. In the end we all pay too dearly for our wish to avert our gaze from such truths, for ignoring such distinctions in our attempts to coin words to cover *all* that we long for, in short for our desire to be deceived.

THE ESSENCE OF
EUROPEAN ROMANTICISM

INTELLECTUAL HISTORY is a field in which English writers, in general, have taken less interest than those of other countries. There are notable exceptions to this rule; but they are few. The history of English thought, even in the nineteenth century, when it had greater influence than that of any other country, still remains to be written.

The controversy about the relation of ideas to action is, perhaps for this reason, an issue, but not a live issue, in the writings of British historians, philosophers and critics. The examination of the interplay of ideas with social, economic and technological development has (especially in the last two hundred years) largely been left to writers of other nations; and even then more attention has been paid in England to their conclusions than to their methods. It may be that the particular pattern of social and political development in the British Isles has served to concentrate the attention of modern British historians (those of the eighteenth century and after) on the causes and effects of the great social upheavals – the Industrial Revolution, the French Revolution and their consequences – and has led to a relative neglect on their part of the other great movement, contemporary with these, which, no less than the Renaissance, the Reformation and the rise of the natural sciences and technology, has altered ways of thinking and behaviour in the West. Perhaps it should not be described as a movement – which implies some degree of organisation – so much as a set of attitudes, a way of thinking and acting that is loosely described as romantic.

This topic is usually left to the history of literature and the arts. Yet it is a wider force, which for two hundred years has deeply, and indeed decisively, affected European life. The word 'romanticism' is vague, and like most terms of its kind, tends to be too general to be of use. 'It is impossible to think – *seriously* – with

words like "classicism", "romanticism", "humanism", "realism",'
said a famous French poet and critic in the early years of the
twentieth century. 'One cannot get drunk or quench one's thirst
with labels on a bottle.'[1] Yet it is scarcely deniable that during the
period that begins in the late Renaissance and ends with the full
development of industrial capitalism, a vast transformation of
ideas, language, attitudes, ways of thinking and acting took place.
Any student of the eighteenth century is bound to notice that
towards its end the beliefs of two millennia were, if not destroyed,
at any rate challenged on an ever-widening scale; and that many of
them were undermined.

Since the Greeks, and perhaps long before them, men have
believed that to the central questions about the nature and purpose
of their lives, and of the world in which they lived, true, objective,
universal and eternal answers could be found. If the answers could
not be discovered by me, then perhaps by someone more expert or
wiser than I; if not in the circumstances in which I found myself,
then in others more propitious: in an innocent and happy past – a
Garden of Eden from which our ancestors had for their sins been
expelled, or perhaps in a golden age that still lay in the future,
which posterity (perhaps after much labour and suffering) would,
or at any rate could, one day reach. It was assumed that all the
truly central problems were soluble in principle even if not in
practice. Somewhere true answers to all genuine questions must
exist, if not in the minds of men, then in the mind of an omniscient
being – real or imaginary, material or ideal, a personal deity, or the
universe come to full consciousness of itself.

This presupposition, which underlies most classical and Christian thought, orthodox and heretical, scientific and religious, was
connected with the belief that, whether men knew it or not, the
whole of life on earth was in some sense bound up with the search
for answers to the great, tormenting questions of fact and of
conduct; of what there is, was, will be, can be; of what to do, what
to live by, what to seek, hope for, admire, fear, avoid; whether the
end of life was happiness or justice or virtue or self-fulfilment or
grace and salvation. Individuals, schools of thought, entire civilisations differed about what the answers were, about the proper
method of discovering them, about the nature and place of moral

[1] Paul Valéry, *Cahiers*, ed. Judith Robinson (Paris, 1973–4), vol. 2, pp. 1220–1
(from a notebook dated 1931–2).

or spiritual or scientific authority – that is to say, about how to identify the experts who are qualified to discover and communicate the answers. They argued about what constitutes such qualifications and justifies such claims to authority. But there was no doubt that the truth lay somewhere; that it could in principle be found. Conflicting beliefs were held about the central questions: whether the truth was to be found in reason or in faith, in the Church or the laboratory, in the insights of the uniquely privileged individual – a prophet, a mystic, an alchemist, a metaphysician – or in the collective consciousness of a body of men – the society of the faithful, the traditions of a tribe, a race, a nation, a social class, an academy of experts, an élite of uniquely endowed or trained beings – or, on the contrary, in the mind or heart of any man, anywhere, at any time, provided that he remained innocent and uncorrupted by false doctrines. What was common to all these views – incompatible enough for wars of extermination to have been fought in their name – was the assumption that there existed a reality, a structure of things, a *rerum natura*, which the qualified enquirer could see, study and, in principle, get right. Men were violently divided about the nature and identity of the wise – those who understood the nature of things – but not about the proposition that such wise men existed or could be conceived, and that they would know that which would enable them to deduce correctly what men should believe, how they should act, what they should live by and for.

This was the great foundation of belief which romanticism attacked and weakened. Whatever the differences between the leading romantic thinkers – the early Schiller and the later Fichte, Schelling and Jacobi, Tieck and the Schlegels when they were young, Chateaubriand and Byron, Coleridge and Carlyle, Kierkegaard, Stirner, Nietzsche, Baudelaire – there runs through their writings a common notion, held with varying degrees of consciousness and depth, that truth is not an objective structure, independent of those who seek it, the hidden treasure waiting to be found, but is itself in all its guises created by the seeker. It is not to be brought into being necessarily by the finite individual: according to some it is created by a greater power, a universal spirit, personal or impersonal, in which the individual is an element, or of which he is an aspect, an emanation, an imperfect reflection. But the common assumption of the romantics that runs counter to the *philosophia perennis* is that the answers to the great questions are not to be discovered so much as to be invented. They are not something found, they are something literally made. In its extreme Idealistic form it is a vision of the entire world. In its more familiar form, it confines itself to the realm of values, ideals, rules of conduct – aesthetic, religious, social, moral, political – a realm seen not as a natural or supernatural order capable of being investigated, described and explained by the appropriate method – rational examination or some more mysterious procedure – but as something that man creates, as he creates works of art; not by imitating, or even obtaining illumination from, pre-existent models or truths, or by applying pre-existent truths or rules that are objective, universal, eternal, unalterable; but by an act of creation, the introduction into the world of something literally novel – the unique expression of an individual and therefore unique creative activity, natural or supernatural, human or in part divine, owing nothing to anything outside it (in some versions because nothing can be conceived as being outside it), self-subsistent, self-justified, self-fulfilling. Hence that new emphasis on the subjective and ideal rather than the objective and the real, on the process of creation rather than its effects, on motives rather than consequences; and, as a necessary corollary of this, on the quality of the vision, the state of mind or soul of the acting agent – purity of heart, innocence of intention, sincerity of purpose rather than getting the answer right, that is, accurate correspondence to the 'given'. Hence the emphasis on activity, movement that cannot be reduced to static segments, the flow that cannot be arrested, frozen, analysed without being thereby fatally distorted; hence the constant protest against the reduction of 'life' to dead fragments, of organism to 'mere' mechanical or uniform units; and the corresponding tendency towards similes and metaphors drawn from 'dynamic' sciences – biology, physiology, introspective psychology – and the worship of music, which, of all the arts, appears to have the least relation to universally observable, uniform natural order. Hence, too, celebration of all forms of defiance directed against the 'given' – the impersonal, the 'brute fact' in morals or in politics – or against the static and the accepted, and the value placed on minorities and martyrs as such, no matter what the ideal for which they suffer.

This, too, is the source of the doctrine that work is sacred as such, not because of its social function, but because it is the imposition of the individual or collective personality, that is, activity, upon inert stuff. The activity, the struggle is all, the victory nothing: in Fichte's words, 'Frei sein ist nichts – frei werden ist der Himmel' ('To be free is nothing – to become free is very heaven').[1] Failure is nobler than success. Self-immolation for a cause is the thing, not the validity of the cause itself, for it is the sacrifice undertaken for its sake that sanctifies the cause, not some intrinsic property of it.

These are the symptoms of the romantic attitude. Hence the worship of the artist, whether in sound, or word, or colour, as the highest manifestation of the ever-active spirit, and the popular image of the artist in his garret, wild-eyed, wild-haired, poor, solitary, mocked-at; but independent, free, spiritually superior to his philistine tormentors. This attitude has a darker side too: worship not merely of the painter or the composer or the poet, but of that more sinister artist whose materials are men – the destroyer of old societies, and the creator of new ones – no matter at what human cost: the superhuman leader who tortures and destroys in order to build on new foundations – Napoleon in his most revolutionary aspect. It is this embodiment of the romantic ideal that took more and more hysterical forms and in its extreme ended in violent irrationalism and Fascism. Yet this same outlook also bred respect for individuality, for the creative impulse, for the unique, the independent, for freedom to live and act in the light of personal, undictated beliefs and principles, of undistorted emotional needs, for the value of private life, of personal relationships, of the individual conscience, of human rights. The positive and negative heritage of romanticism – on the one hand contempt for opportunism, regard for individual variety, scepticism of oppressive general formulae and final solutions, and on the other self-prostration before superior beings and the exaltation of arbitrary power, passion and cruelty – these tendencies, at once reflected and promoted by romantic doctrines, have done more to mould both the events of our century and the concepts in terms of which they are viewed and explained than is commonly recognised in most histories of our time.

---

[1] Quoted without a reference in the article on Fichte in *Entsiklopedicheskii slovar'* (St Petersburg, 1890–1907), vol. 36, p. 58, col. 2.

MEINECKE AND HISTORICISM

THE TRANSFORMATION of the writing of history in the nineteenth century is to a large degree the work of the great German
masters from Niebuhr and Boeckh to Mommsen and Burckhardt,
from Savigny and Ranke to Max Weber and Troeltsch. Ideas are
not born of ideas by parthenogenesis. The process which led to the
new historical vision, and even more to its dominant influence over
much of the political and intellectual life of the West, has its roots
in great social and cultural changes which go back to the
Renaissance and the Reformation, if not beyond. The rise in
historical consciousness, the best-known and most notorious
outgrowths of which are the ideologies of nationalism and power
politics, responded to the need at once to explain and to justify the
open struggles of nations and classes in its day. Its beginnings can
be traced to many lands, but it first found systematic expression
among German thinkers and was historically connected with the
rise of the national German State. Radical political developments
are often preceded by a ferment in the realm of ideas, and it is in
the German-speaking lands that the new sense of historical
development grew into a powerful and influential current of ideas.
Individual thinkers, and, after them, wider groups – academic,
political, artistic, religious – began to conceive of all human
activities as elements in unified, 'organic' social wholes, not static
institutional structures, but dynamic processes of development of
nations, cultures, classes – social 'organisms' held together by
impalpable and complex relationships which characterised living
social wholes, quasi-biological entities which defied analysis by the
exact quantitative methods of chemistry or physics. Such forms of
life, it was held, could be felt, or intuited, or understood by a
species of direct acquaintance; they could not be taken to pieces
and reassembled, even in thought, like a mechanism compounded
of isolable parts, obedient to universal and unaltering causal laws.

The thinkers who revolted against the central classical and Christian concept of a world governed by a single, static natural law, in any one of its many forms, Stoic or Aristotelian, or Thomist, or the causal-mechanistic patterns of the French Enlightenment, were seldom unworldly philosophers. They were, for the most part, deeply involved with the political societies and nations to which they belonged; and they saw their intellectual activity as bound up with the rise of a new order of things in which the German peoples played a leading part. They were acutely conscious of their own German roots in the Reformation, in pietism and the mystical and visionary movements that preceded it, in the localised, provincial, tradition-bound social, political and religious life of German cities and principalities. Above all, they were acutely aware of the differences between their world and the universalism and scientific rationalism deeply embedded in the outlook of the civilisations west of the Rhine. As scholars, critics, historians, they investigated, collected, described, analysed, explained; as men and citizens they were caught up in the social and political questions and struggles of their society. Whatever their convictions, they did not isolate these functions from one another: in varying degrees they were identified with the activities of parties and movements, and were often linked by direct personal relationships with their leaders. This gave particular life and force, as well as, at times, considerable public influence to the points of view that they were held to represent. It is the political commitment of some of the major figures of the new historical school that (despite the earnest efforts of some of them to preserve a degree of detachment) communicates to their historical works a sense of moral and political direction, whether they are dealing with their own times or with remote cultures and situations. While this may have been equally true of historians in other countries – Macaulay and Grote, Michelet and Guizot cannot be described as politically neutral writers – in Germany this acquired the status of an almost official national philosophy of history. This applies, for all their differences, as much to Niebuhr and Mommsen, Droysen and Max Weber as to such violently partisan writers as Treitschke or Sombart; and it is, in a measure, no less true, for all his agonised desire to rise above immediate and ephemeral considerations, of the last great representative of this tradition, Friedrich Meinecke.

In his three celebrated masterpieces,[1] Meinecke addressed

[1] The two volumes that preceded *Die Entstehung des Historismus* (Munich

himself to some of the central issues of his own time, and traced their origins and development. In particular he described with exact and unassailable learning the gradual waning of the older European outlook dominated by the notion of a timeless, unaltering natural law (disobeyed by wilful rulers, individual or collective, only at a fearful cost) and its supersession by the concept of the nation, conscious of its unique individuality and its overriding claims, and answerable only to itself. He gave a classical account of the tensions which this brought to light between, on the one hand, commonly accepted universal human values, the rights of individuals or groups and the general moral principles that governed human conduct, and, on the other, the claims of the State which, in moments of crisis, comes into violent conflict with the rules of common human morality – claims the satisfaction of which alone, at whatever price, will ensure the security, the power and the greatness of the nation to which statesmen owe their primary allegiance.

His discussion of this issue is throughout dominated by his awareness of the unresolved problem of the relationship of what Savigny had called 'silently operating forces',[1] which, in the end, determine the direction of a society and of the development of its members, to what he recognises as the freedom of action, within historically determined limits, on the part of human beings, and, consequently, of the corresponding degree of historical responsibility which must be attributed, or denied, to this or that individual or group or policy. But the *idée maîtresse* that obsesses him, as it obsessed his forerunners, concerns the properties of those – for him the only genuine – associations of men which possess each its own individual laws of growth, its own unique 'organic' character

---

and Berlin, 1936), translated by J. E. Anderson as *Historism: The Rise of a New Historical Outlook* (London, 1972) [to which the present essay was originally a foreword] are *Weltbürgertum und Nationalstaat: Studien zur Genesis des deutschen Nationalstaates* (Munich and Berlin, 1908) – in its English version *Cosmopolitanism and the National State*, trans. Robert B. Kimber (Princeton, 1970) – and *Die Idee der Staatsräson in der neueren Geschichte* (Munich and Berlin, 1924) – in its English version *Machiavellism: The Doctrine of Raison d'État and its Place in Modern History*, trans. Douglas Scott (London, 1957). [The German term 'Historismus' is more usually translated 'historicism', though in this piece IB naturally follows Anderson in his choice of 'historism' to render Meinecke's central concept. Ed.]

[1] Friedrich Carl von Savigny, *Vom Beruf unsrer Zeit für Gesetzgebung und Rechtswissenschaft* (Heidelberg, 1814), p. 14.

– social wholes which develop like plants, obedient each to its own specific nature, and which can, therefore, neither be explained, nor understood, nor maintained in the light of laws or principles which falsely assimilate them to some generalised pattern that ignores their own peculiar essence, the individual goals in terms of which they live and act, values incommensurable with those of other societies or periods, in terms of which alone all that they are and do can be explained or justified. Inevitably he came to be profoundly troubled by the evident irreconcilability of the moral relativism to which this seemed to lead, and the allied notion that success alone – at times mere power – is the sole arbiter of what truly counts and is worth living (and, it may be, dying) for, with the need for something more than such subjectivism; something more than values revealed to the capricious individual intuition of an individual thinker or poet or statesman – the need for common ground between men, a common purpose which, even if not universally accepted, is at any rate valid for many men for long stretches of history, and can provide some approach to objectivity in determining basic values – greatness and littleness, good and evil, progress and retrogression. Meinecke saw the rise of the notion of the individuality and variety of paths of development on the part of States – independent social organisms – as the greatest break in the continuity of European thought since the Reformation. And indeed, in retrospect, it can scarcely be denied that the great movements by which the last two centuries have been violently swayed – traditionalism and pluralism, romanticism and the Promethean conception of man, anarchism as well as nationalism, individualist self-realisation no less than imperialism, racism and all kinds of social and political irrationalism – all stem in varying degree from this vast revolt against what Meinecke calls 'the generalising view' – belief in scientific uniformities, or the sway of natural law, as well as the varieties of positivism, utilitarianism, rationalism, but above all the great monistic conception of the universe as a single, unvarying system, intelligible in the light of reason to all men – if only they have eyes to see – at all times, in all conditions, everywhere.

In the volume devoted to the origins of the new historical consciousness, Meinecke sets himself to trace the new outlook from Leibniz and Voltaire, Montesquieu, Vico and Burke to its final triumph in the works of the great German founders of the new historical method. Meinecke was a man of vast and disciplined erudition, with a degree of intellectual scruple and sensitiveness to the finest nuances of ideology and outlook uncommon even among his great predecessors: his essays on his three heroes, Möser, Herder and especially Goethe, which form the greater part of the last panel of the great triptych, distinguished as they are by a delicate interweaving of description, ideas and historical circumstance, of the personal temperament of individual thinkers with the quality of life of the society in and for and about which they wrote, demand a good deal more of the reader than the sweeping generalisations of bolder and often more superficial historians of ideas. His style, like the subject-matter, is complex and, at times, opaque, the method sometimes unfocused and impressionistic. Meinecke is intensely anxious not to fall into the errors he castigates in the hated natural-law, mechanistic, all-levelling, eighteenth-century Encyclopaedist tradition. He is fearful of oversimplifying, of concepts that cut into the living flesh of social or individual sentiment or ideology – which calls for all the powers of the most responsive 'individualising observation' (to use his phrase) – of vivisecting it with the surgical knife of some dogmatic theory or ideology. He is anxious to convey what Möser called 'the total impression', which cannot be obtained by mere analysis of the parts, still less by the application of some Procrustean historical pattern which fails to convey the tone, the unique colour, what the German historicist thinkers referred to as the *Zeitstil* or *Volksstil* which permeates all the activities of an individual or a society, its sciences as much as its arts, Richelieu's dispatches as much as his love-letters – he wishes to avoid constricting and distorting formulae, fanatical faith in laws that social change must obey, into which all the facts must be compressed, no matter how much the subject-matter may resist such schematism. Meinecke draws his portraits with an infinity of tiny strokes; and even though the main lines emerge, those who are accustomed to histories of ideas composed by analytic thinkers who operate with sharp definitions of terms, divisions into types, lines of ideological descent boldly and vividly presented, may occasionally be lost in this great forest, even though the general shape traced by the author need never, in fact, be lost sight of. Those who are prepared to follow Meinecke's carefully qualified, but never prolix or repetitive, prose will be handsomely rewarded. What this method serves to keep alive is an unbroken sense of reality – of the flow of social, political, artistic, religious, personal life and its complex patterns as it affects, and is affected by, beliefs, ideals, their vision of themselves and their past on the part of individuals and communities – a sense of the concrete, many-faceted, changing, never completed life of societies.

No doubt the view of history as the development of social, political and moral organisms, of Aristotelian entelechies the interplay of which constitutes the growth of the human spirit – a Neoplatonic-Hegelian vision – is only one of many conceptions of what men live by, and likely to be found wanting by those who demand the stricter methods of verification by the application of empirical or scientific tests, even if the results so obtained do not answer all our questions, or do not answer them at a sufficiently profound level of imaginative enquiry. Nevertheless, there is no doubt that, apart from its historical and political influence and its transforming impact on general ways of thought and feeling in the West, this approach (whatever its metaphysical shortcomings) did more to enlarge the horizon and perspectives of historians than the positivist doctrines against which it reacted so strongly. Meinecke was brought up in the faith of this movement, and used its own canons, like Dilthey (by whom he was profoundly impressed) and Max Weber and Rickert, to describe and resurrect its origins for scientifically minded generations which had begun to be exceedingly sceptical about its validity.

What gives extraordinary vitality to Meinecke's account of the revolution of the historical consciousness at the beginning of the last century is the fact that he himself was no less deeply agonised by the problems that he treated than those who first addressed themselves to them. He grew up in the heyday of Prussian nationalism, by which he was deeply affected. Such problems as the relation of values (both of historians and of men in general) to objectively established facts and to the conclusions of the natural sciences; the relativity of different outlooks and of the values that they embody; the conflict between the claims of the national and international order, of the State as against those of other associations, or of individual rights; the justification of the use of force, in particular of war; the apparent incompatibility between the methods of the natural sciences and those of humane studies, and the implications of this for political and individual morality – all these problems arose for him not merely as a historian or as a student of historical method, but as a German and a human being; he was tormented by them all his life. His conscience on these matters is never wholly clear: he does not try to evade painful issues; he patiently searches for solutions; he hopes to find some man of genius who will solve or resolve these problems of theory and practice, to which he does not pretend to have found a final answer.

The time at which he wrote *Historism* was one of crisis, which consciously or unconsciously offered a parallel to that earlier critical turning-point in German history, when the German *Geist* was hemmed in on one side by the levelling spirit of French revolutionary and Napoleonic centralisation and rational organisation, contemptuous of tradition and of the individuality of different societies – together with the complementary influence of British industrialism and its destruction of ancient ties – and, on the other, threatened by the menacing, barbarous great power in the East. If the German 'spirit' had won this war on two fronts, and established the great unified German State, it had done so at what might be thought by some to have been a fearful cost in moral values. After 1918, with Bolshevism in the East, and once again what he regarded as a shallow liberal universalism in the West, Meinecke put all his hopes in a mysterious synthesis of the claims of individual liberty and morality with the needs and values of public life in the majestic historical march of the great organic whole – the national State. For him it represented the central educative, spiritualising agency which shaped men and alone made possible the development of all that they lived for – moral goals and feelings, art, personal relationships, the conquest of brute nature within and without. He spoke about Western civilisation; but what he cared for most was, of course, Germany, her culture and her survival: he feared equally the Scylla of timeless, abstract principles that took no account of life and change, and the Charybdis of relativism that destroyed morality or reduced its goals to matters, in the end, of subjective temperament or inclination. This conflict shaped itself in his mind as the tension between men and historically evolving institutions that are the same men conceived in social and historical terms.

Historismus is the conception that with passionate, but at times painfully uncertain, hope he looked to as the solution; as it was in 1815 and 1848, so it must be in 1918 and 1932. This is the vision that communicates an almost religious fervour to his entire conception of history, and infects his prose style; it derives from Herder and Ranke rather than from his idolised master, the calm, unhistorical Goethe. For a time he seemed to believe that Hegel had managed to heal the wound that Machiavelli had inflicted upon the body politic of Europe by demonstrating the irreconcilability of personal and political morality; he almost managed to persuade himself that the great metaphysician had somehow succeeded in satisfying the claims of political and personal – human – morality in a sublime synthesis; or if Hegel did not succeed, then this was achieved, in his own intuitive, unsystematic but concrete and miraculous fashion of which only a man of genius is capable, by the incomparable Goethe. He worshipped Bismarck, whose policies seemed to him – as to so many German academics of the time – to have created conditions in which alone the German nation could realise its character and destiny. In 1914 he was among those who looked with mounting hope to the fulfilment of the great Prussian dream; 1918 brought home the consequences of such views. Cautious and conservative by temper, he was not a chauvinist; he accepted the Weimar Republic and supported it loyally to the end. He was a patriot and a nationalist, but he was not prepared for inhumanity. State authority had its limits; a very old man, he did not bow before Hitler or Hitlerism.

His bitter reflections after the final débâcle make a sad and depressing document. Read objectively, it is a statement of the bankruptcy of much of what he and his generation of German scholars had stood for. Meinecke was an unswervingly honest man, and although the prejudices of his time and class shine through, his unerring – sometimes painful – consciousness of where the true moral centre of gravity of a given social or moral situation lies seldom fails him. This, together with his prodigious learning and his feeling for the complex web of ideas, movements, institutions, events and personalities of the principal actors, makes his account of the rise of German historical thought a still unsuperseded classic.

In the dark days that followed the German defeat in 1918 he plainly found relief in returning to the finest hour of German cultural life and the new vision of history which is its heart. His task, in theory, was only to describe, only to record, the achievements and aspirations of others; but in fact they were his own. The story is told by a participant, not by a mere observer. The paean to Goethe, even the excuses Meinecke offers for the declared distaste for history and the distinct lack of veneration for the authority of the State on the part of that otherwise almost perfect being, seem to spring from a pathetic wish to save what he can from the shipwreck of the German culture in which he was brought up, to return to the heritage of poets and scholars, the degradation of which sends him back to a scrutiny of its beginnings in happier and better times. The period of which he writes is the springtime of the great development which, by the time he completed his three great treatises, had ended in darkness and an unimaginable disaster. In the period with which *Historism* is concerned the romantic German dream is still distant from the terrible nightmare into which it would later turn: hence the fresh and glowing colours with which he paints the pioneers of genius in whose society he delights to move, founders of the school of which he was, and probably knew himself to be, the last authentic master.

GENERAL EDUCATION

EDUCATION, even if it cannot by itself knock down the barriers by which human beings are divided, should at any rate not add to them. Whatever else the task of education, it should not drive the intellect and the imagination of students into channels that seem to become narrower as our century grows older;[1] consequently, it should do everything possible to make it easier for those engaged in one discipline to understand the methods, achievements, hopes, ambitions, frustrations, the intellectual and emotional processes, of those working in other fields. The obstacles to this are familiar: the disparity of subjects and methods, the fact that some persons are temperamentally uninterested in, or unfitted for, uncovering the secrets of nature; or disinclined to investigate how men came to be what they have become; or averse to, or incapable of, analysing the concepts and categories of thought or imagination, or reflecting critically on what is and what is not worth doing or thinking or being. Moreover, students do need to be qualified for professions, and this entails some degree of specialisation, without which there can be no skills or knowledge or, save in exceptional cases, any intellectual discipline at all.

None the less, wider knowledge is worth striving for. It is not necessary to believe that all knowledge always makes men happier or freer or morally better. The applications of modern science, it may be argued, have increased oppression, danger, misery in some spheres, as well as vastly diminished them in others. It need be accepted only, firstly that the discovery of the truth is a great good in itself, and secondly that the only real remedy for the evil consequences, whether of ignorance or of knowledge, is more knowledge: clearer understanding of what is involved, of what is worth pursuing, of means and ends, consequences and their value. Unless men are given the chance to find out what kind of world

[1] This was written in 1969.

they live in, what they have made, are making, and could make of it – and this can be done only if they have some notion of what other men are thinking and feeling, and doing, and how and why – they will continue to walk in darkness and be faced by the unpredicted and sometimes appalling consequences of one another's activities – faced by this beyond the degree which seems inescapably imposed on us all by our imperfections. The fact that we are never likely to know enough is no reason for not seeking to know as much as we can; to settle for less than this is gratuitous defeatism: blind surrender to forces which can be controlled.

The difficulties are not insuperable. Alliances between cognate subjects in British universities – say politics and economics, or history and literature, or philosophy and physics, or those other recognised combinations which our less hidebound academic establishments permit – have always been feasible. But more doors can be opened: even if the student cannot be expected to proceed through more than a very few of these – and he would usually be ill-advised if he did – he can at least be encouraged to look out upon vistas which would do much to liberate him from the narrow confines in which at present he seems to be expected to exist. Much waste and nonsense can be avoided, and much positive harm too: in particular, liability to systematic misunderstanding of others and of oneself, and of one's world, past and present, and, connected with this, philistinism, much (often resentful) boredom, irrational fears and hatreds of forms of knowledge (and of life) which are felt to be alien, puzzling, and therefore hostile, with a consequent tendency to absurdities in theory which at times lead to barbarities in practice.

The educational problem is not new: it has been in the forefront of interest since at least the days of Comenius. The last three centuries are full of controversy about what it is that will produce the widest understanding, the fullest human life. Such controversy has been particularly lively in the United States; and if the general education courses or 'core subjects' provided in a good many American universities are not examples of unqualified success, this does not mean that we should not appreciate the difficulties or the achievements of the educators of, say, Harvard or Chicago or Columbia, in particular their eagerness to make it possible for students to escape out of ancient straitjackets towards a freer intellectual life. The mere proliferation of remedies is a symptom of the reality of the disease.

In what follows I shall assume that to understand the world in which we live is (for the reasons given above) good rather than bad; that most men cannot achieve this without much conscious effort or, as a rule, without help, in particular the help of teachers; and therefore such obstacles to this process as indolence, ignorance, dogmatism, obscurantism, active dislike of the intellect and rational argument, hatred of novelty, and especially jealous fear of neighbouring disciplines suspected of expansionist ambitions, are vices to be exposed and fought. I shall assume also that human beings are in general entitled to have their capacities for thought and feeling developed even at the cost of not always (or even often) fitting smoothly into some centrally planned social pattern, however pressing the technological demands of their societies; that public virtues and social peace are not necessarily preferable to, still less identical with, the critical intellect, the unfettered imagination, and a developed capacity for personal relationships and private life. To these ends education, and in particular university education, can and should be a powerful means, or, at least, not a positive hindrance.

What are the characteristics of our time to which education should be made relevant? Let me add one or two further truisms. Educational needs spring from the pattern formed by the permanent – or, at any rate, relatively widespread – needs of human beings, modified by the predicament of the particular society in which they live. To understand his needs a man must know something of the times he lives in – here is a truism if ever there was one; yet it tends to be ignored or else interpreted too narrowly. When the present century comes to be viewed from some relatively remote and calm perspective – say a century or two after our time, if humanity survives till then – our age, it seems to me, will be notable not for a revolution in the visual arts and sensibility, like the Italian Renaissance; nor for the rise of bold and ruthless individualism; nor for optimistic faith in the new weapons of reason and empirical science; nor for the achievements of poets, painters, composers and novelists; nor for belief in the liberating powers of science or democracy; nor for mounting expectation of universal peace, harmony and the progress of all mankind under the rule of a wise, beneficent and gradually widening élite. It seems to me more likely that the salient characteristics of our age will be attributed to two phenomena: on the one hand, the Russian

Revolution and its consequences, and, on the other, the unparalleled progress of natural science and its application to human lives.

These developments of Western civilisation have dwarfed all others, and have radically altered and are still transforming the entire world. Yet to some degree they are in conflict with one another. On the one hand they have led to increased belief in reason, and, in its name, in destruction of privilege rooted in irrational convictions, resistance to traditionalism and to transcendent and impalpable values – all that goes by the name of the faith of the Enlightenment. This has given birth to egalitarian principles and practice; to demands for recognition and general self-assertion by the victims of the old order – the claims of individuals, classes, age groups, submerged nations, races, minorities; democratic revolt against the very notion that human beings should (whether or not they can) be moulded by paternalist or any other authoritarian groups; violent rejection of the notion that men should be manufactured like bricks for social structures designed by, or for the benefit of, some privileged group or leader; the desire for the breaking of chains and throwing off of burdens which inspires every revolution in some degree, and militates against the élitist notion that societies or States are works of art to be shaped by statesmen – leaders – a class or group of master minds.

This is one trend. On the other hand the very same forces, both scientific and social, make for rational organisation; for the rationalisation of production, distribution, consumption; and consequently for concentration of power and centralisation as the most effective method of getting things done. And this, as the early socialists all too clearly foresaw, leads to the creation of new hierarchies of technical experts, 'engineers of human souls',[1] deliberate creators and moulders of the 'new man', the emergence of the *Massenmensch*, the reduction of men to 'human material'; to 'the life of the anthill', with all its, by now, notorious consequences – the mechanisation, alienation, dehumanisation of entire societies, manipulated by hidden (and sometimes not so hidden) persuaders; and technocratic or commercial despotism. And as a result of this a reaction inevitably follows – various forms of passionate protest, pleas for return to a more human life, to 'organic' society, *Gemeinschaft*; sometimes fed by backward-looking fantasies, at other times fired with dynamic nationalist or racist passion equally

---

[1] See p. 17 above, note 1.

menacing to individual liberty or the free use of the imagination
and the critical faculties. Or again, the reaction may take the form
of indignant defence of menaced individual values, or of a romantic
rebellion against 'the machine' or 'the system', by anarchists,
students, artists, men in revolt not disciplined by knowledge who
wish to opt out of conventional social life or any ordered existence
– beatniks, hippies, flower children, irrationalist radicals, terrorists,
devotees of the use of purifying violence against a corrupt society,
or alternatively of total rejection of power; or yet again, by various
Marxist and quasi-Marxist oppositions (most of all in their
'revisionist' or 'humanist' forms).

But if men are to be enabled to control their lives in the light of
knowledge of what it is that they are dealing with, and not simply
to regard disturbing changes of this kind with mere bewilderment,
or fatalistic resignation, or fanaticism, or the disdain of the elect, or
a self-destructive desire to surrender to the irresistible, it is
desirable that the young, in particular, should be furnished with
weapons against such helplessness. They should be given sufficient
knowledge both of the genesis of the new order which is rising,
and of its character; and since a dominant element in this order is
constituted by the vast, swift progress of the natural sciences, and
of the consequences, intended and unintended, of simultaneous
advances on scientific and technological fronts, they must acquire
some understanding of it if they are to exercise a degree of
conscious control over it. These may be social issues, and the
sociology of the role of the sciences in human lives may seem
remote from, say, questions which preoccupy theoretical physicists. But the vast amount of ignorance about what technology is,
about its relation to pure research, about the degree to which its
methods transform men, including scientists, and finally about
what is common and what is not to scientific, and literary, and
critical or historical thought, is so great (and growing) that this
alone puts both statesmen and the elected representatives of the
people, and the electorate itself, at the mercy of experts, who are
often themselves, at best, one-eyed. This situation breeds systematic misunderstanding, and leads to the accumulation of power by
the experts – scientific middlemen – whom the awe of both public
and politicians renders relatively immune to democratic control.

It is absurd to regard this state of affairs as irremediable. The
irresistible, as Justice Brandeis once observed, is often simply that
which is not resisted. This may seem a merely utilitarian reason for

a programme of general education in universities, but it is nevertheless a crucial one for mankind at large. If to it are added the claims of disinterested intellectual satisfaction, and the exhilarating prospect of understanding the forces at work in one's world, it offers, to say the very least, sufficient reason for supposing that such a programme is worth attempting.

Where are we to begin? Merely to preach, merely to encourage scientists to study history or sociology or philosophy, or the great works of man – the classics of literature and art – or (as has been suggested often enough) simply to encourage students of literature or sociology to grasp the methods and the goals of molecular biologists or solid state physicists, seems plainly useless. Useless, because it does not work. Natural scientists may be bored by, or have no time for, Homer or Michelangelo (even if some among them, not nearly as few as is commonly supposed, were and are highly civilised human beings). Historians and students of literature find it difficult to understand expositions of scientific disciplines. What can be done is something different. To assist scientists or mathematicians towards some understanding of how historians or critics arrive at their judgements (which involves an uncertain but indispensable type of imaginative insight), and how they justify them (an exercise in logic, although at times an unorthodox kind of logic), however it is done, is at once more feasible and far more intellectually valuable than an attempt to 'civilise' a chemist by dwelling on the properties of *The Divine Comedy*, or of the ceiling of the Sistine Chapel, or of the *Agamemnon*, or to try to talk a Greek scholar into taking a canter past the principal landmarks of elementary physiology or the theory of numbers. The problem is one of grasp of mental processes, what Whitehead correctly calls adventures of ideas, not of throwing up hastily constructed bridges between 'cultures'. If this task is to be performed, it can be accomplished not by precept but only by example – by the discovery or training of teachers of sufficient knowledge, imagination and talent to make the student see what they see: an experience which, as anyone knows who has ever had a good teacher of any subject, is always fascinating, and can be transforming.

How, it may be asked, is this to be achieved? By what educational reform? The notion that the picture of the world had changed, and that education must change with it, presented itself dramatically to the first advocates of 'modern education' and led to excesses which hold lessons for reformers. In the eighteenth century more than one *philosophe* urged radical reform of education in the direction of reason and enlightenment. The study of dead languages, of history (save as a collection of cautionary examples of the follies, crimes and failures of mankind), of the field of the humanities in general, must be discontinued forthwith, and the new instruments for the discovery of truth – natural sciences, including the social ones from which much was expected – and the inculcation of civic principles of a utilitarian kind, must immediately be substituted. This, for example, was the programme of conscientious French reformers, Helvétius and his friends, and to some degree of Condorcet. This unhistorical radical positivism, understandable enough during the *ancien régime* in France (or indeed in Germany, Italy or Spain), provoked a violent reaction on the part of the insulted human spirit, of the neglected life of the imagination. This led to the romantic rebellion; to a return to the study of the past, the remote, the peculiar, the irrational, the uncharacteristic; to the rejection of systems, generalisation, symmetry, timeless serenity, rationality itself; to the cult of eccentricity and ugliness as expressions of the revolt of the passions against the 'cold' classifications and abstractions practised by the natural sciences. The *lumières* were accused of spreading darkness: of closing the mind to insight into the inner life and of promoting the atrophy of the will and the emotions, and thereby philistine attitudes to the great masterpieces of art and thought and religious feeling. It is, in part, this nineteenth-century war between the advocates of the humanities and of the sciences, in which intransigent positions were taken, that led finally to a situation which can be called only neither peace nor war – something like a condition of armed neutrality between scientific and humane studies, with an ever widening gulf between them, which it is the business of modern education, if not to abolish, at least to narrow.

Can this be done? It was, I think, Tolstoy who once observed that what a man perceives clearly – really clearly – he is able to expound simply, and that what is clearly understood (even, I suppose, if it is false) can therefore be communicated by a teacher to a pupil of average responsiveness. He believed that allegations of the impossibility, or acute difficulty, of communicating the technical details of a discipline to untrained minds (not that he thought this particularly important in comparison with central moral truths – the grasp of the real ends of life – but this is not relevant here) were, as often as not, due to the fact that the teacher sought to conceal from himself that he did not begin to see the wood for the trees. Tolstoy was convinced that the salient features of any problem can always be conveyed; and that pleas of difficulty, although sometimes well founded, too often disguised the mentor's own intellectual confusions and insecurity. This, as so much in Tolstoy, may be vastly oversimplified; but, again as so often in the ideas of this devastating thinker, it expresses a disagreeable truth. If even a few serious and imaginative teachers with a knack for clear exposition tried to convey what they knew to students on the other side of the barrier, and persisted until they obtained a response, he could not believe that the results would be disappointing. And in this I strongly suspect he was right.

Pretentious rhetoric, deliberate or compulsive obscurity or vagueness, metaphysical patter studded with irrelevant or misleading allusions to (at best) half-understood scientific or philosophical theories or to famous names, is an old, but at present particularly prevalent, device for concealing poverty of thought or muddle, and sometimes perilously near a confidence trick. Nevertheless, the increasing effort to drag in scientific notions into the realms of art or ideology, or literary ones into those of the sciences, is itself a pathetic symptom of the craving to bridge a gulf. Impostors, both literary and scientific, or poorly equipped popularisers offer counterfeit commodities because there is a mounting demand for the genuine article, and their shameful activities are as good an index as any to what many in their societies need and search for as best they can. The proposition that education cannot help, that good money cannot drive out bad, seems to me defeatist nonsense: the history of thought from the Greeks onwards testifies against it.

Everyone knows what effect even the informal casual talk of a gifted, enthusiastic and sympathetic schoolmaster can have upon his pupils, both for better and for worse. A capacity for discovery and invention, for basic research and original work, is not always allied to either a desire or a gift for teaching. But sometimes it is. There are times when middlemen – those who understand something and tell others, like Voltaire with his not very perfect exposition of Newton, or, a century and a half later, those other great *vulgarisateurs*, Jules Verne and H. G. Wells, in their own highly imaginative way – have an immensely liberating effect. There is no reason why this kind of exposition should not be integrated into academic disciplines, without woolliness or dilution or superficiality or degradation of learning; provided that those who are engaged in it are themselves of sufficient intellectual calibre, and believe in their task, and do not regard it as a chore and a bore to be performed only as an obligation to the age and society in which they live, as a peripheral and undignified labour involving a loss of time that might otherwise be dedicated to their own original work.

I do not mean to imply that a gift for exposition is as valuable as a capacity for original thought, still less that all academic disciplines are of equal intrinsic or pedagogical worth. To maintain that they are is a vulgar educational egalitarianism which does violence to the truth and harm to educational practice. A gifted expositor can put life into virtually any topic: nevertheless there are indices of intellectual power. The academic value of a subject seems to me to depend largely on the ratio of ideas to facts in it. 'Interplay' would doubtless be a better word than 'ratio' to indicate the relationship; nevertheless the latter brings out more clearly the danger of underrating the component of ideas, whether intuitive, empirical or logical (that is, deductive, hypothetico-deductive, inductive, and so forth). Thus, in subjects where the factual component is virtually non-existent, for example in logic or pure mathematics, expertise infallibly connotes a high degree of intellectual power. Whatever may be thought of the value of these disciplines, it is plain that only a very gifted man can be a good pure mathematician or a good logician. It could be argued that an accurate account of the rise and fall of export figures for Danish cheeses during a given decade of the nineteenth century might offer material useful to an economic historian capable of valuable original work in this field, or function as an illustration for some new and revolutionary technique for estimating economic change. Consequently the labours of the expert on the sales of Danish cheese might well be more socially useful than an elaborate topological fantasy. Nevertheless our respect for the specialist on cheeses is not high: we value his work but not him; and the sole reason for this is the low content of ideas – hypotheses, powers of reasoning, capacity for general ideas, awareness of the relationship of elements in a total pattern – in such painstaking but intellectually undemanding work. If the interplay of ideas and facts in subjects so disparate as, say, economic history and theoretical chemistry as a branch of applied mathematics, or in social psychology and metallurgy, could be compared by someone who knew one of these subjects well and professionally, and the other through the illumination obtained from a good teacher, this alone would be an enormous source of intellectual exhilaration and profit: it would make a student of this type not only feel, but be, far more at home in the intellectual world of his time. It is the capacity for rising to a clear perception of structures of thought and knowledge, of their similarities and differences, of their methods of discovery and invention and their criteria of truth and validity; above all a grasp of their central principles – and therefore of what is the nerve and muscle and what the surrounding tissue in any human construction, what is novel and revolutionary in a discovery and what is development of existing knowledge – that lifts men intellectually. It is this that elevates them to that power of contemplating patterns, whether permanent or changing, buried in, or imposed on, the welter of experience, which philosophers have regarded as man's highest attribute; but even if they are mistaken in this, it is surely not an unworthy goal for what we like to call higher education.

INDEX

Compiled by Douglas Matthews